Work

opposing viewpoints®

Other Books of Related Interest in the Opposing
Viewpoints Series:

America's Future
Economics in America
Education in America
The Family in America
Immigration
Japan
Male/Female Roles
Politics in America
Poverty
Social Justice
Trade

Work

opposing viewpoints®

David Bender & Bruno Leone, *Series Editors*

Scott Barbour, *Book Editor*
Karin L. Swisher, *Assistant Editor*
Charles P. Cozic, *Assistant Editor*

OPPOSING
VIEWPOINTS
SERIES®

Greenhaven Press, Inc., San Diego, CA

Greenhaven Press, Inc.
PO Box 289009
San Diego, CA 92198-9009

Cover photo: Owen McGoldrick

Library of Congress Cataloging-in-Publication Data

Work : opposing viewpoints / Scott Barbour, book editor. Karin L. Swisher and Charles P. Cozic, assistant eds.
    p.   cm. — (Opposing viewpoints series)
    Includes bibliographical references and index.
    ISBN 1-56510-219-3 (lib. :alk. paper)   — ISBN 1-56510-218-5 (pbk. : alk. paper)
    1. Work—Social aspects. 2. Work—Social aspects—United States. 3. Labor market—United States. 4. Hard-core unemployed—United States. 5. Public welfare—United States. [1. Work. 2. Labor. 3. Public welfare.] I. Barbour, Scott, 1963-   . II. Swisher, Karin L., 1966-   . III. Cozic, Charles P., 1957-   . IV. Series: Opposing viewpoints series (Unnumbered)
HD6955.W667   1995
331—dc20   94-16100
                                                                    CIP
                                                                    AC

Every effort has been made to trace the owners of copyrighted material.

"Congress shall make no law . . .
abridging the freedom of speech,
or of the press."

First Amendment to the U.S. Constitution

The basic foundation of our democracy is the First Amendment guarantee of freedom of expression. The Opposing Viewpoints Series is dedicated to the concept of this basic freedom and the idea that it is more important to practice it than to enshrine it.

Contents

	Page
Why Consider Opposing Viewpoints?	9
Introduction	12

Chapter 1: How Should the U.S. Workforce Be Educated?

Chapter Preface — 16

1. The Education System Should Emphasize Work Skills — 17
   Ray Marshall & Marc Tucker

2. The Education System Should Not Emphasize Work Skills — 24
   Peter Shaw

3. A German-Style Apprenticeship Program Would Be Effective — 29
   Wilfried Prewo

4. A German-Style Apprenticeship Program May Not Be Effective — 34
   Kenneth A. Couch

5. Training Programs Will Benefit U.S. Workers — 41
   Robert B. Reich

6. Training Programs May Not Benefit U.S. Workers — 48
   John B. Judis

Periodical Bibliography — 53

Chapter 2: Should Government Intervene in the Job Market?

Chapter Preface — 56

1. Government Intervention Causes Unemployment — 57
   Lowell Gallaway & Richard Vedder

2. Government Intervention Can Foster Full Employment — 66
   Wallace C. Peterson

3. Government Regulations Have Created a Contingent Workforce — 74
   William Tucker

4. Government Regulations Are Needed to Protect the Contingent Workforce — 82
   Chuck Williams

5. Increasing the Minimum Wage Reduces Employment — 91
   Stephen Chapman & Doug Bandow

6. Increasing the Minimum Wage Does Not
   Reduce Employment   96
   Alan B. Krueger
Periodical Bibliography   101

Chapter 3: What Role Should Labor Unions Play in the Workplace?

Chapter Preface   103
1. The Influence of Labor Unions Is Declining   104
   Richard Edwards
2. The Influence of Labor Unions May
   Be Increasing   113
   John B. Judis
3. Unions Are Still Necessary   122
   Kevin Clarke
4. Unions Are Outdated   130
   Leo Troy
5. Labor-Management Partnerships Are Beneficial   137
   Barry Bluestone & Irving Bluestone
6. Labor-Management Partnerships Are Harmful   146
   Mike Parker & Jane Slaughter
7. Business Should Not Be Allowed to Permanently
   Replace Striking Workers   154
   Robert B. Reich
8. Business Must Be Allowed to Permanently
   Replace Striking Workers   158
   David Warner
Periodical Bibliography   164

Chapter 4: How Should Equality in the Workplace Be Achieved?

Chapter Preface   167
1. Affirmative Action Promotes Equality   168
   Gertrude Ezorsky
2. Affirmative Action Does Not Promote Equality   177
   Herman Belz
3. Comparable Worth Policies Can Be Effective   186
   Elaine Sorensen
4. Comparable Worth Policies Are Ineffective   194
   Steven E. Rhoads
5. Diversity Management Is Beneficial   203
   Ann M. Morrison
6. Diversity Management Is Counterproductive   212
   Frederick R. Lynch

7. Apprenticeships Would Increase Opportunities
for Youths   219
    Edward E. Barr

8. Apprenticeships Would Reduce Opportunities
for Youths   228
    Harvey Kantor

Periodical Bibliography   237

Chapter 5: How Should Work and Society Be Reconciled?

Chapter Preface   240

1. Welfare Reform Should Require Recipients
to Work   241
    Donna E. Shalala

2. Welfare Reform Should Not Stress Work   248
    Neil Gilbert

3. Business Supports Work-Family Programs   254
    John L. Adams

4. Business Does Not Adequately Support
Work-Family Programs   262
    Jaclyn Fierman

5. Working Mothers Benefit Families   269
    The Myers family, interviewed by Judith Valente

6. Stay-at-Home Mothers Benefit Families   278
    Elena Neuman

Periodical Bibliography   286

For Further Discussion   287
Organizations to Contact   290
Bibliography of Books   298
Index   302

Why Consider Opposing Viewpoints?

"The only way in which a human being can make some approach to knowing the whole of a subject is by hearing what can be said about it by persons of every variety of opinion and studying all modes in which it can be looked at by every character of mind. No wise man ever acquired his wisdom in any mode but this."

John Stuart Mill

In our media-intensive culture it is not difficult to find differing opinions. Thousands of newspapers and magazines and dozens of radio and television talk shows resound with differing points of view. The difficulty lies in deciding which opinion to agree with and which "experts" seem the most credible. The more inundated we become with differing opinions and claims, the more essential it is to hone critical reading and thinking skills to evaluate these ideas. Opposing Viewpoints books address this problem directly by presenting stimulating debates that can be used to enhance and teach these skills. The varied opinions contained in each book examine many different aspects of a single issue. While examining these conveniently edited opposing views, readers can develop critical thinking skills such as the ability to compare and contrast authors' credibility, facts, argumentation styles, use of persuasive techniques, and other stylistic tools. In short, the Opposing Viewpoints Series is an ideal way to attain the higher-level thinking and reading skills so essential in a culture of diverse and contradictory opinions.

In addition to providing a tool for critical thinking, Opposing Viewpoints books challenge readers to question their own strongly held opinions and assumptions. Most people form their opinions on the basis of upbringing, peer pressure, and personal, cultural, or professional bias. By reading carefully balanced opposing views, readers must directly confront new ideas as well as the opinions of those with whom they disagree. This is not to simplistically argue that everyone who reads opposing views will—or should—change his or her opinion. Instead, the series enhances readers' depth of understanding of their own views by encouraging confrontation with opposing ideas. Careful examination of others' views can lead to the readers' understanding of the logical inconsistencies in their own opinions, perspective on why they hold an opinion, and the consideration of the possibility that their opinion requires further evaluation.

Evaluating Other Opinions

To ensure that this type of examination occurs, Opposing Viewpoints books present all types of opinions. Prominent spokespeople on different sides of each issue as well as well-known professionals from many disciplines challenge the reader. An additional goal of the series is to provide a forum for other, less known, or even unpopular viewpoints. The opinion of an ordinary person who has had to make the decision to cut off life support from a terminally ill relative, for example, may be just as valuable and provide just as much insight as a medical ethicist's professional opinion. The editors have two additional purposes in including these less known views. One, the editors encourage readers to respect others' opinions—even when not enhanced by professional credibility. It is only by reading or listening to and objectively evaluating others' ideas that one can determine whether they are worthy of consideration. Two, the inclusion of such viewpoints encourages the important critical thinking skill of objectively evaluating an author's credentials and bias. This evaluation will illuminate an author's reasons for taking a particular stance on an issue and will aid in readers' evaluation of the author's ideas.

As series editors of the Opposing Viewpoints Series, it is our hope that these books will give readers a deeper understanding of the issues debated and an appreciation of the complexity of even seemingly simple issues when good and honest people disagree. This awareness is particularly important in a democratic society such as ours in which people enter into public debate to determine the common good. Those with whom one disagrees should not be regarded as enemies but rather as people whose views deserve careful examination and may shed light on one's own.

Thomas Jefferson once said that "difference of opinion leads to inquiry, and inquiry to truth." Jefferson, a broadly educated man, argued that "if a nation expects to be ignorant and free . . . it expects what never was and never will be." As individuals and as a nation, it is imperative that we consider the opinions of others and examine them with skill and discernment. The Opposing Viewpoints Series is intended to help readers achieve this goal.

David L. Bender & Bruno Leone,
Series Editors

Introduction

> *"The American work force is being downsized and atomized."*
>
> Lance Morrow, Time, *March 29, 1993*
>
> *"Security will be found not by burrowing into a single job, but through . . . flexibility."*
>
> Robert B. Reich, Los Angeles Times, *March 27, 1994*

For most of the post–World War II period, one main feature of American jobs was security. In exchange for loyalty to their company, employees were typically rewarded with lifelong employment, generous benefits, and guaranteed pensions. This form of employment remained the norm for many people into the early 1970s, when the nature and role of work in American culture was portrayed in Studs Terkel's book *Working*. According to *Time's* Lance Morrow, "*Working* explored the lives of Americans with jobs that seemed like long-term marriages. . . . It began with something like apprenticeship and then, in the ideal model, proceeded through hard work and merit to raises, promotions, success and eventual retirement with pension." Morrow noted that in the past, workers' identities were closely linked to the companies they worked for: "There were Sears men and GM workers and Anheuser-Busch people."

By the early 1990s, various economic forces had drastically altered the structure of industry and the nature of work in America. The end of the cold war had resulted in massive cuts in government defense spending, leaving tens of thousands of defense industry workers jobless and equipped with skills that were in low demand. Economic globalization had increased competition from foreign countries and had led many U.S. businesses to relocate their production facilities overseas to cut overhead and labor costs. Technological advances had dramatically altered industrial processes, enhancing efficiency and reducing the number of workers required in production.

The economic constraints resulting from these forces have led many corporations to "downsize," eliminating many positions—especially middle-management jobs—and vastly reducing their overall numbers of employees. According to *Business Week*, between early 1991 and May 1994, four of the nation's largest corporations—IBM, AT&T, General Motors, and Sears—shed over

50,000 employees each; and in the first quarter of 1994, "employers announced an average of 3,106 cutbacks per day." While downsizing in the past had been a short-term strategy for businesses to survive recessions, many analysts agree that the downsizing of the early 1990s was part of a "reengineering" of the workplace, and that most of the job losses will be permanent. According to Noel M. Tichy, a management professor quoted by *Business Week*, "There still remains this naive view that . . . these jobs will come back. That's nonsense."

Beyond downsizing, reengineering refers to attempts by businesses to alter their management and production processes in order to increase their "flexibility"—their ability to respond quickly to market demands. Previously, management authority was usually arranged in a vertical hierarchy, and production workers were divided into rigidly delineated departments in which they performed a single task repeatedly. Now, according to U.S. secretary of labor Robert B. Reich, "The old hierarchy of mid-level managers, lower-level supervisors and low-skill drones is blurring into a broad class of workplace problem-solvers. Experience and authority sweep away from the front office and are dispersed throughout the productive team." Similarly, according to Steven Pearlstein of the *Washington Post*, the production process is decreasingly departmentalized: "Teams of workers—each trained in several jobs and equipped with computer-driven machinery—[are] given responsibility for significant chunks of the manufacturing process. . . . Designers . . . work with marketers and production engineers."

The increasing flexibility within corporations has created a demand for flexibility throughout the workforce. One of the most widely remarked on developments in recent years is the dramatic growth of the contingent workforce, which consists of temporary, part-time, freelance, and other workers who are not traditional, full-time employees at one company. *Time* contends that in 1988, such workers made up one-fourth of the labor force, and that by the year 2000, the number could be one-half. Reporting on this trend, Jaclyn Fierman, a writer for *Fortune*, notes that "a profound, wrenching, and permanent change in the nature of employment is taking hold in the American workplace."

Critics argue that the growth of the contingent workforce hurts the economy and is unfair to workers. According to Heidi Hartman, director of the Institute for Women's Policy Research, the growing use of contingent employees harms the economy in two ways: first, contingent workers receive low pay, which leads to a reduced demand for goods and services; second, because businesses using contingent workers profit through the payment of low wages rather than through high productivity, the use of such workers encourages maintaining a low-productivity workforce.

Besides harming the economy, according to critics, the use of contingent workers is also unfair to workers. Hartman argues that "these [alternative employment] arrangements . . . may provide more flexibility to the employer to deal with changes in demand or production techniques, but they also generally provide less job security, lower wages and fewer fringe benefits to the workers." According to Bennett Harrison, a professor of political economy, "This is the dark side of flexible production."

Others contend that the growing use of contingent workers is beneficial for the economy as well as for workers. *Fortune* magazine reports that 48 percent of Fortune 500 companies (those included on its annual list of the 500 largest U.S. manufacturing companies ranked by sales) say that the trend toward using more contingent workers is good for the United States, while only 25 percent say it is bad for the country. Proponents contend that the use of contingent workers not only allows businesses to cut costs and remain competitive, but also benefits workers. According to *Fortune*, "Supporters argue that greater use of contingent workers, by increasing companies' flexibility, lowering costs, and lifting competitiveness, will enable them to provide greater job security—and fatter paychecks—for the far larger number of permanent workers who remain." Others insist that contingent workers themselves benefit from contingent employment. For example, Samuel Sacco, executive vice president of the National Association of Temporary Services, argues that temporary work, which is often the target of criticism of contingent employment practices, "offers a critical safety net to displaced workers, providing skills training, wages comparable to similar full-time work and exposure to and experience with a variety of potential employers."

Whether increased reliance on the contingent workforce is beneficial for workers and the economy or not, it appears to have become an integral part of American culture. The world of secure, lifelong jobs described in Terkel's book has largely given way to a work culture whose definitive feature is impermanence. According to Lance Morrow, "America has entered the age of the contingent or temporary worker, of the consultant and subcontractor, of the just-in-time work force—fluid, flexible, disposable." The ideas, policies, and conditions that affect this workforce are discussed and debated in *Work: Opposing Viewpoints*, which contains the following chapters: How Should the U.S. Workforce Be Educated? Should Government Intervene in the Job Market? What Role Should Labor Unions Play in the Workplace? How Should Equality in the Workplace Be Achieved? How Should Work and Society Be Reconciled? These chapters examine the myriad forces shaping the contemporary workforce and workplace.

How Should the U.S. Workforce Be Educated?

Work

Chapter Preface

In their book *Thinking for a Living*, Ray Marshall and Marc Tucker argue that America's poor economic progress relative to that of other industrialized countries since the 1970s is due to the failure of both the business sector and the education system to produce a highly educated and skilled workforce. They insist that "the key to both productivity and competitiveness is the skills of our people and our capacity to use highly educated and trained people to maximum advantage in the workplace." U.S. secretary of labor Robert B. Reich agrees, noting that technological advances have turned many previously low-skill jobs into high-skill jobs and have created new high-skill occupations. Reich asserts that "workers without skills . . . find their options shrinking. More than ever before, what you earn depends on what you learn."

Others argue that the U.S. economy and labor market do not require greatly increased numbers of high-skill workers. For example, in an article in *Issues in Science and Technology* magazine, Ruy A. Teixeira and Lawrence Mishel review data on changes in the job structure and conclude that changes in neither the job mix nor the content of jobs have significantly raised the demand for workers with greater skills. On the contrary, they conclude that "the skills-shortage thesis considerably exaggerates the limited upgrading actually happening in contemporary workplaces. . . . The job structure is changing rather slowly and irregularly." Examining patterns in wage data, Teixeira and Mishel also find that the wages of highly skilled workers have not increased in recent years, as they would have if such workers were in great demand. They argue that "conclusions made from the wage data are quite consistent with the analysis . . . that there has been only moderate growth in skill requirements in recent years."

The ability of U.S. workers to function in an increasingly technological workplace has profound implications for the economic future of the country. Whether and how to match skills training to the needs of business are among the strategies for educating the nation's workforce that are discussed and debated in the following chapter.

"The economic future of the United States depends mainly on the skills of the front-line work force."

The Education System Should Emphasize Work Skills

Ray Marshall and Marc Tucker

Ray Marshall, formerly secretary of labor under President Jimmy Carter, is a professor of economics and public affairs at the University of Texas in Austin. Marc Tucker is president of the National Center on Education and the Economy in Rochester, New York. In the following viewpoint, excerpted from a *Technology Review* article adapted from their book *Thinking for a Living*, the authors argue that if the United States is to compete economically with other industrialized nations, the country's education system must be reformed to provide students with the technical and professional skills demanded by today's "high-performance" workplaces in which workers are given management responsibilities.

As you read, consider the following questions:

1. According to the authors, how do most American children now learn about what goes on at work?
2. Why do the authors insist that their proposed certificate program must be a national system rather than a state or local one?

American enterprise has been organized on the principle that most workers do not need to know much, or be able to do much, beyond what's necessary to perform narrowly defined tasks. The high productivity growth that the United States enjoyed until recently was made possible by giving our workers the most advanced equipment on the market. Today, however, the same equipment is available to low-wage countries that can sell their products all over the world—including here in the United States—at prices way below ours. If we continue to compete with them on wages and hours, as we are now doing, real wages will continue the decline that began in the 1970s and hours will increase until they match the low-wage competition. In short, the U.S. standard of living will plummet.

High-Performance Work Organizations

The alternative is to join the ranks of countries such as Germany, Japan, Sweden, and Denmark that promote high-performance work organizations. In such businesses, highly skilled, well-paid front-line workers are given many of the responsibilities of managers—tasks such as scheduling production, ordering parts, and attending to quality control.

The advantages of this form of work organization are enormous. The ranks of middle management and many support functions are thinned out, creating a large productivity gain. Quality improves dramatically. There is better coordination of the myriad functions involved in manufacturing a product, and far fewer mistakes. Improvements in design and construction are made constantly, instead of waiting for new model introductions, creating a strong market advantage. It becomes possible to go after small market segments, because success no longer depends on producing thousands or millions of identical products. Worker motivation and morale are greatly enhanced, because workers take real pride in their work. Taken together, these changes give firms a decisive edge over low-wage, low-skill competitors.

The Importance of Skills

Unfortunately for the United States, high-performance work organizations hinge on a well-educated work force. The U.S. system of educating and training workers has been shaped around the meager demands of "scientific management," where employers design the jobs of their front-line workers so that they require little knowledge or ability. U.S. skill requirements look more like those of Third World countries than those of the leading industrial nations.

Third World skills are fine for companies that choose to compete with South Korea, Mexico, and the Philippines. But firms that want to take on Germany and Japan are finding themselves at a disadvantage. The scant minority—fewer than 5 percent—of American firms that are embracing high-performance forms of work organization report that they are experiencing or expect to face a shortage of skilled labor. If the vast majority of employers were to adopt high-performance organization, there would be a skilled-labor shortage of epic proportions.

Workers Lack Crucial Skills

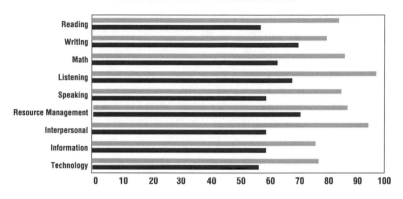

Employers who believe skill is important
Employers who believe finding workers with skill is a problem

Source: National Alliance of Business.

The economic future of the United States depends mainly on the skills of the front-line work force, the people whose jobs will not require a baccalaureate degree. Success, then, depends on developing a program to prepare close to three-quarters of our work force to take on tasks in restructured workplaces that, up to now, have been assigned mainly to the college educated. The idea that Americans just turning 19 or 20 would come to the job equipped for such tasks might sound like the stuff of fantasy, but it is increasingly common in many European countries. If it does not happen here, the United States will simply be unable to attain the rates of productivity growth and deliver the quality that it must achieve. . . .

Constructing a U.S. System

It is doubtful that we would serve this country well by replicating any of the systems of other industrialized nations. We can certainly learn from their successes, but we must keep in mind their different cultural contexts—and outright shortcomings. . . .

The United States must construct its own system for developing strong technical and professional skills in high-school students not going directly to a four-year college—a system that builds on the best practices of the leading industrial nations. Specifically, that means:

Setting aside several weeks each year for grade-school students to visit work sites and learn about the range of career opportunities.

All students need this exposure, not just those headed for the workplace right out of school. Most of our children learn about what goes on at work from movies and television, which give a highly distorted picture. The problem is particularly severe for poor and minority children, but it applies in some measure to almost everyone. There is no substitute for visiting workplaces and talking to the people who work in them.

Many U.S. educators reject the idea that schools exist in part to prepare people for work. This view partly accounts for the primacy of college as the only goal worth working for in school—but this has to change. Teachers themselves will have to be persuaded that work not requiring a college degree can be challenging, rewarding, and the source of real status. That task should become easier as the number of high-performance work organizations grows.

Youth Centers for Dropouts

Creating a system of youth centers through which municipalities recover dropouts.

No nation in which a quarter of the students fail to complete secondary education can hope to have a world-class work force. South Korea's dropout rate is only 10 percent, and Sweden's rate—thanks to its Youth Center program [which provides training and job opportunities for those who leave school]—is even less. Every state should require its municipalities to operate alternative education and work-experience programs based on the Swedish model. Whenever a student dropped out of school, the school district would have to notify the nearest youth center, which would then actively recruit that student.

Many existing programs—ranging from the Job Corps [a training program administered by the federal government] to programs run by churches and community organizations—already have the capacity to do some or all of the functions we would assign to youth centers. The youth centers would contract with such organizations and with school districts to get the job done. The point is not so much to create new institutions as to designate one local agency to take sole responsibility for recovering every dropout.

How to fund such a program? Every local, state, and federal dollar earmarked for a student's education in a regular high school should follow the dropout to the youth center. While this will not be an easy requirement to meet for states and localities experiencing hard fiscal times, there is overwhelming evidence that the nation would save far more in reduced welfare and prison costs.

Academic Skills

Building the vocational education system on a base of real academic accomplishment.

Without exception, the countries with the most successful vocational education systems realize that job training must be complemented by solid academic skills. In most U.S. school districts, one can get a high-school diploma if one shows up most of the time and does not cause any trouble. The states that do impose some sort of performance requirement rarely set the standard above seventh-grade equivalency.

We urge adoption of "certificates of initial mastery," to be awarded to most students around age 16 when they pass an appropriate examination. The subject matter would encompass reading, writing, listening, and speaking, as well as mathematics, the sciences, history, and the social sciences, the arts, and work skills, but the examinations would place a premium on the capacity to integrate knowledge from many of these disciplines in solving problems. Students would be able to take the performance exams as often as they liked until they passed them.

By setting a single standard for everyone, we break ranks with the Europeans, who use their exams to sort students out, dividing those who will go to college from those who will not. Students who get their certificate would be able to choose whether to begin a technical and professional certificate program, enroll in a college preparatory program, or go directly into the work force.

A Certificate System

Providing access for all students who want it to a high-quality on-the-job learning experience leading to a universally recognized qualification.

The United States ought to create a system of technical and professional certificates covering most trades and occupations not requiring a four-year college degree. The certificates would be awarded when students completed a three-year program of combined schooling and structured on-the-job training and passed a written and practical examination. Programs could be offered by many kinds of institutions—high schools, vocational schools, employers, community colleges, and for-profit technical schools among them—working singly or in combination, but always teamed with employers offering the job-site component.

21

These institutions would compete for students' tuition.

Much of the money required to meet this commitment would come from a repackaging of government funds now spent on the last two years of secondary school and the first two years of college. But other funding could come from employers, especially if—as we recommend below—firms are required to contribute to the continued education and training of their employees.

Each state and industry should have a strong voice in constructing the system and an equally strong role in administering it, but it must be a national system, with national standards, nationally recognized certificates, and a system of occupational classifications that do not vary by jurisdiction. Anything less will lead to a system that will reduce the mobility of our work force or lower individuals' incentive to train, or both. The country will almost surely begin to create this system industry by industry and state by state, but the aim from the start must be to make it truly national.

Emphasize Advanced Forms of Work Organization

Designing the work-based portion of the program so it develops the qualities needed for high-performance work organizations.

The United States faces something of a dilemma. On the one hand, a system of technical and professional standards is urgently needed, and it is only common sense that these standards should be largely set by employers. On the other hand, most employers today would design standards around jobs that ask little of the people who have them

Perhaps the United States should rely mainly on employers who are using advanced forms of work organization to formulate the new standards and then devise a curriculum . . . explicitly to prepare our youth to function in the new work milieu. No doubt many young people will be employed at first by organizations that are not prepared to give them all the responsibility they have been trained to exercise or take advantage of all the skills they bring to the job. But these new employees can be powerful agents of change and can make it easier for forward-looking employers to restructure their workplaces.

Providing incentives to employers to invest in developing their employees.

Most advanced nations and many newly industrialized countries require employers to invest a sum equal to at least 1 percent of salaries and wages for continuing education and training. The United States should require companies to do likewise—or, if they are unable or unwilling, to contribute to a government-operated Skills Development Fund, which would supply the education and training. Only expenditures on programs leading to state educational certificates, industry-wide training certificates, or recognized degrees would satisfy the requirement.

The situation is urgent. If we continue on our low-performance work track, real wages will fall much faster until 2010 than they have since 1970. As that happens—and as the proportion of our population in the work force continues to drop—tax revenue will fall, and the investment capital required to educate and train our front-line workers will be increasingly hard to come by. Many states already find themselves in just such a bind. If we do not change course before 2010, when the baby boomers—77 million people—begin turning 65, and straining our pension and health resources, we could truly reach a point of no return.

If ever there was a time to make the choice for a high-skill work force, it is now.

"Workers in factories lack not the specific skills to do their jobs, but rather the ability to analyze their places in the larger scheme of things."

The Education System Should Not Emphasize Work Skills

Peter Shaw

In the following viewpoint, Peter Shaw criticizes commentators who wish to reform education in order to improve national economic competitiveness. This approach, according to Shaw, by focusing on training in job skills, ignores the "civilizing mission" of education. Shaw contends that, contrary to popular belief, automation and technology have reduced the demand for highly skilled workers by simplifying job tasks. Consequently, rather than skills, the education system should focus on the basics—reading, writing, and arithmetic—which would contribute to a civilized society by producing "citizens capable of thinking on their own." Shaw, author of *Recovering American Literature*, is a member of the National Council of the Humanities and of the National Association of Scholars.

As you read, consider the following questions:

1. What does Shaw conclude from the fact that the growth of the United States as an industrial power has been accompanied by a decline in reading levels?
2. According to the author, why are educators really opposed to "rote learning"?

The universally acknowledged decline in American education is said to have given rise to a debate over how to improve the schools. Yet virtually all those active in the so-called debate are in firm agreement on both the nature of the crisis and what should be done about it. The problem, it is agreed, is that America stands in danger of not being able to compete in the highly technologized twenty-first-century world. The solution, it is also agreed, is educational reform emphasizing skills like computer literacy.

Under the heading of "training," this approach has come to dominate the educational thinking of the Clinton Administration. Labor Secretary Robert Reich is identified with training, and he is confident that the education establishment can produce internationally competitive workers. That establishment's approach, though, no matter how dressed up to sound forward-looking, dynamic, and innovative, only repeats the same orthodoxy that brought about the crisis in the first place.

The twenty-first-century competitiveness argument is at once a measure of the cultural impoverishment of the education establishment and a sure indicator of its determination to keep in place the most deleterious educational practices of the recent past. In saying nothing about the civilizing mission of education, this establishment exposes the poverty of its approach. And in barely mentioning reading, writing, and arithmetic, it ensures that American children will continue to lack what they and their society truly need. One is tempted nevertheless to endorse any argument, even a crudely utilitarian one, if it promises to direct resources to education. But the distortions inherent in the false pragmatism of most educational reform promise to continue eroding, rather than to improve, education.

Technology Requires Less Education

The technological society does not particularly depend on education. A glance at the record shows us that the rapid growth of the United States into the world's greatest industrial power coincided with a steady drop in reading levels running from 1930 to the present. Regna Lee Wood, a teacher, pointed out in an article in *National Review* [September 14, 1992] that this falling off was followed by a related, long decline in SAT scores beginning in 1941.

Technological society turns out to work in the opposite way from that usually supposed: namely by actually requiring less rather than more education of its workers. This is because modern industry depends on reducing human error, which means reducing dependence on the individual worker's expertise and judgment. In building or maintaining electronic devices, workers who once installed or rewired electrical circuits now plug in modular components consisting of machine-printed circuit boards.

Office workers now routinely service office machines like copiers simply by inserting and removing self-contained cartridges. When other parts of the machines malfunction, signal lights instruct the user to "replace paper" or to remove paper caught at a specified point inside the works. Facsimile machines print out both an explanation and a cure for failed transmissions. Problems not explained by the machines themselves can still be corrected without summoning a technician by phoning so-called help lines.

A Dangerous Myth

In the last decade, a popular myth has been created: the declining economy in the United States is the result primarily of poorly educated workers who can't compete in today's high-tech world of international competition. . . .

This myth is not only wrong, I believe, but dangerous. . . .

It is dangerous because it encourages the public to see schools as solely serving the needs of the economy. Thus it ignores other, more fundamental reasons for compelling parents to send their children to school.

Larry Cuban, *Rethinking Schools*, Summer 1993.

Devices that require professional maintenance and repairs of course continue to exist. But as they grow more complex, service personnel are called upon to master ever smaller portions of the whole. Engines still require mechanics. But like the general practitioner in medicine, the auto or truck mechanic has had a number of his functions taken over by specialists—in muffler replacement, tires, tune-up and oil changing, rustproofing, wheel balancing, transmissions. In what remains of his own realm, the mechanic no longer disassembles and repairs engine parts. He replaces an entire master brake cylinder, carburetor, water pump, or motor running the windshield wipers, seats, or other internal moving parts of a car.

Advancing technology means that complexity is accompanied by simplification. Truck loading and routing become more complex as these processes are analyzed, computerized, and conducted in ever more efficient ways. But on the loading docks workers using hand-held computers make fewer decisions than in the past. Nor do they need computer literacy. They need only the ability to recognize numbers. And in most cases the passing of the computer's electric eye over a bar code renders even number recognition unnecessary.

An article in the *Wall Street Journal* titled "Computer Use by Illiterates Grows at Work," reveals that, "In some warehouses, fork-lift drivers who can't read the labels on a soda machine get directions from talking computers on their belts. . . . Instead of writing up work reports, construction workers can touch pictures on a portable pen-based computer screen to store records." The computers worn by these workers, like the printed circuits being plugged in by auto and television repairmen, are manufactured by still less skilled workers, many of them women just off the farms in South Korea or Mexico. More advanced products are fabricated by workers who need literacy and skill levels only very little higher: "with the touch-screen system that displays cylinders, slots, and cones, the machinist can place a measuring probe next to the part and touch the axis to be measured. The computer then figures out whether the part meets specifications."

The future role of literacy in the workplace has been succinctly stated by Pierre Dogan, the president of Granite Communications, a company that is now "developing software for hotel housekeeping." It seems that "so long as maids can read room numbers, they will be able to check off tasks completed or order supplies by simply touching pictures on the screen." Dogan points out that "you can create a work program with prompting, including iconic messages." In fact, he logically concludes, "you can use an illiterate work force."

Do We Need Education?

Even as computers are rendering literacy unnecessary for a large number of jobs, the education establishment remains convinced that society is moving toward a need for increasing rather than decreasing skills at the lower levels. In classic bureaucratic fashion, it sustains its self-regard by initiating apparently forward-looking initiatives but succeeds only in neglecting its fundamental responsibilities. The truly forward-looking question to ask about education is not what it can do for competitiveness in the twenty-first century, but why we should have education at all when it is not truly needed by a technological society.

The answer might seem to be that education is needed to turn out the experts who can develop computers for hotel maids and aerospace-parts assemblers. Yet the same decline in good teaching that has affected the unskilled has accompanied the flowering of inventiveness that has marked the computer age. Somehow, again despite the shortcomings of education, enough people of high accomplishment have emerged to run a technological society and supply personnel for the learned professions. Just as advanced technology requires less expertise at the lower levels, it requires fewer innovators at the top. The output of both groups is enhanced by the power of the machines and systems they work with. . . .

Skills v. Knowledge

Of course it would be far better to have a workforce and citizenry literate and sophisticated, capable of making decisions and innovating. The successes of technology are a recourse, not something desirable in themselves. But to suggest an alternative approach in the presence of an educationist—for example, that students should be able to add up columns of figures, locate the major countries of the world on a map, parse a sentence, display comprehension of a paragraph of English prose, and know the leading events of world and national history—is to stir up dire warnings about the soul-destroying effects of "rote learning." What educationists really mean when they invoke this phrase is that they experience teaching the basics as a form of drudgery for themselves. Far more pleasant is it to take their students on an outing, show a video, set them to making mobiles expressing the concept of an interrelated world, or discuss the environment, AIDS, world peace, or the student's personal feelings and aspirations.

In practice, interestingly enough, these diversions have proved to engage student interest far less than learning dates and places and grammar ever did. But more importantly, diversion from the basics has made the remainder of life less interesting as well. Workers in factories lack not the specific skills to do their jobs, but rather the ability to analyze their places in the larger scheme of things in their industry, region, country, and historical period. To gain such awareness it is necessary to be a reader and to have developed such habits—by rote, where necessary— as rhetorical analysis, which can help one to understand a variety of phenomena from industrial systems to the exhortations of politicians. What the educationists direly and exaggeratedly denominate rote learning is actually the basis for escaping from the unexamined life that Socrates called a life not worth living.

Indeed, much-maligned rote learning is the best basis for deriving the civilized outlook that formal education has become incapable of fostering. Education concerned chiefly with competitiveness degenerates into the vacuities of "enrichment" programs—global awareness, undifferentiated deference toward other cultures, and the like. But education concerned with the basics produces citizens capable of thinking on their own. . . . To aim education at twenty-first-century competition is to perpetuate the failures of the current education crisis; to aim education at civilizing students through imparting basic skills and knowledge would be to achieve both competitiveness and a civilized polity.

"The German [apprenticeship] system has big attractions."

A German-Style Apprenticeship Program Would Be Effective

Wilfried Prewo

Sixty-six percent of the German labor force is composed of graduates of that country's youth apprenticeship program. In the following viewpoint, Wilfried Prewo describes the German system and argues that such a program would benefit the United States. He contends that apprenticeships would reduce the underemployment of young Americans by equipping non–college bound students to enter well-paying, skilled jobs immediately following high school. To support his position, Prewo notes that in Germany the youth unemployment rate is lower than the national average, while in the United States youth unemployment is double the average. Prewo is chief executive of the Chamber of Industry and Commerce in Hanover, Germany.

As you read, consider the following questions:

1. According to Prewo, how many days a week does the typical German apprentice spend at his or her training company?
2. Why is the American "pro-college bent" counterproductive, according to the author?
3. According to Prewo, why does youth training work best when based in the workplace?

President Bill Clinton has talked about youth training, or apprenticeship programs, as part of his larger U.S. investment program. In this thought Mr. Clinton is right on target. But building an apprenticeship program need not mean an extensive widening of federal or state bureaucracy. To see how this is so, it is worth taking a moment to review the German apprenticeship model.

The German economy today is productive largely because of one outstanding factor: a highly skilled labor force. That labor force is the product of systematic youth training: Some 66% of our labor force is represented by certified graduates of the nation's youth training system. The strength of this asset is reflected in the fact that the economy is productive despite some major disadvantages—such as world-class income-tax rates and labor costs that per hour are 60% higher than those of the U.S.

Government Not Involved

The German youth apprenticeship system may be large, but it is based in the private sector. Training takes place on the job. The typical apprentice spends four days a week at his training company and one day in public vocational school. Apart from states funding schools and federal law setting broad guidelines, government is not involved.

In 1992, some 595,000 German teenagers between the ages of 15 and 19 left school and entered an apprenticeship program. Some 1.6 million young people, or 6.5% of the labor force, are enrolled in apprenticeship programs.

Typically, teenagers leaving school sign a contract with an employer who will train them for two to three years in any one of some 380 occupations: 36% become craftsmen, 22% industrial blue-collar workers (for example, machinists or chemical lab assistants), 32% are in office, trade, and other service-sector occupations (salespersons, secretaries, bankers), 8% in the public sector, and 1% in agriculture. Apprentices receive a salary of $500 to $800 a month, or 20% to 25% the salary of a certified employee who has "graduated" from an apprenticeship program.

Together city and regional chambers of industry and commerce organize the system. They register the apprenticeship contracts, certify training companies, regulate and supervise the program, settle disputes, establish examination boards staffed by volunteers, organize midterm and final exams (88% pass), and issue certificates recognized all over Germany and, increasingly, across Europe.

In the Hanover Chamber of Industry and Commerce, where I work, we administer 29,000 apprentices in 166 occupations (18,700 white-collar; 10,300 blue-collar); 7,400 supervisors train the trainees in 5,300 participating companies. In 1992, we administered 12,750 final exams with 6,000 volunteer examiners, and enrolled 13,000 new apprentices. Of our total chamber staff of 215, 40 work in the training department.

Education in Context

To prepare young people for the world of work, there must be an active connection between school and workplace learning. Schools are intended to provide students with a foundation of basic skills. However, many students do not take the courses required for performing in today's work settings because they are unable to appreciate the future usefulness of these courses. Moreover, students do not have an opportunity to apply these skills in actual work settings. As a result, they often are unable to transfer this knowledge once they enter the business environment. Schools are unable to capture the culture of the work setting, and therefore, students do not develop the employability skills needed to operate within business.

Youth apprenticeship raises the performance expectations for students and provides support for their skill development by establishing a direct connection between school and work.

Most students learn best when what they are being taught is placed in an applied context. Thus, in youth apprenticeship programs, academic subjects are taught within the context of concrete, real world examples. Business people work alongside educators to develop curricula that reflect the academic and technical skills needed in work settings.

It is the application of academic knowledge that ensures the attainment of high skills. In a youth apprenticeship program, an academic curriculum would have math courses teach students to prepare budgets and calibrate machinery, rather than solve problems that seem unrelated to anything existing outside the classroom walls. Science courses lead to the understanding of systems, rather than the memorization of unrelated facts that students forget over time. Students in rigorous youth apprenticeship programs not only take advanced algebra and physics, but they appear to understand the contexts better. Having gained the ability to apply the material to the world outside the classroom, they have learned more, and better. Perhaps most importantly, we have found that a student's interest in learning is rekindled in a youth apprenticeship program.

National Alliance of Business, "How School to Work Works for Business," May 1994.

For Mr. Clinton, who focuses on the underemployment of young people, the German system has big attractions. One is the seamless transition from school to training to work. Some 70% of young Germans sign up for apprenticeships—and, if they perform well, guaranteed jobs. Contrast this with the aimless wandering from minimum-wage job to minimum-wage job of many American high-school graduates. At age 25, Americans who have not attended college often find themselves no higher up the job ladder than they were at age 18. Their German counterparts, by contrast, usually hold well-paying skilled jobs.

Americans traditionally have wanted a college education for their children. An important factor in the German success, though, is recognizing that college is not always the answer. Many jobs, in fact, do not call for a costly college education. The America pro-college bent often yields overqualified and directionless people: An otherwise unemployed biologist works as a chemistry lab assistant. In Germany, a lab assistant is a person trained as such. There's no wasteful academic detour.

The German system, however, does not close the door on education. In their late 20s, about 10% of ex-apprentices enroll in further training to become supervisors. In 1991, 17,000 such Germans received such higher certification in industrial jobs; 16,000 in office jobs. The cream of the alumni crop then trains the apprentices in the workplace.

The system strengthens the tradition of internal advancement. Hilmar Kopper, the chief executive of Deutsche Bank, the largest in Germany, does not have a university degree. He joined his bank after high school as an apprentice. Werner Niefer, retiring president of Mercedes, started there 50 years ago as a mechanics apprentice.

For the jobs-oriented Mr. Clinton, it might be worth noting that youth training is the best unemployment insurance. In May 1992, German unemployment was at 6.2%, but for those with occupational training only 4%. Here, youth unemployment is below the general jobless rate, a relationship that is the reverse in most other countries. In the U.S., youth joblessness is double the average.

What works and what doesn't? Germany's centuries-long experience in apprenticeships has shown youth training works best when it is based in the workplace. Teenagers, particularly less-gifted teenagers, have strong doubts about the relevance of high-school classroom work. In the workplace, young apprentices are among adult workers, so they have models to emulate. The reward for their successful work is a clear one—after certification, a quadrupling of their paychecks.

For employers, the system has many advantages. Curricula change in a bottom-up process with technology, not top-down when school boards think so.

Worthwhile Investment

Training does cost dearly. In 1991, German industry spent $27 billion for equipment, company supervisors, and salaries for training the 1.6 million apprentices. Subtracting their contribution to an output of $10 billion, the net cost was $17 billion or $10,500 per apprentice. But for industry, this is a worthwhile investment promising lower turnover. The evidence: Of their own accord, businesses offer 22% more apprenticeship slots than there are applicants.

Germany, of course, is not the only mass model; Denmark, Austria and Switzerland also have good systems. Not every detail can be transposed to America, a country whose companies would probably require a substantive tax credit to be enticed into undertaking training in significant numbers. Concentrate, though, on the salient features: The administration should set a national framework, offer tax credits and, on the state or local level, provide vocational schools. Otherwise, it can—and should—keep its hands off.

"Emulating the German approach may . . . give us an education system that will not perform better but will cost more than our current one."

A German-Style Apprenticeship Program May Not Be Effective

Kenneth A. Couch

In Germany, most high school–age students participate in an apprenticeship program, which includes on-the-job training in specialized skills. In the following viewpoint, Kenneth A. Couch argues that such a system has not proven to be more effective than America's more general form of education. Comparing statistics from the two countries, he concludes that the apprenticeship program has not benefited Germany's manufacturing sector, nor has it increased employment among young Germans. Moreover, he points out that between 1983 and 1988, despite Germany's apprenticeship program, growth in both employment and Gross Domestic Product was greater in the United States than in Germany. Couch is an assistant professor of economics at Syracuse University in New York.

As you read, consider the following questions:

1. According to Gary Becker, cited by Couch, why do expenditures on education lead to higher wages for workers?
2. According to the author, would a system more "gender-neutral" than Germany's improve the net earnings of apprentices as a whole? Why or why not?

From Kenneth A. Couch, "Germans and Job Training, Education and Us," *The American Enterprise*, November/December 1993, ©1993, The American Enterprise Institute. Distributed by The New York Times Special Features. Reprinted with permission.

During the 1992 [presidential] campaign, candidate Bill Clinton outlined . . . a system of apprenticeship and certification similar to Germany's much-vaunted youth apprenticeship program. Writing in *Phi Delta Kappan*, the magazine of the professional education society, Bill Clinton stated that "in our administration, we'll establish a national apprenticeship program, like those in Europe." . . . Of the possible European models, Germany clearly came closest to the Clinton approach. . . .

In August, 1993, Secretary of Education Richard Riley commented that "we are the only major industrialized nation with no formal system for helping our young people—particularly the 75 percent of high school youth who don't go on to finish a four-year college—make the transition from the classroom to the workplace. That translates to lost productivity and wasted human potential." The administration's goal is to enhance individual productivity through a restructured education system. But while it is hard to be against efforts to improve U.S. productivity and competitiveness, it is not at all clear that embracing the German apprenticeship model is going to provide the solution. Emulating the German approach may in fact give us an education system that will not perform better but will cost more than our current one. . . .

Human Capital

The intellectual basis for improving education stems from the work of University of Chicago economist and Nobel Laureate Gary Becker on investments in human capital. Becker believes that individuals use experiences, such as their years of education, to increase their workplace productivity. In a competitive economy, the pay of workers is a direct reflection of their productivity. The amount each person produces multiplied by its market price equals that person's wage rate. More or higher-quality schooling improves productivity and leads directly to improved earnings and a higher standard of material well-being. Thus expenditures on education represent an investment in "human capital," which yields a return to the individual over time in the form of increased earnings. . . .

A system emphasizing general education, such as we have in the United States, would theoretically produce individuals who think about a great variety of topics because they have been trained to do so. Thinking across disciplines, the argument goes, fosters among the most able an intellectual freedom that encourages innovation and invention. For average workers, a general education provides a general set of skills useful to a variety of employers. When faced with layoffs, workers with more general skills should have less trouble moving into new occupations. . . .

While a more general education may prove useful in a dy-

35

namic economy, a formal educational system such as Germany's, which focuses on the transmission of skills related to a specific occupation, also has theoretical advantages. When young people leave school, they should already have skills particular employers find valuable in order to smooth their transition to work. Once at work, individuals who possess skills needed by employers should have a better chance than others of not being laid off. In theory, the higher workplace productivity acquired through this kind of education system helps offset the relatively higher wage rates paid in industrial nations and helps these nations retain high-productivity, high-wage jobs.

Average Rate of Increase of Employment 1983–1988

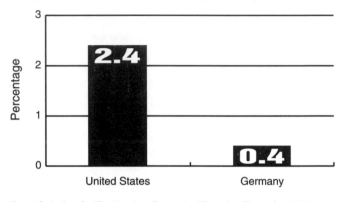

Source: Kenneth A. Couch, *The American Enterprise*, November/December 1993.

The major disadvantage for workers who possess very specific skills is that if laid off, they may lack general skills that would make it easier to move into a different occupation. One way of viewing this is that their individual productivity, except in the job for which they were originally trained, is too low to justify hiring them. In a dynamic economy characterized by significant job turnover, individuals who are the product of an education system that emphasizes a specific set of work skills would be expected to experience longer-term unemployment than individuals with more general skills.

The issue of specific versus general skills has become a familiar topic of debate in Germany. While many in the United States worry that the education system here does not provide workers with a specific set of skills that can raise productivity, Germans face the problems of workers who are often left without a usable set of workplace skills when they lose a job in a declining industry. Anyone contemplating bringing our education system more in line with Germany's should be aware of these reservations.

Germany's Approach

There are theoretical advantages and disadvantages to both the U.S. and German systems of education, but theory does not reveal which system is preferable. Nonetheless, many in the United States have concluded that a system such as Germany's, which emphasizes education aimed toward a specific occupation, is superior to ours, which emphasizes the development of a more general set of skills. Before examining whether existing evidence warrants such a conclusion, let us examine the high school education of a typical German.

The high school system in Germany prepares students for various certification exams. Certifications are usually received by age 19 since school is normally begun at age 6. This matches the 12 years of education most U.S. students have prior to high school graduation. Two broad tracks exist within the German high school system: one for individuals who are expected to attend a college, university, or advanced technical school, and one for those expected to enter an occupation directly following high school. For students headed for postsecondary education, high school experiences in Germany are similar in most respects to those in the United States. One clear difference is that since a smaller proportion of German high school graduates attend postsecondary schools, selection of students for the college-preparatory track is quite competitive, and the classes are more rigorous than the typical classes in U.S. public high schools.

Selection for the college-preparatory track is based upon the results of a single test taken at age 13. Those who do not qualify (the majority of German young people) are tracked into apprenticeship programs. Companies offer apprenticeships that must lead to jobs at the end of a training period when the certification exam is passed. Students normally enter training at ages 15–17, so they may be apprentices for as long as four years. During the period of apprenticeship, students typically spend up to four weekdays at a work site and the remainder in the classroom. The government, industry, and unions jointly determine the content of the training at the work site. The classroom setting provides courses intended to reinforce the work experience. For example, apprentices in manufacturing might take courses in economics to help them understand the constraints faced by their employers. Trainees are paid a proportion of the wages of permanent workers in their specific industry. At the end of training, the apprentices take an occupational certification exam; pass rates are over 90 percent.

Data from the German Socio-Economic Panel (GSOEP) show

37

that, of all high school certifications held in Germany in 1988 (the year before unification [which resulted in economic instability] and therefore the most appropriate year for this analysis) by individuals older than 25, 69 percent came from this mixed system of apprenticeship and classroom education often referred to as the dual system. Seventy-nine percent of the individuals in the 24–33 age cohort who completed a high school level certification but did not have any further formal education were occupationally certified following an apprenticeship. Contrast this with the United States, where data from the National Longitudinal Surveys of Youth (NLSY) indicate that 70 percent of an identical cohort described their own educational curricula as general in nature. These figures show the differences in emphasis of the two systems. Adoption of a national system of apprenticeship would dramatically alter the emphasis of the U.S. educational system, although the extent of that change would be related to the size of the program. *Business Week* has estimated that a national apprenticeship program could affect 56 percent of high school students.

Two common misperceptions exist concerning apprenticeships. The first is that they are all in manufacturing. In fact, apprenticeships cover a broad spectrum of job types, from cashiers at retail stores to specialists in electronics. Second, the assumption is often made that because apprenticeships can only be offered if a full-time job is available following certification, former apprentices typically go to work at the workplace of their former employer. In fact, one year after certification, less than half of the newly certified workers in Germany were employed by the same company they worked for as apprentices. This change in employment can largely be explained by social circumstances. Apprentice wages are typically not enough for independent living, so most apprentices reside at home. Certification in Germany implies a breaking of home ties and mobility much as high school graduation does in the United States.

Comparing Results

Proponents of a national apprenticeship program believe that the United States is failing in international competition because of shortcomings in our educational system. But while there are areas where Germany is outperforming the United States economically, the evidence is not completely one-sided. A careful examination of the experiences of young people in the two systems reveals many similarities in areas where a "superior" education system may have been expected to produce differences.

Consider again 1988, the year prior to German reunification, and compare the same cohort of young workers described by the GSOEP and NLSY data. These 24- to 33-year-old high school graduates with no further education have had time to make the transition to the world of work. For these young workers, the German system has not produced a more robust manufacturing sector. Approximately 18 percent of the U.S. cohort was working in manufacturing compared to 16 percent of the German cohort. Nor did it produce a higher level of employment for this age group; about 82 percent of both cohorts were working. Levels of socialization were similar too. In the cohorts considered, 58 percent of the Germans and 56 percent of the Americans were married. Thirty-four percent of the German households had children; so did 35 percent of the American households. These and other data indicate how similar the experiences of Germany and America are, not how dissimilar.

Comparisons of aggregate indicators of economic well-being tell a similar story. Organization for Economic Cooperation and Development data for the six nonrecessionary years prior to German reunification (1983–1988) show that the rate of employment growth in the United States exceeded that of Germany each year. The average rate of increase in this period was 2.4 percent in the United States versus 0.4 percent in Germany. Over the same period, the rate of growth in real Gross Domestic Product in the United States surpassed Germany's each year. The average rate of increase over the period was 3.9 percent in the United States and 2.3 percent in Germany. These data illustrate that in some important respects the economic performance of the United States has exceeded that of Germany.

More Earnings?

All of these observations suggest that an apprenticeship program by itself is unlikely to have widespread positive effects either on economic measures such as employment or on indirectly related social problems. But then again, Becker's human capital theory never suggested that all of the ills of society would be solved, only that additional or higher quality time spent in education would translate into higher worker productivity and thus higher wages. If a program of apprenticeship is indeed superior to a classroom curriculum, then individuals who are occupationally certified should be paid more than individuals who are educated in the general curriculum. Is this true?

Again consider the youth cohort from Germany, as analyzed in 1988. Now separate those who successfully completed a high school apprenticeship from those who successfully completed another high school level curriculum. Also, subtract individuals whose highest level of certification was less or more than a high school level in order to evaluate comparable groups of individuals. The only available study, completed in 1993 by the author, indicates that, on average, earnings of successful apprentices in

Germany were no different from those of nonapprentices 5 to 14 years following certification.

Evidence from this study shows that training results in substantial increases in earnings for males but not for females. When averaged, however, there is no positive net effect on earnings. One common explanation among researchers for this phenomenon is that the apprenticeship system in Germany perpetuates a gender-based segregation of occupations. It is possible that the United States might enact a program characterized by less bias. But apprenticeships are offered by firms, not selected from a hypothetical high-wage job structure designed by a government economist. If some women are apprenticed in trades formerly reserved for men and vice versa, gender differences in earnings might narrow. But introducing a more gender-neutral system of apprenticeship is unlikely to affect net earnings of apprentices taken as a whole, because the existing distribution of jobs as well as the wages attached to them would remain unchanged. This raises some doubt about the advantages in terms of wage gains of adopting a national system of apprenticeship in the United States.

A German-Type Program Is Not Merited

A considerable body of evidence shows that improved education is related to higher earnings. A reasonable national goal would be to see to it that all workers have the necessary skills to engage in productive employment. Reform could be as simple as returning meaningful literacy and numeracy standards to high schools and having the collective will to achieve them. Alternatively, improvement might involve a national scheme of apprenticeship and occupational certification. If achieving national educational goals costs more money but increases the earning ability of citizens, such a program might very well be merited. This appraisal suggests that the apprenticeship program used in Germany would not pass this test.

"More than ever before in this country, what you earn depends on what you learn."

Training Programs Will Benefit U.S. Workers

Robert B. Reich

Formerly a professor of political economy at the John F. Kennedy School of Government at Harvard University, Robert B. Reich was appointed U.S. secretary of labor under President Bill Clinton in 1993. He is the author of several books, including *The Work of Nations: Preparing Ourselves for 21st-Century Capitalism.* In the following viewpoint, Reich argues that due to the growth of technology in the workplace, specialized skills—particularly the ability to identify and solve problems—are increasingly required of U.S. employees. To help workers develop these skills, Reich advocates job training as a central component of all employment-related government programs, including the education, welfare, and unemployment systems.

As you read, consider the following questions:

1. According to Reich, how did the change in the earnings of college graduates between 1980 and 1991 compare to the change in the earnings of high school graduates in the same period?
2. Why has trade adjustment assistance been ineffective, in the author's view?
3. Reich asserts that the debate over government programs is often "a collision of two philosophical caricatures." What are these two perspectives?

From "Getting America to Work: What's Working and What's Not Working in Workforce Policy," Robert B. Reich's speech to the Center for National Policy, Washington, D.C., January 27, 1994. Courtesy of the U.S. Dept. of Labor.

On January 25, 1994, the President [Bill Clinton] spoke eloquently about the challenges still facing this nation, and his Administration's determination to meet them head on. The overarching goal is to enable all Americans to have full and productive lives: to eliminate the fear of loss of health care that so often accompanies joblessness, to move people off welfare and into work, to provide new jobs and skills for people who need them, and to ensure that our kids have a chance to prosper and become responsible members of our society even if they come from our toughest neighborhoods.

As the President said, the pillars of society are family, community, and work. Work does more than put structure in our days and money in our pockets. It also grants dignity and independence—and can even provide meaning to our lives.

But many Americans cannot get work, keep work, or advance in a career. Although the economy has been adding an average of 165,000 new jobs each month, the pathways to these jobs are not always clear. More than ever before in this country, what you earn depends on what you learn.

If you have the skills that come with a college degree or other training beyond high school, you'll probably find a job and earn a good wage. But if you don't have the skills, you're more likely to be without a job or stuck in a job that pays substantially less than the one you once had. For example, from 1980 to 1991, the real earnings of full-time workers over age 25 who had graduated from college rose by 9%. But earnings for similar workers who had completed high school but not gone to college *dropped* by 7%.

New Kinds of Jobs

Within a century, Americans have moved from the farm to the factory, and now to the computer workstation. Mass production manufacturing jobs, which used to pay good wages to people without much education or formal training, are disappearing— just as farm jobs began to vanish a hundred years ago.

Fortunately, what is disappearing is being replaced by hundreds of thousands of new kinds of jobs—jobs that, at their heart, require workers to identify and solve problems. Not all of these jobs are in high-tech industries. And not all require a college degree.

There's the truck driver who has a computer and modem in his cab so that he can time deliveries to exactly when the customer needs them, and then can help assemble complex machinery. He's not a trucker in the old sense of the term. He's a technician, and he's making good money.

There's the salesperson in a department store who has complete responsibility for her section of the sales floor. She advises customers about new products in her specialty. And she orders the latest and best merchandise, in a sense managing the area she knows best. She too is earning a good living.

There's the factory worker in a new kind of factory. She sits behind a computer, programming and reprogramming a robot that does the pulling and twisting that humans once did. She earns a good income. And a man in the same company who maintains and repairs computers, continually upgrading them and linking them together in ever more efficient ways. Like the rest, he too has a good job.

A National Training Strategy

A national strategy must be pursued that will restructure work-places so that front-line employees can effectively utilize newly acquired skills. The system must provide workers with benefits and training services that will lead to high-wage, high-skill jobs and that will establish governance structures ensuring equal input from unions, employers and the community.

Sheldon Friedman and Jane McDonald-Pines, *North American Outlook*, September 1993.

And there are many others. In fact, most of the 2 million new jobs that were added to the economy in 1993 required some education and training beyond high school. And *all* of the good jobs of the future will require problem-solving skills and the capacity to continuously learn on the job.

Although the core duty to develop such skills rests with each citizen, government has a role to play in *easing* their workforce transitions—in helping them move from school to work, from welfare to work, and from work to work.

But here's the problem: the system we have in place to ensure that every worker learns and constantly upgrades his or her skills is not a system at all. It's a rag-tag collection of programs—a hodgepodge of initiatives, some of which work, many of which don't. In its place this country needs . . . a true system of lifelong learning. We'll scrap what doesn't work, and build on what does.

What Does Not Work

Here, for example, is what we know *does not* work:

• *Conventional short-term training for disadvantaged teenagers.* At federal expense, tens of thousands of low-income, out-of-school young people receive three to six months of job training. An exhaustive study completed by the Department of Labor shows that recipients of such training experience no discernible benefit compared to low-income young people who don't get the training—no improvements in job prospects, no gain in earnings.

• *Targeted jobs tax credit.* In 1982, Congress established a tax credit to encourage employers to hire certain groups of disadvantaged workers. In 1991, to cite one typical year, some 428,000 employees were covered and claimed under this provision. But according to recent studies by Cornell University's John Bishop and Grinnell College's Mark Montgomery, at least 70% of these workers would have been hired even *without* their employers' receiving a tax break.

• *Small training stipends for food stamp recipients.* During the 1992–93 fiscal year, the Agriculture Department's Food Stamp Employment and Training Program provided $165 million in job training to 1.5 million food stamp recipients—or about $100 worth of training for each participant. Studies show zero impact on employment prospects and earnings.

• *Income support without training.* Trade adjustment assistance is supposed to provide income support and training to workers displaced by foreign competition. But the Labor Department's Inspector General determined that about half the workers who qualify never enroll in training, and thus fail to develop skills they need for the next job.

• *Training for only particular groups of displaced workers.* Along with trade adjustment assistance, there is a special retraining program for workers displaced by defense downsizing, another for workers displaced due to logging restrictions in the Northwest, and yet another for workers whose job loss is connected to the Clean Air Act. Each of these programs expends vast resources trying to determine whether an applicant qualifies. Displaced workers who don't meet the requirements are out of luck.

• *Training for the wrong occupations.* Our researchers have found that U.S. training, vocational, and loan programs turn out 80,000 certified cosmetologists per year—for a job market that each year has room for only 17,000.

This is a disturbing list. Investing scarce resources in programs that don't deliver cheats workers who require results and taxpayers who finance failure.

What Does Work

So here's what we're going to do:

We're going to recommend against renewing the targeted jobs tax credit. We're going to require training as a condition of receiving trade adjustment assistance. We're going to consolidate all programs for displaced workers so they qualify for help regardless of why they lost their job. We're going to use a national jobs data bank to link job retraining tightly to where jobs exist.

We will also shift money away from what doesn't help Americans get jobs to what *does*. Here's a sample:

• *Job Corps.* According to studies by a set of economists at Mathematica Policy Research, young people who have entered this intensive one-year, highly structured training program earn 15% more per year thereafter than their counterparts. They're twice as likely to attend college, less likely to commit serious crimes, and will spend more of their adult lives in jobs and less on welfare. The combined benefits of this program, after only five years, are one and a half times its costs—a 50% return on the public's investment.

• *Combined classroom instruction with intensive on-the-job skill-training.* Another success story for disadvantaged youth is the Center for Employment Training, based in San Jose, California, with 28 branches around the country. CET connects what teenagers learn in school with what they will do on the job by placing local employers on CET's board and fostering close ties to the local business community. According to research by the Rockefeller Foundation and the Manpower Demonstration Research Corporation, CET graduates earned $6,500 more, in the two years after their graduation, than members of a control group.

• *Job training for disadvantaged adults.* According to a recent study by a panel that included many of the nation's most prominent labor economists, even relatively short-term training is helping the approximately 300,000 low-income adults who enroll each year in federal job training programs. Their earnings are, on average, 10% to 15% higher than earnings in control groups without training. Here again, earnings gains substantially exceeded program costs.

New Approaches

• *Combining supportive services like child care and job search assistance with job training to get people off of welfare and into work.* Evidence from pilot programs in California and Massachusetts shows that job training combined with child care, continued health insurance, and job search assistance sped welfare recipients into the workforce. And once employed, participants saw their annual earnings increase by an average of $500.

• *A year or more beyond high school.* You don't need a degree to reap the benefits of investments in skills. A study by Thomas Kane of Harvard University and Cecilia Rouse of Princeton University shows that every year of skill training beyond high school boosts future incomes by 5% to 10%.

• *New approaches and new incentives.* Researchers compared unemployed workers in Massachusetts and Washington state who received training in starting a new business with those who did not receive such training. Eighteen months after completing a program that trained the unemployed in entrepreneurial skills, participants were more likely to be working and less likely to be collecting unemployment benefits. In addition, a study by Bruce Meyer of Northwestern University showed that when unemployed workers received a portion of the remaining weeks of their insurance in a lump-sum payment—often enabling them to settle for lower starting wages in the next job—they got re-employed faster.

• *Job search assistance.* Pilot programs in six states show that unemployed workers who received not just an unemployment check but early help in searching for the next job were re-employed, on average, one to four weeks more quickly.

Building on Successes

The Clinton Administration will build on these successes. We proposed—and Congress passed—legislation to identify workers at risk of long-term joblessness and provide them with early search assistance.

We are proposing an expanded Job Corps. And we're combining classroom learning with on-the-job training. The School-to-Work Opportunities Act will tie the classroom to work-based learning during the last two years of high school and for at least a year after graduation.

We will help move the poor from welfare to work, and help them stay at work. The President's welfare reform proposal will provide child care, job retraining, and, where necessary, transitional employment.

Finally, we're converting the unemployment system into a genuine re-employment system. The Administration is proposing legislation to create "one stop" job centers providing not only unemployment checks but also job-search assistance, job counseling, and up-to-date job information. Jobless workers who want to start their own businesses will be able to do so without giving up unemployment benefits. Lump-sum benefits will be available to those who get jobs quickly. And regardless of why a person loses his or her old job, he or she will receive up to a year and a half of instruction in competitive job skills, backed by extended unemployment benefits.

Programs Can Work

I've seen evidence that programs can work and produce results. In Sunnyvale, California, the NOVA program provides a one-stop center where displaced workers have successfully upgraded their skills and gotten back on the job.

I've been to Baltimore, where a program called Baltimore Works has succeeded in identifying and profiling displaced workers early and matching their skills to real job opportunities in the area. The program provides comprehensive services that help workers prepare for, and get, their next job.

I've been to Louisville, where the Job Link Center brings together business, labor, education and community groups to evaluate workers' needs, provide them new skills, and help them find new work.

These efforts, which are springing up around the country, show that we can make programs work—that we can do the right things to get Americans working.

Beyond Simplistic Caricatures

Too often in American politics, the debate over government programs has been a collision of two philosophical caricatures—opposite in direction, equally simplistic. One perspective, often associated with Republicans and conservatives, holds that the difficulty of making programs work justifies surrendering all hope for making government a force for good in people's lives. The other perspective, often associated with Democrats and liberals, holds that the nobility of a program's intentions justifies surrendering responsibility for results.

Both these ideologies, I believe, amount to a retreat from the hard, vital work of designing programs that deliver. And neither is worthy of America's workers and families. They expect better. They deserve better.

If we are truly to make the fundamental changes Americans seem to crave, we must get beyond this sterile, childish game of "government-works-no-it-doesn't-yes-it-does." We must respect the real need for helping Americans navigate their workforce transitions, and respect the evidence about what's working and what's not. And we must accept the burden of proof in spending the taxpayer's hard-earned money, and recognize that effective programs require clear-eyed, relentless assessment and reform.

Where a program works and meets a real need, we'll make it happen. Where it doesn't, we'll eliminate it. And where it's broken, we'll fix it. Build on what's working, get rid of what's not.

"Most studies . . . demonstrate that retraining has little effect in raising wages."

Training Programs May Not Benefit U.S. Workers

John B. Judis

In the following viewpoint, John B. Judis questions the effective-ness of job training programs—specifically retraining for workers displaced by free trade practices, technological advances, and corporate downsizing. To support his position, Judis, a Washing-ton correspondent for *In These Times*, a liberal news and opinion magazine in Chicago, Illinois, cites a study that concludes that one retraining program (Trade Adjustment Assistance) does not improve the employment and wage rates of its participants. Moreover, the retraining concept is based on the assumption that the demand for high-skill workers is growing, while in fact, Judis contends, the demand for such workers is declining.

As you read, consider the following questions:

1. According to the study by Mathematica Policy Research, cited by Judis, why did workers who received Trade Adjustment Assistance training fare worse than those who merely received unemployment insurance?
2. Why will retraining not help middle-aged workers, according to the author?
3. What responsibility does Judis say the government is avoiding by promoting retraining?

Retraining for dislocated workers has become the clarion call of the Clinton administration's program on jobs and wages. It's the answer to workers who feel the White House doesn't care about runaway factories or about the growing disparity between economic classes. It's also the answer to liberal critics who charge that the administration has betrayed its promise of public investment.

As Secretary of Labor Robert Reich explained during a congressional hearing on the effects of the North American Free Trade Agreement (NAFTA): "In order that Americans embrace the challenge of change, in order that Americans reduce [their] feelings of anxiety . . . it is absolutely necessary [to create] a comprehensive program for dealing with dislocated workers, regardless of cost." . . .

According to Reich, who is the administration's spokesman on these matters, retraining is designed to accomplish two important objectives. First, it is supposed to provide better, higher-wage jobs for workers who lose their jobs because of imports, NAFTA, automation, or corporate downsizing. Second, it is expected to generally reduce unemployment by allowing workers to satisfy the rising demand for highly skilled employees.

Argues Reich: "Technology is demanding and rewarding people who can solve and identify problems. Less and less are people being rewarded for their muscle or their stamina. More and more they're being rewarded for their ability to solve and identify problems."

Retraining Has Little Effect

But is Reich correct? There is no question that worker training can be useful, especially on the job. But the administration may be vastly overstating the importance of retraining—both in its ability to increase the wages of dislocated workers and to mute the threat of structural unemployment.

Reich says, "All of the studies show that if you get long-term training, a year or more, you're going to affect your future incomes by increasing that future income by an average of 5 to 6 percent." Experts I consulted disagree. Said one government official who specializes in labor demographics, "Reich wouldn't know a study if it came and bit him on the nose."

Most studies show exactly the opposite of what the labor secretary claims: they demonstrate that retraining has little effect in raising wages. The most important study was done for the Labor Department itself by Mathematica Policy Research Inc., a highly respected research group from Princeton. The results were submitted in April 1993 and were officially made public in the fall of 1993, but when I asked the Labor Department for a copy, officials claimed that the department had only one copy in the entire building. I finally secured a copy from the research organization itself. After reading the report, I could understand why the Labor Department was not eager to hand it out.

The Failure of TAA

Mathematica Policy Research studied the training program instituted under the Trade Expansion Act of 1962. In exchange for labor union support for tariff reductions, the Kennedy administration established a program of Trade Adjustment Assistance (TAA). The program gave Trade Readjustment Allowances (TRAs) to workers who could demonstrate that they were laid off because of imports. Workers were encouraged to use these grants for training, but many did not. To fix this problem, the 1988 Omnibus Trade and Competitiveness Act required TRA recipients to participate in a retraining program unless none was available.

Toles. Copyright 1994 *The Buffalo News*. Reprinted with permission of Universal Press Syndicate. All rights reserved.

The research group discovered, however, that even after training, TRA recipients failed to maintain their former living standards. "More than three-quarters of the re-employed TRA recipients earned less in their new job three years after their initial unemployment insurance claim than they did in their pre-layoff job," the study found.

Moreover, the study found that manufacturing workers who received TRA training actually *fared worse* than those who merely received unemployment insurance. "Wage losses were significantly higher among TRA recipients than among unemployment insurance exhaustees," according to the study.

The study found that TRA recipients who were retrained actually "received slightly lower wages on average than those who had not participated in training." Mathematica Policy says this is because "TRA trainees were more likely to have switched industry or occupation on their new job, and industry- and occupation-switchers suffered greater wage and benefit losses than did stayers."

The study concluded, "We did not find strong evidence that training had a substantial positive effect on employment and earnings, at least in the first three years after the initial unemployment insurance claim."

This study's conclusions directly undermine Reich's case. And retraining under TAA is the most important and relevant government training program to look at. It was designed for the same group of workers Clinton and Reich want to help with their new training efforts.

A Gross Oversimplification

Reich and the administration's argument is also based on a broader fallacy about the relation between wages and training. Reich argues that the growing wage gap between workers with only high school educations and workers with college diplomas is caused by a mismatch of skills: too many semi-skilled workers are seeking too few jobs, while too few college-educated workers are available for positions that require advanced training. Retraining laid-off manufacturing workers will therefore lead them to get jobs at higher wages, the theory goes.

But the theory doesn't fit the reality of jobs and wages. It's a gross oversimplification to deduce that the growing salary gap between high school- and college-educated workers means that a laid-off 45-year-old worker can substantially raise his or her salary by taking one year of intensive training. In reality, that middle-aged worker—now with the equivalent of a year in community college—will be competing in the job market against 20-year-olds who require fewer benefits, are subject to fewer illnesses and disabilities, and are likely to be capable of working longer shifts and more days.

Even on a more general level, Reich's argument doesn't fit the facts. First, there has not been—and will not be—a surplus of high-skill jobs awaiting workers who undergo training. According to Daniel Hecker of the Bureau of Labor Statistics (BLS), writing in the June 1992 *Monthly Labor Review*, one in five college graduates during the '80s ended up working at a job that *did not require a college degree*. That's compared to one in 10 during the '70s. Hecker concludes that during the '80s, "an oversupply of college graduates existed."

In the same issue, BLS researcher Kristina Shelley writes that employment projections for the 1990–2005 period indicate that "average annual openings in jobs requiring a [college] degree will be fewer than the opportunities available in the 1984–90 period." Meanwhile, the number of annual college graduates is expected to grow. This suggests that, if anything, the wages of college-educated workers can be expected to decline or remain stagnant over the next decade.

On the other side, the wages of workers with high school diplomas fell precipitously—12.7 percent from 1979 to 1989—but not because of an oversupply of blue-collar employees. As Larry Katz, the Labor Department's chief economist, has argued, the fall in working-class wages has been primarily due to the shift from higher-paying manufacturing jobs to lower-paying service jobs—and to the 15 percent decline in union membership. In the past, unionized workers have typically earned 25 percent more than their non-unionized counterparts.

A "Field of Dreams" Approach

Retraining is far from futile, and there are many reasons to go to college besides vocational education. But by imputing miracles to education and retraining, the administration is avoiding its responsibility to create jobs for workers and not merely to create workers for jobs. Writing in the summer 1993 *Issues in Science and Technology*, Ruy Teixeira and Larry Mishel call the administration's strategy a "field of dreams approach to the jobs issue: If we build the workers, jobs will come."

What the studies of training show is that if the administration wants to retrain workers, then it had better make sure those workers have something to do after they receive their diplomas and certificates. . . . And if Clinton and Reich want to raise working-class wages—while strengthening the Democratic Party—they better figure out how to halt the decline of the labor movement.

Periodical Bibliography

The following articles have been selected to supplement the diverse views presented in this chapter.

James Bovard — "Clinton's Summer Jobs Sham," *The Wall Street Journal*, March 5, 1993.

The CQ Researcher — "Worker Retraining," January 21, 1994. Available from 1414 22nd St. NW, Washington, DC 20037.

Larry Cuban — "Are Public Schools to Blame?" *Rethinking Schools*, Summer 1993. Available from 1001 E. Keefe Ave., Milwaukee, WI 53212.

Hans Decker — "Dual System for Vocational Education," *Vital Speeches of the Day*, May 15, 1991.

Nathan Glazer — "A Human Capital Policy for the Cities," *The Public Interest*, Summer 1993.

Janet S. Hansen — "Making Sense of Worker Training," *Issues in Science and Technology*, Winter 1993-94.

Paul Harrington — "Market Demands Higher Education," *Insight on the News*, July 4, 1994. Available from 3600 New York Ave. NE, Washington, DC 20002.

James J. Heckman — "Is Job Training Oversold?" *The Public Interest*, Spring 1994.

Bob Herbert — "America's Job Disaster," *The New York Times*, December 1, 1993.

International Economic Insights — "The Global Workforce: Toward the 21st Century," September/October 1992. Available from 11 Dupont Cir. NW, Washington, DC 20036-1207.

David A. Kaplan — "Dumber Than We Thought," *Newsweek*, September 20, 1993.

Edwin Kiester Jr. — " 'Germany Prepares Kids for Good Jobs; We Were Preparing Ours for Wendy's,' " *Smithsonian*, March 1993.

Paul Krugman — "The Myth of Competitiveness," *Harper's Magazine*, June 1994.

Jay Mathews — "Helping Students Work It Out," *The Washington Post National Weekly Edition*, March 21-27, 1994.

George McGovern

"'Good' Jobs Start at the Entry Level," *Los Angeles Times*, November 10, 1992.

Ann McLaughlin

"Help Wanted: Crisis in the Work Force," *Vital Speeches of the Day*, January 15, 1992.

National Alliance of Business

"How School to Work Works for Business: A Report on Business Involvement in School to Work," May 1994. Available from 1201 New York Ave. NW, Suite 700, Washington, DC 20005-3917.

Lewis J. Perelman

"Academic Bubble Handicaps Economy," *Insight on the News*, July 4, 1994.

Virginia I. Postrel

"Training Wreck," *Reason*, December 1992.

Robert B. Reich

"Jobs: Skills Before Credentials," *The Wall Street Journal*, February 2, 1994.

Robert B. Reich

"Workers of the World, Get Smart," *The New York Times*, July 20, 1993.

Hobart Rowen

"Reich's Solution," *The Washington Post National Weekly Edition*, January 10-16, 1994.

Michael A. Stoll

"Teaching Trades," *Dollars & Sense*, November/December 1993.

Frank Swoboda

"Teaching Tomorrow's Work Force," *The Washington Post National Weekly Edition*, March 21-27, 1994.

Ruy A. Teixeira and Lawrence Mishel

"Whose Skills Shortage—Workers or Management?" *Issues in Science and Technology*, Summer 1993.

Rick Wartzman

"Learning by Doing," *The Wall Street Journal*, May 19, 1992.

Should Government Intervene in the Job Market?

Work

Chapter Preface

In March 1993, *Time* magazine reported that Manpower Inc., a temporary employment agency, was "the largest private employer in America." This observation illustrates one of the most dramatic employment trends of the 1990s: the rapid growth in the number of temporary, part-time, freelance, and contract workers—collectively referred to as the "contingent" workforce. *Time* states that in 1988 one-fourth of the labor force consisted of contingent workers and that by 2000 the number could be one-half.

Many argue that the growth of the contingent workforce is the result of too much government intervention in the labor market. Critics contend that the costs of providing employees with increasing government-mandated benefits are becoming too great for companies (especially small businesses) to bear; in order to avoid these costs, businesses are forced to use contingent workers, who are not entitled to most benefits. For example, a company with more than fifty employees falls under the jurisdiction of the Family and Medical Leave Act of 1993 and is thus required by law to provide certain benefits to its workers. Claire Ansberry of the *Wall Street Journal* writes that "by turning to temporary agencies, smaller employers may fall below the magic number and be exempt from providing those benefits."

Others believe that more government intervention in the labor market would benefit the contingent workforce. These critics attribute the growth of the contingent workforce to corporate greed and indifference to workers. By using contingent workers, argues Camille Colatosti, a writer for *Labor Notes*, companies seek to create "a vulnerable and cheap work force—one that makes do with little job security." Trade unionist Chuck Williams agrees that the increasing use of contingent employees is a deliberate attempt on the part of businesses to exploit workers by providing them with low wages and no benefits. In response, he urges that labor laws and government regulations be reformed so that contingent workers are guaranteed basic benefits, rights, and inclusion in the bargaining process.

The growth of the contingent workforce has changed the way millions of Americans work and earn a living. The government's responsibility for this development is one of the issues discussed in the following chapter on government intervention in the job market.

"Patterns of unemployment in current American society reflect the distinct impact of outdated public policy decisions."

Government Intervention Causes Unemployment

Lowell Gallaway and Richard Vedder

Throughout the twentieth century, the federal government has instituted various fiscal, monetary, and public policies intended to stabilize the U.S. economy. In the following viewpoint, Lowell Gallaway and Richard Vedder argue that these government interventions have consistently resulted in economic downturns, including high levels of unemployment. Moreover, the authors assert that the long-term effect of these governmental intrusions into the marketplace is a rise in the "natural" rate of unemployment—the rate below which unemployment cannot go without causing serious inflation. Gallaway and Vedder are the authors of *Out of Work: Unemployment and Government in Twentieth-Century America.*

As you read, consider the following questions:

1. What is the theory of "underconsumptionism," according to the authors?
2. According to Gallaway and Vedder, what six types of public policy account for the origins of the rise in the "natural" rate of unemployment?
3. What segments of the population do the authors say have been hurt the most by government intervention?

From Lowell Gallaway and Richard Vedder, "What Causes Unemployment?" This article appeared in the June 1994 issue and is reprinted with permission from *The World & I*, a publication of The Washington Times Corporation, copyright ©1994.

Whenever there is a business cycle downturn in the United States, such as we have been experiencing in the early 1990s, pressure mounts for government to do something. Several things account for this situation. First is the American conviction that anything can be made better if we just put our minds to it. This is the ethic of perpetual progress. Second, numerous twentieth-century developments have greatly enhanced the possibility of government intervention in the economy. Once relatively small, with a limited capacity to influence the economy, government has been transformed into a behemoth capable of dramatically altering the course of economic events.

Together, these developments have fundamentally altered the psychology of the relationship between government, the public, and the economy. Among the populace there has been an increasing tendency to look toward government for the solution to any economic difficulties. Thus, as the twentieth century has unfolded, people have become prone to assigning to the government responsibility for what happens to themselves and the economy, whether it be at the national, state, or local level. Of course, viewing government, in the abstract, as being responsible for the flow of economic events means attributing to the people in charge, particularly those holding elective office, the blame or credit for what happens. This affects the behavior of actual and would-be public servants. . . .

Inevitably, a situation of this sort shifts the emphasis in economic policy-making toward short-run problems and outcomes. What becomes important is today—not tomorrow. For the typical citizen, the attitude becomes "What have you done for me lately?" For the economic policymaker in the political arena, the focus becomes the short-run one of doing something now to assist in either acquiring or maintaining power. Historical perspective, the long view, becomes less and less significant. Worse yet, when historical events are considered, they are interpreted to fit the demands of the short run.

Early Government Intervention

Nowhere is the effect of this sequence of events better illustrated than in twentieth-century America, in the history of government policies that affect unemployment. There has been a trend toward greater amounts of government intervention. The move in this direction began early in the century. After the economic downturn that drove the unemployment rate to 8 percent in 1908, agitation for the creation of a central bank became intense. The result was the Federal Reserve System, created in 1913 for the specific purpose of stabilizing the economy by controlling movements in the supply of money.

How successful was it in this respect? Not very. In the first ten

58

years of its existence, annual growth in the money supply ranged from a negative 12 percent to a positive 30 percent. Of particular importance were the events during and immediately following World War I. In the five-year period 1917–21, the annual rate of growth in the money supply ranged from plus 16.2 percent in 1917 to minus 8.9 percent in 1921. The result of these wild swings in money-supply growth was an interval of severe price inflation, followed by a sharp deflation.

These gyrations in prices triggered an economic downturn. The reasons are very simple. Important determinants of whether business is profitable are the cost of labor, the productivity of labor, and the prices at which labor's output is sold. The inflation during World War I had pulled up wage rates. When the sudden deflation of 1920–21 came, it was something of a surprise, and wages did not adjust downward immediately. Nor were the price declines fully compensated for by increases in the productivity of labor. Profits were squeezed, employment fell, and unemployment rose. In short, the relationship between wages, prices, and productivity had become discoordinated as the result of the substantial swings in prices. The business cycle that followed was a sharp one. Unemployment averaged 11.7 percent in 1921. Wage rates adjusted downward, however, and the unemployment rate fell, first to 6.7 percent in 1922 and then to 2.4 percent in 1923.

Inherent Mischief

The 1920–22 business cycle is the first major example of the potential for mischief that is inherent in government attempts to manage the national economy. Although market adjustments resolved the immediate problem, the experience of 1920–22 was to have a substantial effect on public policy when the next significant economic downturn occurred. What was particularly important was the interpretation ultimately imposed upon the 1920–22 business cycle by people who would be quite influential in years to come. The tendency was to blame the severity of the cycle on the rigors of the marketplace. Then Secretary of Commerce Herbert Hoover was especially impressed by this event, viewing the adjustment process that produced the economic recovery as the "liquidation" of labor, which he opposed on humanitarian grounds.

Reactions such as Hoover's would become commonplace in the remainder of the twentieth century. If an act of government intervention in the economy produced unanticipated and unwelcome results, some other factor or institution, more often than not the marketplace, was assigned responsibility for the undesired events; thus the stage was set for even more extensive government intervention at the next sign of an economic problem.

59

The crisis of 1920–22 was found unacceptable by many people who had just witnessed a substantial amount of government intrusion into the national economy during World War I. It seemed almost natural to carry over the planning mentality that marked the war period into the postwar era. Consequently, for all that the adjustment process of 1920–22 provided a striking testimonial to the effectiveness of market mechanisms in correcting a fundamental problem, its aftermath saw a turning away from the type of adjustment mechanism that required reductions in wage rates to reduce the unemployment created by government's attempts at stabilizing the economy.

Reprinted by permission of Chuck Asay and Creators Syndicate.

In its place was substituted just the opposite view of the role of wage rates in the economy. Hoover, industrialists such as Henry Ford and Edward Filene, social commentators W.T. Foster and W. Catchings, intellectuals such as John Hobson, labor union leaders, and others embraced the idea that employment could be increased by the simple act of raising wage rates, rather than lowering them. The idea was very simple. Wages represent purchasing power, and greater purchasing power means more goods produced and more workers hired. Known as *underconsumptionism*, the idea is an appealing one for many, but it ignores the fact that wages are the major cost of producing goods and services. Nevertheless, it became a popular notion subsequent to the 1920–22 business cycle.

Underconsumptionist thinking had little impact on the American economy through 1929. There had been a very mild business cycle that showed a peak unemployment rate of 5.0 percent in 1924. This did not afford much of an opportunity for government intervention. When the pace of economic activity began to decline late in 1929, however, things were different. The underconsumptionist view of the world came to the fore. The immediate cause of the economic downturn was a combination of an unexpected fall in prices, attributable in large part to actions of the Federal Reserve that slowed the rate of growth in the money supply, and a decrease in the average productivity of labor. The productivity decline may well have resulted from previous actions of the Federal Reserve, which led businessmen to make inappropriate investments in productive facilities.

The Great Depression

At the first indications of the economic downturn, public policy actions of an underconsumptionist nature were taken. In late 1929, President Hoover convened conferences of business leaders and urged them not to cut wages. His argument was the by-then familiar one that reducing wages would decrease purchasing power and just make things worse. All the evidence indicates that he was successful in his efforts. In 1930, wage rates were about 8 percent greater than they would have been if adjustments of the type that occurred during the 1920–22 business cycle had taken place. That wages had been kept unusually high during a business cycle downturn was widely recognized. Business leaders, the press, labor union officials, and scholars all made this observation.

In effect, what the United States had done in response to the economic decline that began in late 1929 was conduct a controlled experiment to test the validity of the underconsumptionist idea. The result was a disaster. As wage rates remained high while prices and labor productivity were falling, business profits all but disappeared. With profits in decline, making loans to business became riskier for banks. Interest rates rose, and the value of various claims on business held by commercial banks deteriorated sharply. This weakened the banking system and led to a secondary collapse of prices beginning in 1931. New investment in capital facilities became almost nonexistent, and the total stock of capital available to the economy began to contract. What had seemed to be a moderately severe recession had become the most traumatic economic event of American history, the Great Depression of the 1930s.

61

There was a lesson to be learned from this experience. Apparently, the underconsumptionist approach to stimulating economic activity does not work very well. Yet, in the wake of its obvious failure, the responsibility for the debacle of the 1930s was laid at the feet of the market mechanism. The inability of markets to override the impact of the meddling that characterized the initial years of the Great Depression still is widely interpreted as providing definitive evidence of the inability of market adjustments to produce economic recovery. . . .

Government Activism and Unemployment

A brief description of the relationship between public policy and levels of unemployment in twentieth-century America indicates that periods during which government played an active role in managing the economy alternated with periods in which it did not. It is worthwhile to observe the effects of these cycles of activism and nonactivism on the severity of business cycles. The first two unemployment peaks in the century, those of 1908 and 1915, occurred in a relatively nonactivist era. The unemployment rates in these two years were 8.0 and 8.5 percent, respectively.

The next cycle, 1920–22, is an activist-induced one with a peak unemployment rate of 11.7 percent in 1921. There follows a nonactivist cycle in which the unemployment rate rises to 5.0 percent in 1924. Then come the two major downturns associated with the activist era of the Great Depression, the slide from 1929 through 1933, during which unemployment rose from 3.2 to 24.9 percent, and the 1938 recession, which saw unemployment rise from 14.3 percent in 1937 to 19.0 percent in 1938. Next are the relatively nonactivist cycle troughs of 1946, 1949,1954,1958, and 1961, with their respective peak annual average unemployment rates of 3.9, 5.9, 5.5, 6.8, and 6.7 percent, respectively. Finally, we have the cycle downturns that may be attributed to government actions during the last great activist era, those of 1970–71, 1974–75, 1980–81, and 1982. The peak annual average unemployment rates during these cycles are 5.9, 8.5, 7.6, and 9.7 percent, respectively.

There is an obvious pattern in these cycles. The four that show the highest peak unemployment rates, 1929–33, 1937–38, 1920–21, and 1981–82, all may be traced in some substantial way to the effects of governmental activism. In the case of the fifth-largest unemployment peak, there is a tie between a year from an activist-era cycle, 1975, and one from a nonactivist cycle, 1915. Clearly, the periods in which governmental influence on aggregate economic events was strongest are those marked by the poorest economic performance. As far as the business cycle is concerned, a strong case can be made that government intervention in the economy has made things worse, not better.

62

There is more to the impact of government intervention on levels of unemployment than its influence on the magnitude of business cycles. The trend through time toward greater government involvement in economic affairs has produced some important long-term effects. The business cycle is the short run, and that has been the primary emphasis in public policy. This is reflected in John Maynard Keynes' famous dictum that in the long run we are all dead. That remark is only partially correct. Long runs do come, and when they arrive they are greeted by large numbers of people who are still alive and who are forced to deal with the consequences of the short-run–oriented policy decisions of the past. Thus it is that defunct academic scribblers and political dilettantes from distant ages continue to wield their influence on contemporary life, more often than not for the worse.

Unemployment and Public Policy

Unemployment is a striking example of this. The level and patterns of unemployment in current American society reflect the distinct impact of outdated public policy decisions, some taken more than a half century ago. Go back in time once more, to the early years of the century, to the years before government intervention in the economy began to rear its head, to the years before the Great Depression. Typically, unemployment was in the 4 to 4.5 percent range, with extreme values of 1.4 and 11.7 percent. The Great Depression decade (1930–39) is, most certainly, an aberration from the long-term trend in unemployment, and thus it is appropriate to disregard this period when assessing what has happened since 1929. Picking up the long-term unemployment story after the Great Depression had largely run its course, the normal unemployment experience of the 1940s and '50s is not measurably different from that of the pre-Depression decades. Thereafter, however, the typical (or median) unemployment rate begins to drift upward over the next three decades, a half percentage point in the 1960s, another percentage point in the '70s, and an additional 1.3 percentage points in the '80s. Systematically, the equilibrium, or "natural," rate of unemployment has been creeping upward for at least a quarter century.

The origins of the rise in the "natural" rate of unemployment can be traced to a wide variety of public policies that have significantly affected the labor market behavior of individuals in the United States. The legislation establishing collective bargaining between employers and workers as national policy, prevailing wage laws, the establishment of the Social Security system, unemployment compensation programs, minimum wage laws, and the whole apparatus of the modern welfare state have combined to make people more selective in their search for jobs, driving upward the unemployment rate that is recorded through our data collection process. Today, the usual unemployment rate is perhaps 50 percent greater than it was for the bulk of this century. In fact, the median unemployment rate for the 1980s is about 65 percent higher than that for the '50s. This increase in the natural rate of unemployment represents a pure deadweight loss to the economy. This is ironic, given that so many of the public policies that produced it were justified at the time of their enactment by underconsumptionist arguments. They were supposed to be a positive stimulus to economic activity but have been just the opposite.

Intervention and Unemployment Differentials

The effect of government policies on the structure of unemployment is equally disconcerting. For example, prior to the development of the modern welfare state, there were no meaningful racial differentials in unemployment. Throughout the postwar era, however, unemployment among nonwhites systematically has exceeded that among whites, currently by a ratio of more than two to one. Particularly striking has been the deterioration in the relative unemployment position of young black males. In 1954, the first year in which annual unemployment data are available by race and age-group, the unemployment rate for white males aged 16–19 was 13.4 percent. The similar rate for nonwhites was 14.4 percent.

Eighteen years later, in 1972, the unemployment rate for white males aged 16–19 stood at 14.2 percent, 0.8 of a percentage point higher than in 1954. This was the first year in which data became available for blacks as a separate group, rather than for all nonwhites. The rate for black males aged 16–19 was 31.7 percent, more than twice the 1954 rate for nonwhites. Similarly, the female-male unemployment differential grew in the immediate postwar era, although to a lesser extent.

Clearly, government not only has aggravated the problem of unemployment for twentieth-century Americans but has done so differentially. The biggest losers from government intervention have been the very people advocates of activism claim need the most help—nonwhites, women, and unskilled, inexperienced youths. The strong, skilled, and comparatively affluent have managed to adjust to government intervention, although not without cost. Meanwhile, the primary burden of the welfare state has fallen inordinately on those it was supposed to benefit the most.

The Economy of the 1990s

How pertinent is this discussion to the American economy of the 1990s? Given the historical record of extended periods of government activism interspersed with relatively brief periods of nonactivism, it is not improbable to speculate that the swings in the pendulum that brought the relatively nonactivist era of the 1980s into being would bring yet another activist period, during which there would be a move to "do something" about unemployment. Events often move swiftly in the arena of public policy, and this is one of those times. The public rhetoric associated with the relatively mild recession that began in mid-1990 has been escalating rapidly . . . , raising the possibility of a renewed sense of urgency about the national economy, one that will create a consensus supporting government intervention to manage and stabilize it.

The record of the results of attempting such "managing" during this century . . . has been described. It shows that the methods used in the past to shape the course of economic events will not work. Therefore, if we attempt to provide central direction to the national economy, the disappointments that inevitably will be encountered could produce a demand for new departures in economic interventionism, such as some form of industrial policy or, even worse, wage, price, and incomes control. There is no end to the possible forms of mischief that can be practiced in the name of stabilizing the economy. It is well to reiterate the two important lessons that emerge from the history of public policy of this sort. First, previous public policy failures in the realm of economic stabilization generally have been used as the basis for arguing that even greater power to control and manage is required. Second, whenever nonintervention has produced relatively stable outcomes, the pro-interventionists either have interpreted the results as a triumph of government management or have argued that we could do even better if we added some measure of central direction to the policy mix. Sometimes they have adopted both these positions. Whatever the result, the statists in our midst are capable of interpreting it as the rationale for an extension of the government's role in manipulating the economy.

This raises the possibility that the United States, in the early 1990s, is standing on the threshold of a new era of government activism in managing the economy, despite the historical evidence that tells us that such interventionism is doomed to failure, and despite the fact that throughout the twentieth century, the invisible hand of the unfettered market mechanism has consistently outperformed efforts of the highly visible hand of the state in providing economic stability. If that is the case, the coming years almost certainly will add one more example to the already vast collection of incidents that validate [American poet and philosopher] George Santayana's injunction that "those who cannot remember the past are condemned to repeat it."

"Public policies involving full employment and investment will complement and reinforce one another."

Government Intervention Can Foster Full Employment

Wallace C. Peterson

Between 1973 and 1993, according to Wallace C. Peterson, the average American standard of living worsened due to a decline in the number of good jobs and a rise in the unemployment rate. In the following viewpoint, Peterson argues that in response to these trends, the government should institute a "full-employment" policy that provides incentives for companies to create good jobs, offers apprenticeship and job-training programs, and establishes an incomes policy to curb inflation. In addition, Wallace advocates a public infrastructure investment program to create jobs and spur private investment. Peterson is a professor of economics at the University of Nebraska in Lincoln.

As you read, consider the following questions:

1. How does Peterson define a "good job"?
2. What fundamental lesson from John Maynard Keynes does the author cite?
3. According to Peterson, how does an incomes policy work?

Wallace C. Peterson, "Full-Employment Goal Called Realistic Policy," *Forum for Applied Research and Public Policy*, Winter 1993. (Footnotes in the original article have not been included in this reprint.) Reprinted with permission.

Writing in the *New York Times Magazine*, Elliott Liebow, an anthropologist, said, "Work is not only the fundamental condition of human existence, but it is through work . . . that the individual is able to define himself as a full and valued member of society. It is almost impossible to think of what it means to be human without thinking of work."

Liebow's remark underscores a dimension of work missing from conventional economic analysis, where labor is viewed as one of several "factors of production," or a means to the larger end of more output. Viewing work and labor not only as a factor of production, but as something through which people achieve self-expression and self-realization, changes the role that work plays in the economic system.

Economic analysis traditionally views work as irksome, involving "disutility," which must be overcome by wages to secure the labor needed for the production of goods and services. Goods and services have "utility" because they satisfy human wants.

If work, as Liebow suggests, meets a deep human need it must possess utility as well as disutility. Thus, opportunity for productive and useful work is something that the economy should produce, just as it should produce useful goods and services. The work that people do, the conditions under which they work, and the income and benefits they receive from work are worthy economic ends.

"Good Jobs–Bad Jobs"

The nature of the work that the economy ought to produce is a complex question. A useful departure point is the idea of a "good job," as this term is used in the "good jobs–bad jobs controversy" [described by Frank S. Levy and Richard C. Michel]. A good job, in brief, is one that pays enough to support a middle-class standard of living, including a single-family home, one or more cars, paid vacations, job security with a pension and medical care, and an expectation of steady improvement in the family's standard of living.

From the perspective of both "good jobs"and the general level of job creation, the economy not only did badly during the 1990–1991 recession but has done badly since the early 1970s.

Since 1973, the buying power of the average weekly wage for American workers has dropped by 17.6 percent, a major cause for the increasing number of wives and mothers entering the work force. Working wives and mothers, in fact, saved the real income of the typical American family from declining over the past two decades. What's more, median family income measured in constant dollars in 1991 was a mere 3.4 percent higher than in 1973. At the annual rate of increase behind this change (0.19 percent), it would take nearly 250 years for constant-dollar family income to double. No wonder that persons in the "twenty-something" generation doubt they will ever attain their parents' standard of living.

Job Loss and Unemployment

Two major developments account for these dismal trends. One is the persistent loss of jobs in manufacturing, once a major source of "good jobs" for young, non-college-educated, male workers. In April 1993, there were 10.2 percent fewer jobs in manufacturing than in 1973, although the total number of nonagricultural jobs increased by 42.2 percent in the same period. Between 1973 and 1991, output of goods, which includes construction and mining plus manufacturing, increased by 41.6 percent, but labor employed in goods production fell by 2.8 percent.

These figures show that there have been significant productivity gains in manufacturing and the production of other goods, but they also underscore a basic problem that centers on productivity gains in the contemporary economy. Most of the more than 2 million workers who lost "good jobs" in manufacturing since 1973 have not gone on to better-paying jobs in the service sectors of the economy. On the contrary, as a 1988 Senate report indicates, slightly more than 50 percent of newly created jobs in the 1980s paid wages below the poverty level.

Historically, increases in productivity in one sector have released workers for employment in other sectors where demand is growing, resulting in higher wages and incomes. This process seems to have broken down, raising fears of a Luddite scenario in which rapid technological changes boost productivity but also displace workers into [what Douglas Copeland calls] "McJobs"—positions of low pay, low dignity, low benefits, and no future—or, even worse, permanent unemployment.

The second development is a slow but persistent rise in the rate of civilian unemployment, reflecting the failure of the nation to pursue an active policy of full employment since the end of the 1960s. During the quarter-century after the end of World War II, unemployment averaged 4.6 percent, slightly higher than the "full-employment" target of 4 percent set by the Kennedy administration in 1962. Since 1973, unemployment has averaged 6.6 percent.

Following the officially proclaimed "end" of the recession in March 1991, unemployment climbed to a peak of 7.7 percent in June 1992. By May 1993, the rate had fallen to only 6.9 percent. These statistics led observers to describe the years 1992–1993 as "the jobless recovery." If we adjust for the more than 1 million persons who have dropped out of the labor force in recent years because they cannot find jobs, and the approximately 6 million people working part time who want to work full time, the nation's real unemployment rate lies somewhere between 10 and 12 percent.

Beyond these developments, extensive changes have taken place in the workplace that threaten to undermine deeply held attitudes about work in America. Among these are the beliefs that performance should be rewarded, that loyalty between the employee and employer should be cherished, that workers should be a valued and vital part of any enterprise, and that both employees and employers should share a long-term commitment to the enterprise of which they are a part.

Government Intervention to Create Jobs

In order to create permanent public jobs, government should be allowed to enter domains of manufacturing, service and welfare in which it would compete with private companies and nonprofit agencies. This might be a particularly good idea when and where government can be more labor-intensive than the private sector, and at least equally productive and socially useful. . . .

Needless to say, all the imaginative ways of dealing with the labor surplus require more government intervention in the economy. Since such intervention helped make the American economy great in the first place, it could do so again in the future.

Herbert J. Gans, *The Nation*, September 20, 1993.

Reality often falls short of these ideals, yet they represent values underlying the commitment to full-time employment by millions of Americans.

This "Norman Rockwell" portrait of work in America is changing under the relentless pressure of technology, corporate restructuring and downsizing, and merciless global competition. *Time* speaks of "disposable workers" and "the temping of America" in describing the thrust toward the part-time and contingent worker.

As corporations restructure and downsize, full-time workers are replaced by part-time or temporary workers, contract workers, or subcontractors who undertake as many business functions as possible. The result is a shrinkage in the size of the business firm's core of permanent workers, which may save the firm money but is often devastating for the employee. Part-time or contingent workers usually lack pensions, health care, paid vacations, and opportunities for promotions and job-training programs. With employer contributions to employee pension plans and private welfare funds equal to 10.6 percent of outlays for wages and salaries, the financial stakes for the employer are sizeable.

The evaporation of good jobs is not a phenomenon limited to the United States. It has been taking place across the globe since 1973 and has been particularly severe among the European members of the Organization for Economic Cooperation and Development (OECD).

Canadian economist John Cornwall of Dalhousie University in Halifax has analyzed the reasons why unemployment has risen more than three-fold in the OECD since the early 1970s, increasing from 9 to 30 million. Cornwall believes that the answer—inadequate demand—stems from the failure after 1973 of most OECD nations to pursue full-employment policies, a failure rooted in the inflationary bias that exists in market economies as they approach full employment.

Fear of inflation led to restrictive polices, which, having failed, left OECD nations beset by chronic "economic breakdown." The repercussions of this breakdown spread across the globe, because the OECD is the locomotive that pulls the rest of the world along, while the United States is the locomotive that pulls OECD. Since estimates show that at least 40 million new jobs must be created worldwide each year to avoid serious upheaval and social unrest, it is vital that the United States take the lead in bringing the world's major market economies out of the economic doldrums, where they have languished since the early 1970s.

Full Employment and Investment

The needs of the U.S. economy are many, but two are particularly important: first, a return to an effective full-employment policy, and, second, a massive investment program. Both these proposals are Keynesian in nature, but they must differ from similar programs attempted in the past.

Since the early 1970s, the public has lost sight of a fundamental lesson from John Maynard Keynes—that public and private investment is the key to job creation in the modern economy. The bad news is that the climate of political opinion, in combination with the early policy fumbles of the Clinton administration, does not bode well for new initiatives.

The good news is that if properly designed and administered, public policies involving full employment and investment will complement and reinforce one another. Further, there is little else on the economic horizon to bring the nation out of the stagnation that has been around since 1973.

Partial blame for the absence of a full-employment policy lies with the Reagan and Bush administrations, as neither president believed in using government's power to pursue actively the goal of full employment. Blame also rests with mainstream economists and their uncritical acceptance of the curious doc-

70

trine called the "natural rate" of unemployment, defined as a rate below which unemployment could not be pushed without causing serious inflation.

In theory, such a rate exists. In the 1970s and 1980s many economists concluded that the natural rate lay somewhere between 5 and 6 percent, leading them to believe there was little the government could do to bring unemployment down without triggering inflation.

In reality, spending for the Vietnam War, followed by the cost upheavals caused by the Arab oil embargoes, led to the double-digit inflation of the 1970s. Beginning in the early 1970s, wage gains ran ahead of productivity advances, leading to a cost-push inflation that policy makers could not handle.

With inflation at low ebb, the time is right to launch a new full-employment initiative—one that does more than simply seek to stimulate aggregate demand in the private sector through personal income tax cuts or investment tax credits. It also must:

- Recognize that the goal of creating good jobs—jobs that carry an income appropriate to middle-class hopes and aspirations—is a vital part of a full-employment policy. The truth is that we know little about how this can be done effectively through public policy—or if it can be done at all—but recognition of the need for quality work as a legitimate end of economic activity is the place to start.
- Change the adversarial, if not openly hostile, atmosphere that dominates labor-management relations in the United States. Companies need to be persuaded that creating good jobs is one of their major roles, a task in which the cooperative effort of organized labor must be enlisted.

  As *Time* noted in its article "The Temping of America," current corporate strategies represent, in effect, disinvestment in the nation's human capital. A modern full-employment policy should encourage firms to understand that a well-trained and loyal work force is a major asset. Policies should be developed that will encourage firms to upgrade and improve the knowledge and technological skill of their employees. These policies should discourage firms from seeking profitability by shedding workers or even closing plants and moving to low-wage areas in Third World countries.

  Fortune magazine has noted that the more innovative U.S. companies are starting to recognize that only firms with highly skilled employees can meet the intense global competition they now face.
- Fill the training gap that now exists between college-bound and non-college-educated future workers. Public policy provides financial support for college students but does little to

help persons make the transition from secondary school to work. Non-college-bound youths usually are left to flounder for five or six years as they search for a place in the labor force. Policies should be developed for apprenticeship programs and productive on-the-job training for the non–college bound, as happens in other industrialized nations.

- Curb the inflationary bias that exists in the modern market economy. Between 1950 and 1992, consumer prices rose by nearly 500 percent, though, over the same period, unemployment averaged almost 6 percent of the civilian labor force. It does not require great theoretical wisdom to realize that if the economy had been at or near full employment during those years, inflation would have been far more severe. The logical implication is that an incomes policy must be a part of a modernized full-employment package; otherwise, efforts to create decent jobs for all persons wanting to work will collapse because of the fear of rampant inflation.

An incomes policy limits monetary income gains—primarily wage and salary gains—to the rate at which worker productivity advances, thus preventing labor costs from becoming the basis for price increases. Though most economists remain hostile to an incomes policy, the "Wage-Price Guideposts" suggested by the Kennedy administration in the early 1960s should be dusted off and made an integral part of a modern full-employment policy.

- Finally, avoid the easy assumption that the high-technology revolution in communications and information activities will solve the problem of good jobs. In this respect, the experience of Omaha, Nebraska, is instructive.

Because of its location and the quality of its telephone service, Omaha, calling itself the "1-800 capital of America," has become a national center for telemarketing, telecommunications, and computer services. The rub is that most of the 20,000 new "high tech" jobs created since 1980 are low paying or part time, with either meager or nonexistent health and pension benefits. Annual earnings for many workers are not more than $12,000 to $15,000 a year, close to the 1990 poverty threshold of $13,359.

Technology underlies productivity gains, which are essential to both economic progress and a future of good jobs. Yet, unless there is a dependable increase in demand for goods and services, technological change may destroy more jobs than it creates. This is why a modern investment program is an essential complement to a modern full-employment policy.

A full-employment policy becomes operational through measures that raise aggregate demand, but the means chosen to achieve this goal are vital. In the brief experience the nation had with a full-employment policy under presidents Lyndon B. Johnson and John F. Kennedy, the focus was on stimulating demand in the private sector, primarily by tax credits to spur investment and tax cuts to stimulate consumption. This is not needed now, especially after the go-go years of the 1980s when consumption spending as a share of the gross domestic product (GDP) rose to the highest level in the post-World War II era.

A part of the price for the nation's consumption binge of the 1980s was a cumulative neglect of public investment—the nation's infrastructure. In current dollars, the nation's shortage of public capital—roads, bridges, sewer and water systems, airports, rail networks, and mass-transit systems—is at least $1 trillion.

Contrary to laments in the business and popular press about insufficient savings, the problem today is not a shortage of private capital. Investment in equipment, measured as a percent of the GDP, has climbed from an average of 5.3 percent in the 1960s to 6.4 percent in the 1970s and to 7.4 percent in the 1980s. What is required is a massive program of public investment to rebuild and modernize the nation's infrastructure.

With the Cold War over, resources for such a program can be provided through major reductions in military spending. A carefully designed program for infrastructure investment also is the best way to make a start on providing jobs with adequate pay for all persons seeking full-time work. What's more—contrary to conventional economic wisdom—infrastructure investment does not crowd out private investment. In fact, over four to five years, every dollar spent on public investment leads to an increase of approximately 45 cents in private investment.

By its nature, an infrastructure investment program will be highly decentralized, since this spending overwhelmingly takes place at the local level. Most of the financing, however, must come from the federal government. This is not a problem, given the long history of federal financing for state and local government activities through grants-in-aid techniques.

Making the connection between a policy of full employment, based upon the creation of good jobs and investment in the nation's neglected infrastructure, is neither unrealistic nor radical. The resources are there, currently locked up in our oversized military establishment.

Most economists understand that an infrastructure-investment program is good economics. Most economists also understand that investment in capital and people is the proper road to full employment and economic growth. But they must enlarge their horizons to include public as well as private investment in the formula.

"Government regulation has now set up a series of trip wires that discourage small businesses from taking on more employees."

Government Regulations Have Created a Contingent Workforce

William Tucker

Since the early 1980s, American companies have reduced their numbers of permanent, full-time workers and have increased their reliance on temporary, contract, and part-time employees—collectively referred to as a "contingent" workforce. In the following viewpoint, William Tucker reports that the growth of this contingent workforce has been encouraged by government regulations such as the Americans with Disabilities Act of 1991 and the Family and Medical Leave Act of 1993 that raise the economic and legal costs to employers of hiring permanent, full-time workers. Tucker is a freelance writer who frequently contributes to *Insight*, the *American Spectator*, and *National Review*.

As you read, consider the following questions:
1. What company does Tucker say is the nation's largest employer?
2. What two problems does the Family and Medical Leave Act of 1993 cause for employers, according to William Styring, quoted by the author?
3. According to Michael Losey, quoted by the author, what is the cost of firing a white-collar employee?

William Tucker, "The Changing Face of America's Work Force," *Insight on the News*, March 14, 1994. Reprinted with permission.

For 20 years, Ralph Reiland and his wife, Sarah McCarthy, have run Amel's, a restaurant serving Middle Eastern cuisine that has been voted "best ethnic restaurant" for the last 7 years by *Pittsburgh* magazine.

In 1993, Reiland was offered the opportunity to buy two other restaurants in Pittsburgh and expand into a chain. After checking out the possibilities, however, Reiland decided to decline.

"We've now got 45 employees," says Reiland. "Expansion would mean nearly doubling our work force. But that would put us over the 50-employee limit that exempts us from the Family [and Medical] Leave Act of 1993. That would make things very difficult for us—especially since no one knows yet what the implications of the law are going to be. We decided it was better to stay small."

"Too Many Regulations"

Some observers detect a sea change in American employment practices. "More and more, companies are starting to see full-time employees as a last resort," says Jeff McGinnis, a policy analyst at the Labor Policy Association, a Washington think tank. "You contract out, you hire part-timers, you do everything to avoid hiring people full time. I don't think it's a healthy trend, but as long as Congress imposes all these new regulations, it's an inevitable reaction."

"We're seeing a lot of companies stuck at 49 employees because they don't want to come under the Family Leave Act," echoes Diane Generous, director of risk management at the National Association of Manufacturers. "Companies are saying, 'We're not going to expand because there are too many regulations.'"...

A Changed Labor Market

Years into an economic recovery, it has become clear that the American labor market has changed significantly. "The size of the American contingent work force . . . has ballooned over the past decade" John Sweeney, president of the Service Employees International Union told a Senate Labor and Human Resources subcommittee at a special conference Feb. 8, 1994. "Today, temporary, contract and part-time employees represent 25 to 30 percent of the entire work force."

The trend is not uniform. Involuntary part-time labor was steady from 1984 to 1994, but the number of voluntary part-time workers increased from 10 million to 16 million. Self-employment figures have shown little change, but the number of independent contractors actually has declined—primarily because of the ferocious effort by the Internal Revenue Service to secure more taxes from independent workers.

Yet one segment of the labor market is booming: temporary

employees—people who work for agencies that coordinate jobs for them. From 1980 to 1993, the number of "temps" quadrupled, from 400,000 to 1.6 million. Temporary employees compose 1.5 percent of the work force. In fact, positions filled by temps represent one out of every six new jobs created between December 1991 and March 1994.

"The early part of a recovery is usually our most explosive period of growth," says Bruce Steinberg, spokesman for the National Association of Temporary Services. "Companies wait to see if the recovery is real before they hire full time. But there are also some apparent government disincentives to creating full-time work."

All this has created a booming business for Manpower, Inc., Kelly Services (the former "Kelly Girl" company) and the 7,000 other large and small companies that contract independent workers to provide temporary services to other employers. And the industry's annual payroll now is $17 billion.

With 650,000 people on its lists, Manpower is the nation's largest employer (although many of the employees work only a few weeks a year). At 575,000 people, Kelly Services is second largest and at 375,000 people, General Motors is third.

The Effects of Family Leave

Temporary-help employment grew 10 times faster than overall employment between 1982 and 1990. In 1992, temporary jobs accounted for about two-thirds of new private-sector jobs. . . . When taken together, temporary, contract and part-time workers now make up about 25% of the work force.

That percentage could grow with the [passage of the] family-leave bill, which forces firms with more than 50 workers to provide extra benefits. By turning to temporary agencies, smaller employers may fall below the magic number and be exempt from providing those benefits. And while many people, especially women with young children, prefer the freedom of a temporary job, an increasing number are forced into it.

Clare Ansberry, *The Wall Street Journal*, March 11, 1993.

Officials at these firms brush aside the suggestion that they are helping eliminate full-time employment. "We are basically in the business of providing jobs for special projects and contingencies," says Sharon Canter, director of strategic information at Manpower's Milwaukee, Wisconsin, headquarters. "Many of our employees use our services as a route to full-time employment."

"People will fire temporary employees first and then hire them back first when the recovery begins," echoes Eugene Hartwig, senior vice president of Kelly Services. "The only difference is that this time there hasn't been as much job creation as in previous recoveries."

The biggest impact has been on the most dynamic job-creating sector of the American economy—small businesses.

"You have to realize that, as far as job growth is concerned, the Fortune 500 hasn't hired anybody in the last 10 years," says William Styring, research director at Indiana Policy Review. "They're all downsizing. All the job growth comes out of small businesses. But government regulation has now set up a series of trip wires that discourage small businesses from taking on more employees. The result is that a lot of businesses decide to stay small."

Barriers to Growth and Full Employment

Styring points to a series of factors that create enormous barriers to business growth and full-time employment:

- At 15 employees, businesses come under the jurisdiction of the Civil Rights Act and the Americans with Disabilities Act.

   Employees commonly use the Civil Rights Act's Title VII to protest termination. "People can claim discrimination because of age, sex, race, national origin, marital status—you name it," says Sue Meisinger, vice president at the Society for Human Resource Management. "If you can breathe, you can file a lawsuit, and if you can't, then you qualify for the Americans with Disabilities Act." Under the Civil Rights Act, a company also can be sued if its work force does not match the ethnic composition of the local community.

   Since 1991, the Americans with Disabilities Act has fast become a weapon used to challenge dismissals. More than 1,000 new cases are filed with the Equal Employment Opportunity Commission each month. Weight problems, bad backs and unspecified mental and emotional disturbances are the most common disabilities. "A fired employee need only say, 'My boss thought I was overweight so he didn't like me,' and he or she can file a complaint," says Meisinger. "The law says an employee must only be 'perceived' to be disabled by his or her employer in order to qualify for protection."

- At 20 employees, businesses are subject to the Age Discrimination in Employment Act of 1967 and the Consolidated Omnibus Budget Reconciliation Act of 1986, which says that employers must carry employees' health insurance for up to 18 months after dismissal. Until the disabilities act, age discrimination was the most commonly cited statute in wrongful termination cases. "Basically, all the applicants are men over age 40," says Meisinger. "There are also a few people under 25 saying they have been discriminated against because of their age."

- At 50 employees, businesses fall under the jurisdiction of the Family and Medical Leave Act of 1993. The legislative centerpiece of President Bill Clinton's first three months in office, the law allows employees to take up to 12 weeks of unpaid leave to tend to family needs and medical emergencies. "One problem is that the employer must continue health benefits," says Styring. "That can be expensive. But it's also very difficult for a smaller company to maintain continuity if people can leave for three months."

- At 100 employees, the Worker Adjustment and Retraining Notification Act applies. This requires employers to give 60 days' notice to employees and local governments before a plant closing or major layoff. The procedure, of course, opens the possibility for challenges and litigation. At 100 employees, a business also must file a special form with the Equal Employment Opportunity Commission that details the company's ethnic, racial and gender makeup, opening the door to much closer inspection and regulation.

"Europeanization"

Ironically, this heavy regulation of the labor market imitates European trends—at a time when European unemployment soars above rates in the United States.

Europe leads the United States in labor-market regulation, according to David Henderson, professor of economics at the Naval Postgraduate School in Monterey, California, whose article, "The Europeanization of the U.S. Labor Market" appeared in the fall 1993 issue of the *Public Interest*. "In many European countries, hiring is controlled by the state," he says. "For example, in Sweden employers must recruit workers through the government, and employment agencies are government-owned. And in Greece and Spain, employers must notify the government about positions within their own firm."

But in other respects, according to Henderson, the United States is approaching Europe in the number of impediments in the labor market. "Unemployment payments and health benefits are still greater in Europe, but many of the restrictions on firing people are becoming similar. As a result, temporary employment is increasing as much in the U.S. as in Europe."

Manpower, Inc. was reborn when a British company acquired it in 1987. In previous decades, Manpower concentrated on providing day laborers to replace sick or vacationing employees at lumberyards. Then the company underwent a hostile takeover by Blue Arrow, a temporary agency that specializes in working around Britain's arcane employment laws. Mitchell Fromstein, Manpower's longtime chief executive officer, eventually reacquired the company and returned the headquarters to Milwaukee. But Manpower's services have expanded into providing engineers, accountants and computer operators. It also earns half its revenue in Europe. (For Kelly Services, the figure is 12 percent.)

"The temp companies say, 'Part of the reason we do so well in other countries is because their work rules are so much stricter than ours,'" says John Larson, vice president of G2 Securities in Milwaukee, who follows the temp industry. "What's ironic is that we're starting to follow Europe's path. Family leave, mandated health benefits—anything that scares a permanent employer has a tendency to help the temp industry."

Costly Terminations

One emerging factor that influences even the largest industries is the difficulty in firing people, either when their services are no longer needed or when they are incapable of doing the job.

"For roughly the last 100 years, the universal rule in the United States has been that if you had a contract with an employer that didn't have any specifics in it, that contract could be terminated by either party 'at will,'" says Professor Theodore J. St. Antoine, reporting on the model termination act for the National Conference of Commissioners on Uniform State Laws. "In recent years, however, about a dozen states have added a 'covenant of good faith and fair dealing,' which has been interpreted by the courts to mean that you can't fire people, especially long-term employees."

As the "employment at will" doctrine has eroded, employers find themselves embroiled in lengthy proceedings to terminate employees who are incompetent or no longer needed.

In a recent study, the Rand Corporation found that expanding legal definitions of wrongful termination led to a 300 percent increase in lawsuits in California in the 1980s. "Executives and middle managers made up more than half the cases," said James Dertouzos, who conducted the Rand study. "Juries awarded damages in two-thirds of the trials, with the median award about $200,000. Our recommendation to businesses is to meet the dismissed employee's initial demands, rather than going to trial."

In a similar study, Michael Losey, president of the Society for Human Resource Management, estimated that the costs of firing a white-collar employee far exceed the cost of taking one on board. "It costs $9,200 to hire someone, while firing the same employee will cost $30,000 and inducing voluntary retirement runs to $55,000," says Losey. "Costs of termination have become a major contributor to the growing use of a contingency work force."

Only in government itself is termination more difficult. Employees at the federal, state and municipal levels are protected by constitutional rights—"due process" and "fair procedure"—in dismissal proceedings. Consequently, public employees rarely are terminated. The *Washington Monthly* once ran a 12-page article called "Firing a Federal Employee: The Impossible Dream," that chronicled the futile efforts of one supervisor to dismiss a subordinate who repeatedly challenged him to fistfights. Jack Stieber, former director of the School of Labor and Industrial Relations at Michigan State University, estimates that 150,000 private employees would have "causes of action" against being fired if they had the same protection government and union employees enjoy.

"The problem is that the federal government has been operating under the mistaken impression that the purpose of employment is to provide people with a safety net," says Jay Whitehead, who runs Payroll Options, a company that helps employers deal with independent contractors. "That's not the vision Thomas Jefferson saw. He saw a nation of self-employed individuals. The concept that we should all be working for giant corporations is really a 20th century phenomenon. It may not last into the next century."

"Staff Leasing"

As Clinton attempts to mandate employer-provided health benefits, another trend is emerging—"staff leasing," in which temporary firms contract to provide not just individual employees, but entire departments. Kelly Services has acquired Your Staff, Inc., a California employee-leasing firm, as a way to enter the business.

"Employers are taking a hard look at how they use personnel," says Hartwig, vice president at Kelly. "They may let leasing firms take over whole areas, such as the personnel department or the mail room. Our job is to provide the salary, benefits and bookkeeping and attend to all personnel matters. If a contractor requests that a certain employee be dismissed, for example, that's our responsibility.

"Still, an employer shouldn't think they are completely off the hook," Hartwig adds. "They can still be charged with sexual harassment or discrimination for something that happens on the job."

Even when an employer makes every conceivable effort to meet federal standards, a company can still find itself in trouble. Across town from Ralph Reiland's restaurant, a Pittsburgh bar and grill ran into trouble when a former waitress charged that the bartender—her ex-boyfriend—harassed her while she was on the job.

"I took every conceivable step you could take to avoid personnel problems," says Mark Graves, owner of the Sports Garden, which catered to fans of the Pittsburgh Penguins, Steelers and Pirates. "We encouraged direct complaints to our manager. We had a blind suggestion box. I even had an employee council that met once a month to air complaints and discuss personnel problems. We're a very employee-conscious company. I don't know what else I could have done."

Nonetheless, on Feb. 7, 1994, a Pittsburgh jury found Graves's business liable for $85,000 in damages for failing to control the bartender's behavior toward his ex-girlfriend. The day before the verdict came down, Graves announced the Sports Garden would close. Sixty-two employees now are looking for work.

"There is an urgent need for a program to reverse this trend [of exploiting contingent workers]. . . . Legislative action is a vital arena for implementing such a program."

Government Regulations Are Needed to Protect the Contingent Workforce

Chuck Williams

Since the early 1970s, opportunities for permanent, full-time employment have been dramatically reduced as companies increasingly rely on temporary, part-time, and contract employees—collectively referred to as the "contingent" workforce. In the following viewpoint, Chuck Williams argues that the use of contingent workers—who receive low pay, little job security, and few legal rights—exemplifies the exploitation of labor inherent to capitalism. He calls for legislative action to reduce this exploitation by strengthening the rights of contingent workers. Williams is a trade unionist and a member of the National Committee of the Communist Party, USA.

As you read, consider the following questions:

1. According to the author, what two explanations are used to justify replacing permanent jobs with contingent ones?
2. In what four ways do contingent workers enable employers to save costs, according to A.E. Polivka and T. Nardone, as cited by Williams?

From Chuck Williams, "Temporary Workers: A Permanent Feature of Capitalism?" *Political Affairs*, September/October 1993. Reprinted with permission.

Early in 1993, Bank of America announced that it was placing thousands of full-time employees on permanent part-time status. The announcement by the nation's second largest bank, following extensive layoffs as the corporate giant consolidated its merger with former arch-rival Security Pacific National Bank, caused a brief murmur of outrage even in the commercial press. Using this increasingly common device to cheat the bulk of its work force out of already meager non-union benefits—while posting annual profits of over $1.4 billion—seemed excessively greedy even by Reagan-Bush era standards. However, Bank of America's action was only a particularly large-scale example of a dramatic change which has taken place in the U.S. work force over the last two decades: the replacement of millions of steady, full-time jobs with various types of "on demand" employment.

"A wide range of employment practices, including part-time work, temporary work, employee lending, self-employment, contracting out, and home-based work" are generically referred to as contingent employment [according to A.E. Polivka and T. Nardone], although the term used in France, "precarious employment," perhaps better captures the essence of these arrangements.

There are more than 30 million U.S. workers in these contingent categories, a figure far higher than at the beginning of the 1970s. An analysis of U.S. Bureau of Labor Statistics data [by L. Golden and E. Appelbaum] showed that "the number of temporary jobs filled daily by temporary help rose more than two-and-a-half times" from 1982 to 1988. (And this figure apparently does not include those workers who are temporarily hired directly by the employer rather than through a "body broker" agency.) Meanwhile, [according to the *Union Labor Report*] "the number of part-time workers has increased by 40 percent, while almost half of all new jobs have been filled by part-time workers" since the early 1980s.

Who makes up the contingent work force? "Not surprisingly, the bulk of these workers are women, people of color, and immigrants, as well as older workers and teens—the most vulnerable members of the labor force" [according to C. Colatosti]. . . .

Second-Class Employees

What does it mean to be a contingent worker? In the first place, such employment almost never provides sufficient income to support a living standard above the poverty level. Part-time employees often work at several different part-time jobs in an attempt to patch together enough income on which to survive. Thus, for example, a worker may put in 20 hours a week at each of three different jobs, for a total of 60 hours, and receive no overtime premium pay.

Contingent workers are concentrated in sectors of the economy already characterized by low pay—clerical, food service and health care—and increasingly in manufacturing and construction as well. But all sources agree that [in the words of Golden and Appelbaum] ". . . the compensation level of contingent labor is low relative to that incurred with comparable permanent employees." Temporary clerical workers average only $5.11 an hour. "Temporary workers nationwide average $6.38 an hour, compared with $7.87 an hour for permanent, full-time workers in the service industry and $8.54 for full-time workers in manufacturing" [according to Colatosti]. . . .

No Benefits or Security

The second defining characteristic of contingent employment is the virtual absence of employer-paid benefits. In the United States, which has the lowest level of employer-paid benefits of any fully industrialized country in the world, vital benefits such as medical and dental insurance, paid holidays and vacations (when available at all) are almost always conditioned upon full-time permanent employment. Except for some sub-standard benefits provided by certain temporary help agencies to their most regularly employed workers, contingent workers are almost universally denied company-paid benefits.

Third, "Probably the most salient characteristic of contingent work is the low degree of *job security* [according to Golden and Appelbaum]. Unlike permanent workers in layoff-prone industries, temporary workers do not enjoy a reasonable expectation that they will be called back. This has several important implications.

One is that the temporary worker never achieves tenure on the job, and is always on a kind of "super-probation." He or she may be fired at any time, for any reason or for no reason at all. This vulnerability is used to speed-up and tyrannize workers, and bosses use their example to degrade the working conditions of their non-contingent coworkers.

Even more pernicious is the fact that existing legal protections for workers, most of which were legislated with permanent full-time employment in mind, often do not apply or are virtually unenforceable for contingent employees. This includes, among other things, wage and hour laws, safety regulations and anti-discrimination statutes. . . .

In attempting to justify the trend toward replacing permanent full-time jobs with contingent jobs, two types of explanations are commonly offered. The first, which has become a favorite theme in the life-style pages of the popular press, is that workers themselves want greater flexibility in work hours, as well as the "freedom" to come and go.

In a modern version of the old sexist myth that women work to earn "pin money," not because they need to support themselves and their families, we are told that part-time and temporary work is a "life-style choice," and that the startling rise in contingent employment merely follows the entry of more women into the work force.

In an insightful statistical analysis published in 1992 in the prestigious *American Journal of Economics and Sociology,* Professors Lonnie Golden and Eileen Appelbaum categorically reject these assertions:

> There is no support for the hypothesis that changes in the composition of the labor force play a significant role in the expansion of temporary jobs . . . work schedule preferences of women or other groups, do not account for the rise in temporary work since 1982. . . .

The correct explanation is that employers favor contingent arrangements because they are highly profitable. This explanation is usually disguised behind euphemisms such as "flexibility to respond to market conditions," which, in fact, means to transfer the risks of the market from the capitalist to the worker.

A Cost-Saving Arrangement

In a 1989 study, two U.S. Bureau of Labor Statistics economists [Polivka and Nardone] listed the advantages which employers derive from the use of contingent workers. Cost savings, hence higher profits, are achieved by:

- Reducing the cost of maintaining a constant work force while demand for a firm's product varies.
- "Reducing worker compensation and administrative costs; (firms offer lower pay and few or no benefits to workers filling contingent positions . . .)."
- Helping employers "insulate a core of permanent employees from layoffs" in order to "obtain wage and work rule concessions from their permanent staff by offering them employment security."
- "Using contingent arrangements to screen prospective candidates for permanent jobs." (In effect, a pre-probationary period for new employees.)

To be sure, there are some workers who prefer non-traditional arrangements. These include full-time students, parents who prefer (and can afford) to spend more time raising children, and certain highly paid technical and managerial personnel who can earn enough to live on in a part-time capacity. However, these groups constitute a small percentage compared to the number of workers forced into part-time or temporary work by lack of alternatives.

The mushrooming use of various contingent employment arrangements represents a qualitatively new strategy for intensifying the exploitation of labor and extracting super-profits from the U.S. working class. This new strategy marks the maturation of an economic trend described by C. Lane:

> Around 1975, the general deterioration of economic development, the growing uncertainty and instability of world product markets and the introduction of new technology brought about new requirements in the utilization of labor, as well as mass unemployment. The ensuing loss of numerical and/or organizational strength of organized labor resulted in a decisive shift in the balance of power between capital and labor. This shift was accompanied by an ideological reorientation, both at the level of the state and among employers. A model of "free market capitalism," advocating managerial freedom in the use of capital and labor, came to the fore. The model demanded the dismantling of any restraint on the free working of the market, exercised both by organized labor and by the state.

The spectacular growth of this phenomenon since the late 1970s precisely coincides with the unfolding of a systemic crisis of monopoly capitalism; it is part of a multi-faceted effort to place the full burden of this crisis entirely on the backs of workers, especially those who are most vulnerable. . . .

ANOTHER GLASS CEILING

Many employers have developed a two-tier work force strategy: retaining a "core" of permanent full-time employees augmented by a "periphery" of contingent workers. Such arrangements are used to undermine the unity of the workers by buffering the core from layoffs, forced overtime and less-desirable job assignments. For example, one large oil refinery in California continuously augments its unionized maintenance force with several hundred outside contract employees. The core workers are offered all the available overtime, but never forced to work it, while the contractors do the work that is left over or refused.

Laws and Aggressive Organizing Are Needed

To their credit, most unions see the dangers posed by a two-tier workplace and offer strenuous resistance, but some have given in to company pressures to legitimize contingent arrangements. Considering the present power advantages enjoyed by management in the traditional bargaining arena, as well as the small and decreasing percentage of the work force actually represented by unions, laws to restrict the use of contingent employment are urgently needed.

Organized labor must also develop a more aggressive approach to organizing contingent workers. Because the great majority of these workers are women, racially and nationally oppressed, and/or youth, unions must develop approaches to organizing which address their full range of problems.

The Golden-Appelbaum study describes the situation succinctly:

> When labor's bargaining strength is great, firms are hindered in their ability to add temporary rather than permanent employees. Conversely, reductions in labor's power inhibit workers' ability to resist employer imposition of . . . flexibility . . . by substituting temporary for permanent positions.

There is an urgent need for a program to reverse this trend towards pauperization, insecurity and super-exploitation of the growing contingent sector of the working class. In order to address this problem in both unionized and unorganized sectors of the economy, as well as to reinforce the position of unions in their struggles against contingent employment, legislative action is a vital arena for implementing such a program.

At present, to the extent that laws and governmental regulations deal at all with contingent workers they frequently serve to legitimize or even encourage the super-exploitation of these workers. For example, the powerful South Coast Air Quality Management District in Southern California recently adopted an amendment to its car-pooling mandate on employers to provide an exemption for companies using agency-provided temporary employees, thus encouraging the use of such employees over permanent workers.

On the federal level, the Employee Retirement Security Income Act of 1974 (ERISA), the law which controls employment-based benefit programs, expressly permits employers to exclude part-time and temporary employees from most benefits. Similarly [according to D. Nye],

> . . . the 1986 Consolidated Omnibus Budget Reconciliation Act (COBRA) requires employers of 20 or more people to offer continued health care coverage to terminated employees and to survivors, divorced spouses, and dependent children of employees . . . but legislation such as COBRA, combined with employer efforts to cut large parts of their work forces, have prompted some companies to turn to temporary arrangements as a cost-effective alternative to the entanglements of traditional employment relationships.

In yet another example, a U.S. Court of Appeals recently ruled that an employer who shut down a plant with more than 50 workers with no notice had not violated the Worker Adjustment and Retraining Notification Act because the temporary workers who were laid off did not count toward the 50-worker minimum that triggers the employer's obligation to provide 60 days' prior notice of a plant closing.

Ironically, all of the above-cited examples involve laws intended to protect workers or the environment, but have in fact furnished loopholes which encourage profit-driven businesses to prefer the use of contingent work arrangements over permanent full-time jobs.

A Bill of Rights for Contingent Workers

The following legislative program, while not exhaustive, is intended to open a discussion on an effective working-class approach to the problem of contingent employment.

- *Health care reform:* The failure of employers to provide health insurance to temporary and part-time workers is probably the largest source of super-profits from the use of these workers. Hence, the enactment of a national health care plan is one of the most effective steps that can be taken to curtail the use of contingent employees, provided these workers are fully covered by such a plan.

  The best approach is a comprehensive package of complete medical, psychological and dental coverage, not tied to employment and at no cost to the individual. If it is tied to employment, employers of part-time workers should pay on a full, not prorated basis, and employers should be responsible for the premiums of laid-off employees until they are re-employed.

- *Shorten the work week:* A 35-hour work week for 40 hours' pay would dramatically reduce unemployment and underemployment by greatly increasing the need for full-time workers. Forced overtime for non-emergency situations should be made illegal. Reducing the length of the standard workweek with no reduction in pay is crucial to shifting the burden of capitalism's protracted crisis off the backs of the working class.

- *Guaranteed paid vacation for all workers:* All workers should be guaranteed at least four weeks' paid vacation per year, bringing the U.S. in line with other advanced capitalist countries. Employers of temporary workers should pay into a fund to provide this benefit.

Legal Remedies

- *Criminalize violations of worker's rights:* In our capitalist society, an unemployed worker who robs a store faces years in prison, but the store owner who robs employees by failing to pay the minimum wage or overtime premiums faces at worst an order to reimburse and perhaps a fine.

All employer violations of wage and hour laws, safety regulations and anti-discrimination laws should be treated as criminal offenses, with mandatory jail time for repeat offenders. Back pay awards should be double or triple actual damages, as is currently provided under the federal Fair Labor Standards Act [a law that provides for maximum hours and minimum wages].

State and local bodies charged with enforcement of these laws should be beefed up with additional staff and investigatory powers. Routine audits should be conducted of employer records, rather than merely waiting for complaints by workers who are frequently intimidated or unaware of their legal rights.

Workers should have the option of suing in court, with the employer paying all legal fees when found to be at fault, to prevent sabotage of worker protections by deliberately lax enforcement.

- *Labor law reform:* There is a clear relationship between the strength of unions and the prevalence of contingent employment. As part of a comprehensive reform of labor law, the National Labor Relations Act [a 1935 law establishing workers' rights to organize and bargain collectively] should be amended to require the inclusion of all part-time and temporary employees in any bargaining unit. In addition, contract provisions which discriminate against these workers in wage rates, benefits, and the right to accrue seniority or be rehired should be prohibited.

Non-union contract employees should be included in bargaining units and under existing union contracts from the moment they set foot on unionized property. Employer interference with union organizing should be treated as a criminal human rights violation, and back-pay awards should be double or triple actual damages.

- *Improve Social Security:* Social Security benefits should be dramatically increased through higher employer contributions to protect those workers who are unable to participate in an employer-sponsored pension plan. The formula for benefits should not penalize those workers who have suffered long periods of unemployment and underemployment.
- *Improve Unemployment Insurance:* Eliminate qualifying periods of employment for eligibility for unemployment benefits. Such requirements discriminate against part-time and temporary workers as well as first-time job seekers and those working under bogus "self-employment" arrangements. Raise and extend benefits by setting national standards or federalizing the unemployment insurance system.
- *Call-back rights:* Require that laid-off temporary workers be given preference for rehire, and create a presumption of illegal discrimination if they are by-passed.
- *Government-supported child care:* Many parents, especially women, are forced to accept part-time or temporary work because they are unable to find or afford adequate child care arrangements. This is a vicious cycle which condemns millions of children to growing up in poverty.
- *Special minimum wage for part-time:* To discourage the use of part-time employment and to augment the income of such workers, establish a higher minimum wage for those working less than a full work week. This would create an additional incentive for employers to rely on standard full-time job arrangements.
- *Eliminate laws which encourage contingent employment:* Public policy should recognize the various forms of temporary employment as substandard, and laws and regulations should discourage it. The out-of-control growth of contingent employment in the United States has contributed significantly to the impoverishment and precarious living conditions of a large and growing section of the working class. Because this development disproportionately affects minorities, women and youth, it represents an additional dimension of discrimination and super-exploitation in contemporary U.S. society. In the words of Golden and Appelbaum, "Without legislative action, an increasing number of workers and their families are likely to lose access to a stable stream of income and secure standard of living."

An effective class approach to this crisis must have the goal of shifting the burden of business risks and market fluctuations from the backs of workers to the wallets of the bosses.

"The minimum wage destroys jobs."

Increasing the Minimum Wage Reduces Employment

Stephen Chapman and Doug Bandow

In the following viewpoint, Stephen Chapman and Doug Bandow argue that employers only hire people who are worth more as producers than they cost as employees. When the minimum wage is raised, the authors contend, many low-wage workers become more costly than they are worth to employers. Employers respond to these disproportionate labor costs by eliminating positions, according to Chapman and Bandow, thus reducing employment opportunities for unskilled and inexperienced workers. Chapman, author of Part I of the viewpoint, is a nationally syndicated columnist. Bandow, author of Part II, is a nationally syndicated columnist and a senior fellow at the Cato Institute, a libertarian public policy research foundation in Washington, D.C.

As you read, consider the following questions:

1. According to Chapman, what percent of the people employed at minimum-wage jobs live in poor households?
2. What skills does minimum-wage employment instill in workers, according to Bandow?
3. According to the studies cited by Chapman and Bandow, what percent of teens are affected by a 10 percent rise in the minimum wage?

Stephen Chapman, "The Persistent Folly of the Minimum Wage," *Conservative Chronicle*, November 3, 1993. Reprinted by permission of Stephen Chapman and Creators Syndicate. Doug Bandow, "Another Strategy to Destroy Jobs," *The Washington Times*, August 21, 1993. Reprinted by permission of Doug Bandow and Copley News Service.

I

The Clinton administration, which has already shown that improving the economy is harder than it thought, is about to show that damaging the economy is easier than it thinks. Labor Secretary Robert Reich wants to increase the minimum wage, ignoring predictions that it will raise the incomes of some workers by 6 percent only by reducing the incomes of others by 100 percent.

Reich and his allies in organized labor think it's a scandal that the legal minimum wage, now $4.25 an hour, has lagged behind inflation. Since 1968, it has lost nearly a third of its real value.

He and his boss also lament the fact that a worker can labor diligently full-time year-round at the minimum wage and remain mired in poverty. The poverty level for a family of four is $14,335 a year, but a family with just one full-time worker at the minimum wage has an income of less than $9,000 a year (not counting such benefits as food stamps, Medicaid and the earned income tax credit).

Helping the Non-Poor

When it comes to helping the poor, though, raising the minimum wage is the equivalent of tossing $10 bills out of an airplane flying at 5,000 feet. Less than 20 percent of the people employed at minimum-wage jobs live in poor households, and most of those don't work all year. Boosting the minimum wage would help four times as many non-poor people as it would poor people, which even by Washington standards makes it a wildly sloppy way to combat poverty.

Someone getting the minimum wage is less likely to be a long-suffering father in a housing project trying to put food on the table than a high school kid raised in middle-class comfort saving for college or a car. The Congressional Budget Office, reports *Investor's Business Daily*, found that there are only 120,000 minimum-wage employees who are "both full-time, year-round workers and poor"—one one-thousandth of the work force.

Making Do with Fewer Workers

So why not help those 120,000? Because many of them would be hurt, not helped. If you increase the price of anything, buyers will make do with less of it, and the AFL–CIO [American Federation of Labor–Congress of Industrial Organizations] hasn't been able to repeal this inconvenient law as it applies to labor.

Workers are hired because what they produce is worth more to their employer than what they are paid. Otherwise, there would be no reason to employ them. It's easy to decree that every worker will be paid at least $4.50 an hour. It' s not so easy to decree that every worker will be worth at least $4.50 an hour.

Workers who are worth $4.25 but must be paid $4.50 will eventually find themselves not being paid at all because employers have a notoriously consistent habit of abandoning practices that lose money.

The minimum-wage boost, keep in mind, would not be the only new burden for many employers, who may also have to start buying health insurance for every worker.

A Wage Subsidy Program

Suppose that the minimum wage were removed, and in its place the government announced a "target" wage, promising to pay employers a wage subsidy equal to, say, half the difference between the actual wage paid (after announcement of the wage subsidy program) and the target wage. Unlike the minimum wage, which interferes with market forces in a coercive fashion, a wage subsidy program would complement market forces by increasing the demand for low-skilled workers. Unlike the minimum wage, which cannot increase both the wages and the employment of low-skilled workers simultaneously, a wage subsidy program would do precisely that.

Benjamin Zycher, *Jobs & Capital*, Summer 1993.

Companies faced with rising wage expenses have several options besides coughing up the cash. They can replace human beings with machines, which are exempt from the solicitude of the secretary of labor. They can subcontract work to self-employed people, whose compensation isn't fixed by law. They can replace workers in the United States with workers in Indonesia or China. They can reduce output so they need fewer employees. Or they can close down entirely.

A Handful of Studies

Most economic studies of past increases estimate that each 10 percent boost leads to a cut in teen employment of between 1 percent and 3 percent. Reich, however, prefers to rely on a handful of contrary studies, such as those showing that employment in fast-food restaurants in Texas and New Jersey rose as the minimum wage did.

If this data is conclusive, McDonald's can assume that the more it charges for Big Macs, the more it will sell. It can also figure that water will run uphill. Local circumstances may occasionally spur the demand for unskilled labor enough to overcome the effect of a higher wage floor. But even in these unusual cases, there would be bigger job gains without an increase.

Teenagers are the workers most affected by the minimum wage since they are the least likely to have the skills and experience to obtain higher pay. Economist Alan Reynolds of the Hudson Institute notes that when the minimum wage was left unchanged from 1981 until 1990, the number of employed teenagers rose from 41 percent to 48 percent. After Congress lifted the minimum wage in 1990, teen employment dropped back to 43 percent—before the recession began.

Raising the minimum wage is a sure way to destroy jobs. . . . Workers who find themselves unemployed as a result will enjoy the consolation of knowing that the job they no longer have pays better than ever.

II

If the 1992 [presidential] election was about anything, it was about jobs. Indeed, that was the justification for the Clinton administration's proposing, and congressional Democrats' supporting, extra expenditures on summer jobs programs even as they claimed to be committed to cutting the deficit.

Yet Labor Secretary Robert Reich is apparently now pressing the administration to take a step guaranteed to destroy jobs: Raise the minimum wage. In a confidential memo, apparently given to President Clinton in July 1993, Mr. Reich has suggested both increasing the current minimum and indexing it for inflation, measures also supported by leading Democratic legislators. Mr. Reich explains that he wants "to achieve the goal of making work pay." Similarly, Representative Marty Sabo, Minnesota Democrat, argues that an increase is required to put "needed funds in the pockets of millions of working Americans."

The intentions of Mr. Reich, Mr. Sabo, and their allies are good, but there ain't no such thing as a free lunch, as the saying goes. It is one thing for Washington to decree a minimum wage. It is quite another to force employers to hire workers at that wage. Indeed, there are few issues upon which economists are as united as the fact that the minimum wage destroys jobs. In short, a minimum wage increase will hurt the very people it is supposed to help.

The principle is simple. Businesses are normally not charities; for this reason, they usually only hire people who can produce more than they are paid. For the ill-educated, unskilled and inexperienced, that often isn't much.

Reducing Opportunities

While no one can support a family at today's minimum, most people working at that level are second-earners; almost two-thirds are under the age of 24. In such cases, minimum wage employment often represents a person's initial entry into the economy, the first job that teaches important basic skills, such as punctuality, hard work, problem-solving, and people interaction. Indeed, a recent survey of restaurant employees found that 8 of 10 believed their work, often at the minimum wage, had helped them prepare for better jobs in the future.

Even if these sorts of low-paying jobs were "dead-ends," however, they would remain better than none. The lack of opportunity for a person is not solved by reducing the number of his or her opportunities.

That is precisely what the minimum wage does. It tells employers that if they hire someone, they must pay him or her the arbitrary minimum. But nothing requires the firm to hire the person or maintain him on staff. Thus, when the minimum rises, applicants who can't produce more than the minimum will not be hired and employees with only limited abilities will be fired. Companies will leave some jobs undone, rely on fewer, more skilled employees, or automate. Some restaurants, for instance, have introduced mechanical taco and sushi-makers.

There is nothing nefarious about such a result. To the contrary, why should labor-intensive firms, which are providing a service to society by employing the most marginal employees, bear the entire cost of paying them more than they are worth to the business? In effect, Mr. Reich is arguing for higher taxes on the very companies that are hiring the most disadvantaged workers.

Unfortunately, the negative impact of the minimum wage on overall employment is clear. A score of studies over the last 20 years have found that a 10 percent rise in the minimum reduces employment of teens, who are hardest-hit by government wage-setting, by somewhere between 1 percent and 3 percent. The number of hours worked by employees who don't lose their jobs also falls.

Reaching a similar conclusion was a study by the Congressional Budget Office in 1988, which estimated that pending legislation to increase the minimum would destroy between 250,000 and 500,000 jobs. And the Minimum Wage Study Commission, established in 1977 by Congress, found that employment opportunities fall by between 0.5 percent and 2.5 percent for every 10 percent jump in the standard. More recent research, from the Employment Policies Institute, among others, has reached similar conclusions.

In short, increasing the minimum wage will not put "needed funds" into workers' pockets; rather, it will leave many of them out of work. Thus, instead of thinking about raising the minimum wage, Mr. Reich should focus on increasing the number of jobs. It is time policy-makers learned that good intentions are not enough to put food on workers' tables; good consequences of public policies are necessary as well.

"The minimum wage has not had an adverse effect on employment."

Increasing the Minimum Wage Does Not Reduce Employment

Alan B. Krueger

In the following viewpoint, Alan B. Krueger questions the conventional view among many economists that increases in the federally mandated minimum wage reduce employment opportunities—especially among teenagers and young adults. Krueger cites four studies that conclude the minimum wage has little or no adverse effect on employment. He concludes that the conventional view is based on an economics textbook model that fails to account for the complexity of the labor market. Krueger is the Bendheim Professor of Economics and Public Affairs at Princeton University in New Jersey.

As you read, consider the following questions:

1. According to Professor Allison Wellington, cited by Krueger, how is the employment rate affected by a ten percent increase in the minimum wage?
2. What issues does Krueger say are omitted in the textbook model of the labor market?

From Alan B. Krueger, "Have Increases in the Minimum Wage Reduced Employment?" Prof. Krueger's essay was originally published in the summer 1993 issue of *Jobs & Capital*, the quarterly journal of the Milken Institute for Job and Capital Formation and is reprinted by permission.

Nearly 50 years ago George Stigler wrote that economists should be "outspoken, and singularly agreed" that increases in the minimum wage reduce employment. Although the theoretical logic behind this view is impeccable, there is one problem: *the evidence is not singularly agreed*. In fact, a growing number of studies conclude that the minimum wage has not had an adverse effect on employment. In my view, an objective reading of the evidence would lead one to question whether moderate increases in the minimum wage have *any* effect on employment. Here I review four recent empirical studies on the employment effect of increases in the minimum wage.

(1) In the study using perhaps the most convincing methodology, my colleague David Card examined the effect of the increase in the federal minimum from $3.35 to $3.80 in April 1990. Card grouped the states into three categories based on the fraction of teenage workers who fell in the $3.35–$3.80 range just before the minimum wage increased. High-wage states, like California and New York, had few workers in the range where the minimum wage increase would matter, while low-wage states, including Mississippi and Alabama, had as many as 50% of teenagers in the range where the minimum wage increase would matter. If the minimum wage increase adversely affected employment, one would expect to see a greater decline (or less growth) in teenagers' employment in the low-wage states than in the high-wage states. Contrary to this straightforward prediction, Professor Card found no meaningful difference in employment growth between high-wage and low-wage states. If anything, the states with relatively few workers affected by the increase in the minimum wage had less employment growth than in those with relatively many workers affected.

Professor Card's work has been criticized for not waiting long enough after the minimum increased to allow firms to adjust employment. However, an additional year of data can now be analyzed. Moreover, in the course of this additional year the federal minimum increased again, up to $4.25 per hour, which should magnify any employment losses. When he follows up on his original study with an additional year of data, Card's finding becomes even stronger—the states most affected by the increase in the minimum had greater employment growth than those that were hardly affected. Card's results pose a strong challenge to the conventional view that cannot be easily dismissed.

Results Contrary to the Conventional View

(2) In another study Professor Lawrence Katz of Harvard and I examined the effect of the increase in the federal minimum wage on employment in fast food restaurants in Texas. We studied the effect of the increase in the minimum from $3.80 per

hour to $4.25 in April 1991. We surveyed 100 restaurants before the minimum increase and again afterward. Some of the restaurants were located in parts of the state where the entry wage was already above $4.25, so the increase in the minimum had no direct effect on them. Almost half of the restaurants were initially paying new workers $3.80 per hour, and were forced to raise wages to comply with the law. Contrary to the conventional view, we found that employment increased more in those restaurants that were most affected by the minimum wage increase than in other restaurants.

Poverty v. Teen Fashion

Just for argument's sake, say that raising the minimum wage eliminates some jobs. Who is most affected? Teenagers, who make up 30 percent of the minimum wage work force. Because of their short time in the labor market, in theory, they are the first to go when wages rise. . . .

In addition, there's some truth to the old conservative argument that most minimum wage earners aren't poor. More than half of all minimum wage earners are between 16 and 24. Of those, almost one-fifth live in multiworker households with combined incomes greater than $50,000, and the Congressional Budget Office estimates that only one in five minimum wage workers lives below the poverty line. The question about raising the minimum wage, then, may come down to this: Do we want to have more low-wage jobs that impoverish adult families in order to keep middle-class teenagers in high fashion?

Stephanie Mencimer, *The New Republic*, May 23, 1994.

---

(3) Professor Card and I have followed up on the Texas study by examining the effect of a 1992 increase in the New Jersey state minimum wage. Effective April 1992, the minimum wage in New Jersey increased from $4.25 to $5.05 per hour, giving New Jersey the highest minimum wage in the country. This increase created a natural experiment that we use to estimate the effect of a higher minimum wage. Specifically, we conducted a survey of 410 fast food restaurants in New Jersey and eastern Pennsylvania. The stores in eastern Pennsylvania were unaffected by the increase in the New Jersey minimum, and thus provide a control group to compare to New Jersey. Again, contrary to the conventional view, we find that employment grew in New Jersey relative to that in Pennsylvania. Moreover, when we look at stores within New Jersey we find that employment growth was greatest at the stores that were forced to raise their

wages the most by the increase in the state minimum. The New Jersey study has significant advantages over the previous Texas study. Most importantly, we followed up all stores that may have closed. In addition, the increase in the minimum was large, and came on the heels of a recent increase in the federal minimum.

(4) David Card has performed a similar analysis of the effect of the increase in California's minimum wage. In July 1988 California increased its minimum wage from $3.35 to $4.25. Professor Card found that employment of California's teenagers did not change relative to a set of comparison states that had no change in the minimum wage.

All of these disparate studies conclude that the minimum wage has not had an adverse effect on employment. No doubt, each of these individual studies has weaknesses. But the composite of the studies overcomes many of the objections that can be levied against particular studies. A balanced reading of this research suggests that recent increases in the minimum wage have had little, if any, effect on employment.

Contradicting the Conventional Model

The main evidence in support of the conventional view comes from time-series studies conducted in the 1970s that relate changes in teenage employment to changes in the minimum wage over time. A 1983 paper thoroughly surveyed this literature and concluded that the effects tend to be small: a 10 percent increase in the minimum wage reduces teenage employment by 1–3 percent. But if exactly the same models are re-estimated to incorporate more recent data, the effect is much smaller: Professor Allison Wellington finds that a 10 percent increase in the minimum reduces employment by just 0.6 percent, and that this effect could easily have occurred by chance. Even the most favorable evidence for the conventional model now finds negligible effects of the minimum wage on employment. . . .

There are several additional puzzles about the minimum wage that lead one to question the applicability of the conventional model. First, many firms that are *not covered* by the minimum wage pay the minimum anyway. Second, only a handful of firms—less than 2 percent—have taken advantage of the youth subminimum wage [a training wage, equal to 85% of the minimum wage, which employers are allowed to pay teenagers], even though they paid teenagers less than the subminimum before the minimum wage increase. Third, an increase in the minimum wage has a spillover effect in some firms, causing workers earning above the minimum to get a raise. And finally, increases in the minimum wage do not appear to be offset by reductions in fringe benefits. Each of these findings contradicts the textbook model of the minimum wage.

This array of evidence suggests that the low-wage labor market does not conform to the simple competitive model described in most introductory economics textbooks. The failure to find convincing evidence of adverse employment effects of minimum wages should come as no surprise. One should bear in mind that the textbook model, like all theoretical models, is an abstraction; it should be used when its predictions are valid and discarded when they are not. The textbook model assumes that firms can immediately and costlessly fill all vacancies, and that workers earning more than the minimum wage will not suffer unemployment. In actuality the labor market is more complicated. Workers have to search for openings and firms expend resources recruiting, and both are concerned with equity, motivation, and fairness. These issues have no role in the textbook model of the labor market. If a higher wage makes it easier for firms to recruit workers, then appropriate theoretical models predict that modest increases in the minimum are associated with employment gains.

I want to emphasize that my comments should *not* be interpreted as support for the position that increasing the minimum wage is sound public policy. Economics, at best, can provide dimensions of the tradeoffs engendered by increasing the minimum wage. Even the largest disemployment effects of the minimum wage reported in the literature are small, and may not justify much concern. The main effect of a modest increase in the minimum wage seems to me to be redistributive: low-wage workers gain and low-wage employers lose. But there may be more effective ways of redistributing income than by raising the minimum, and the public may decide that it is undesirable to alter the income distribution. Moreover, the effect of the minimum wage on inflation, poverty, and other outcomes must be considered before informed public policy can be made on the minimum wage.

Periodical Bibliography

The following articles have been selected to supplement the diverse views presented in this chapter.

Clare Ansberry — "Hired Out: Workers Are Forced to Take More Jobs with Few Benefits," *The Wall Street Journal*, March 11, 1993.

Michael Barrier — "Now You Hire Them, Now You Don't," *Nation's Business*, January 1994.

Don L. Boroughs — "Business Gives In to Temptation," *U.S. News & World Report*, July 4, 1994.

James Bovard — "The IRS Wages War on the Self-Employed," *Insight*, January 24, 1994. Available from 3600 New York Ave. NE, Washington, DC 20002.

Janice Castro — "Disposable Workers," *Time*, March 29, 1993.

Camille Colatosti — "A Job Without a Future," *Dollars & Sense*, May 1992.

Christopher Cook — "Temps—the Forgotten Workers," *The Nation*, January 31, 1994.

Jaclyn Fierman — "The Contingency Work Force," *Fortune*, January 24, 1994.

Herbert J. Gans — "Making Jobs," *The Nation*, September 20, 1993.

David R. Henderson — "The Europeanization of the U.S. Labor Market," *The Public Interest*, Fall 1993.

Thomas D. Hopkins — "Government Regulation and Jobs: What Are the Consequences?" *USA Today*, May 1994.

Lawrence F. Katz and Alan B. Krueger — "The Effect of the Minimum Wage on the Fast-Food Industry," *Industrial and Labor Relations Review*, October 1992. Available from the Institute for Research on Poverty, 1180 Observatory Dr., Madison, WI 53706.

Stephanie Mencimer — "Take a Hike," *The New Republic*, May 23, 1994.

David Moberg — "Fed Up with the Fed," *In These Times*, May 30, 1994.

Lance Morrow — "The Temping of America," *Time*, March 29, 1993.

David Neumark — "Employment Effects of Minimum and Subminimum Wages: Recent Evidence," February 1993. Available from Employment Policies Institute, 607 14th St. NW, Suite 1110, Washington, D.C. 20005.

Joan C. Szabo — "Contract Workers: A Risky Business," *Nation's Business*, August 1993.

Murray Weidenbaum — "How Government Reduces Employment," *St. Croix Review*, April 1994. Available from PO Box 224, Stillwater, MN 55082.

What Role Should Labor Unions Play in the Workplace?

Work

Chapter Preface

Labor union membership declined from 34.7 percent of the workforce to just under 16 percent between 1954 and the early 1990s. Some corporate heads cheer this decline, hoping it signals the end of unions altogether. Others, however, who believe that unions are still necessary in the workplace, have proposed labor-management partnerships to help unions regain their strength.

Labor-management partnerships rely on mutually beneficial agreements between two long-time adversaries: management and workers' unions. For example, managers agree to include workers in company planning and decision making and to guarantee workers' job security, and union workers agree to accept automation of some jobs and to improve production efficiency. Those in favor of closer ties between labor and management argue that such agreements as these can improve companies' overall competitiveness and at the same time provide workers with a more challenging, rewarding, and secure work environment. According to Irving and Barry Bluestone, professors of labor studies and political economy, respectively,

> Instead of limiting workers' input to the factory floor or outer office, management must bring labor into the inner circle where strategic decisions about the enterprise are made. And instead of viewing the company as its mortal enemy, labor must be willing to focus its energy on improving the competitiveness of the enterprise.

Opponents contend proposed labor-management partnerships are management attempts to undermine the power of unions and the rights of workers. They argue that if unions agree to partnerships with management, workers may begin to trust management more than the unions and may eventually vote their unions out. Critics aver that the resulting lack of union protection would then lead to long hours, reduced wages, and job cuts. Mike Parker and Jane Slaughter of the Labor Education and Research Project in Detroit, Michigan, maintain that in the past such partnerships have harmed workers: "A look at the history of work reorganization programs [such as labor-management partnerships] reveals that management has mapped a clear road to a union-free economic world where most of us have poor jobs and no job security."

Whether or not they succeed, labor-management partnerships are one method envisioned by both labor unions and business supporters to improve employee-employer relations and company profitability. Labor-management partnerships are one topic discussed in the following chapter on the role of unions in the U.S. workplace.

"*Private-sector unionism is in a prolonged state of decline.*"

The Influence of Labor Unions Is Declining

Richard Edwards

Richard Edwards is dean of the College of Arts and Sciences at the University of Kentucky in Lexington. In the following viewpoint, Edwards argues that the influence of labor unions in the American workplace has declined, which he attributes to a variety of internal and external factors. Union membership in the private sector has been falling since 1955, he maintains, without organized union attempts to stop the decline. Current efforts to unionize new industries and those populated by workers without prior union experience, Edwards predicts, will not be enough to reinvigorate unions and restore their influence.

As you read, consider the following questions:

1. What percentage of the private-sector nonagricultural labor force is represented by unions, according to Edwards?
2. According to the author, why have unions fared poorly in National Labor Relations Board (NLRB) elections?
3. What are the four reasons that, Edwards contends, account for the decline of labor unions?

Excerpted from Richard Edwards, *Rights at Work*. Washington: Brookings Institution, 1993. Copyright ©1993, The Twentieth Century Fund. Reprinted with permission from the Twentieth Century Fund.

Unions once enjoyed great industrial strength, and in the political arena they were part of the central power triad of business, labor, and the public interest, what Europeans call the "social partners." Now, in both the industrial and political arenas, the unions have been reduced to special-interest status, one among many players with continuing but limited influence.

The unions' recent decline has been qualitative and moral as well as numerical. During the first years of numerical decline, from the mid-1950s to the mid-1960s, the unions maintained their institutional and organizational presence reasonably well, despite share losses; for these years, share loss was not necessarily a good index of the unions' general strength. But certainly since the mid-1970s, the unions' quantitative decline has mirrored and reinforced their qualitative losses, which include the decay of their institutional infrastructure, a weakening of their cultural links to working-class communities, the disappearance of their organizational presence in many industries, a marked decline in the power of their ideology to attract adherents and to motivate commitment, the erosion of their political influence, and a decrease in their members' militance. The qualitative dimensions of the union decline need to be kept in mind even as one focuses on the numerical losses. . . .

The De-Unionization of the Labor Force

The extent of the unions' decline can be measured by an index of their private-sector share (or density), that is, the percentage of all private employees whose jobs are covered by union contracts. [As of 1992] unions represent less than 12 percent of the private-sector nonagricultural labor force, less than a third of the peak union share achieved during 1952–54 (see figure 1).

Public-sector unions have done much better; indeed, they have provided almost the only area of growth for the union movement. Public-sector unions and employee associations increased their share during the 1970s and 1980s from about one quarter to nearly 40 percent of the public-sector labor force. But in several ways this good news for unions is less heartening for workers: for one thing, the public sector employs only about 15 percent of the total labor force, so quantitatively, private-sector developments dwarf those in the public sector. Moreover, public-sector workers to a far greater extent derive workplace rights from civil-service regulations, and so public-sector collective contract rights are less likely to provide a model for emulation in other workplaces. The at-will doctrine, for example, is highly attenuated in the public sector, and elaborate, explicit, and typically formalized procedures govern promotion, assignment to pay steps and benefits levels, discipline, job training, layoffs, and job assignment. It is in the private sector, where few of these rights or procedures exist by law, that collective bargaining has been crucial in delivering rights to workers.

Because unions historically have had their center of gravity in the private sector, growth in public-sector unions and decline in the private sector promise not only to change the composition of union membership but also to alter more fundamentally the unions' orientation and operations. However, what is relevant is that private-sector unionism is in a prolonged state of decline. Richard Freeman, one of the closest scholars of unionism, calls this "the effective de-unionization of most of the U.S. labor force."

The Arithmetic of Decline

The arithmetic of unionism's declining fortunes is highly revealing. Because the labor force grows between 1.5 and 2 percent each year, overall union membership must grow by an equivalent percent as well, or the union share will decline; if union membership drops, the unions' share will decline even faster. Union membership may fail to keep up with labor-force growth either because union membership in already organized enterprises fails to grow fast enough, or because efforts to organize new enterprises fail to bring in enough new members, or both. In practice there is always some attrition from the already-organized membership because of plant shutdowns, the natural demise of some union industries, and the fact that the workers at new plants are almost always initially nonunion. Unions therefore cannot maintain their share without substantial new organizing.

The evidence on the attrition rate in the already-organized enterprises is not very satisfactory, because reliable data are scarce and notoriously tardy. One estimate suggests that unions would lose roughly 3 percent of their share each year in the absence of new organizing. The attrition rate may have increased recently, but by how much is not clear. William Dickens and Jonathan Leonard calculate that the "automatic" loss of union members (not share) appears to have increased during the 1970s (the latest period they studied), but the rates of attrition were not markedly different from those suffered during the decade 1955–64. Richard Freeman, using admittedly crude calculations, estimated the "net depreciation or appreciation of union density," considering both changes in employment in unionized establishments and the rate of growth of total employment; he found that the net depreciation rate increased from 3.4 percent in the 1960s to 4.7 percent in the 1970s to 6.1 percent in the period 1980–85. Other evidence, more indirect, reinforces these findings.

These relationships can be illustrated as follows (using rounded numbers for ease of presentation). The total number of employees in the nonagricultural private-sector labor force in

106

1990 was about 91 million. Of these, about 10.2 million were union members, and so the union share was between 11 and 12 percent. Assume that private payrolls grow 2 percent per year; to keep up with the growth in the private labor force, every year unions need to attract 204,000 (2 percent of 10.2 million) new members from among private-sector workers. Assume further that the natural attrition rate among union membership is 3 percent of the union share per year; to replace members lost through attrition, unions need to attract 306,000 (3 percent of 10.2 million) new members. Considering both factors together, unions would need to organize about 510,000 new private-sector members each year just to maintain their share around 12 percent; to increase their share, they would need to attract more than 510,000.

Losing the Battle for New Members

What are the chances that the unions can enroll 510,000 new private-sector members every year? They have been losing the battle for new members, losing badly, and doing an increasingly poor job as time goes on. As researcher [Michael Goldfield] said after reviewing the evidence on attrition, "The steady decline in the union density from 1954 to the present is almost totally explained by the slowing down of the rate of new organizing during this period."

The principal means by which unions add new members is recognition elections supervised by the National Labor Relations Board [a government agency that works to correct or prevent unfair labor practices committed by either employers or unions]. When at least 30 percent of a nonunionized firm's workers request an election, the NLRB identifies the employees eligible to be covered by the law (the "bargaining unit") and schedules an election. If a majority of the firm's eligible workers vote to be represented by a union, the union is legally recognized and certified to bargain on behalf of all the workers in the bargaining unit. Hence an election victory, although it does not guarantee that the union will be successful in obtaining a contract, nonetheless constitutes the key step in recruiting new union members.

Unions have fared poorly in NLRB elections. For one thing, fewer workers participate in NLRB elections each year, and because such elections are the principal way that private-sector unions win new members, the declining pool of eligible new members means that even before any ballots are cast, the scope for possible union growth has already greatly narrowed. The percentage of private nonagricultural workers covered by such elections dropped from over 2.4 percent in 1950, to about 1.1 percent in 1965, to 0.5 percent in 1980, to 0.3 percent in 1983.

In 1989, only 273,775 private-sector workers, less than 0.3 percent of nonfarm private-sector workers, had an opportunity to
vote on unionization in an NLRB election. Because 510,000 new
members were needed, but only 273,775 (in 1989) were covered
in the elections, the unions had fallen short of their goal by
some 236,225 workers before the ballots were even counted.

Figure 1. Changes in Union Share, 1945–90[a]

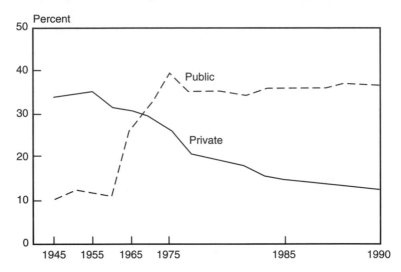

Sources: Leo Troy and Ned Sheflin (1985); Bureau of Labor Statistics, *Employment and
Earnings* (January issues, 1985–92).

[a]*Private* is union members as a percentage of all private, nonagricultural wage and salary
workers. *Public* is union members as a percentage of total public-sector employment. The
increase in public unionization between 1960 and 1970 reflects in part the recategorization
of employee associations as unions.

Within the constricting circle of recruitment opportunity,
unions have been faring much worse at winning new members.
Fewer of the voters in NLRB elections now vote in favor of
unions. The percentage of workers voting for unionization, considering all certification elections together, shrank from 75 percent or more before 1950 to around 60 percent in the 1960s to
less than 50 percent in the 1980s; in 1989, just 49 percent of the
workers eligible to vote in NLRB elections cast their ballots for a
union. Not surprisingly, the union victory rate in these elections
has likewise plunged—from 76 percent in 1950–54, to 55 percent
in the 1960s, to 37 percent in 1975–79. In 1988, unions won

1,839 out of 3,670 elections, for a win rate just over 50 percent; but from these elections they gained just 96,771 workers in the bargaining units they won—fewer than one-fifth of the number needed to maintain their 12 percent share of the work force.

The impact of adverse trends on union presence in the private sector has been devastating. New workers won to unionism through NLRB elections as a percentage of all nonagricultural employees declined from 2.0 percent in 1950 to 0.7 percent in 1965; it dropped to 0.2 percent in 1980 and around 0.1 percent in the 1980s. In NLRB elections during the 1980s, unions enrolled fewer than one new member for every thousand workers employed in the private sector. Thus, by the 1990s the unions' efforts to attract new members through the election process yielded only a small fraction of the number needed to maintain even their anemic 12 percent share. Unions gain a few members in other ways (expanded employment in some already-unionized enterprises, for instance, or union recognition achieved without an election), but NLRB elections remain the unions' primary means of access to the 85 percent of the labor force employed in the private sector. In trying to sign up new members, unions have hit a stone wall.

Structural Changes and Union Decline

In popular discussions, the most commonly cited factor in the decline of unions is change in the kinds of industry now prevalent and in the types of workers increasingly present in the labor force. The national economy has transferred its base from goods produced by heavy industries in the Northeast and Midwest to services and light industries located in a variety of areas besides the so-called Frost Belt. So too, the makeup of the labor force has changed to include more women, more white-collar or other nonproduction employees, and more highly educated and younger workers. Because both the industry and labor-force transformations constitute movements away from the traditional sources of union strength, it has sometimes been argued that these structural changes lie behind the eroding union support.

Recent research tends to cast doubt on the central importance of structural and compositional factors in the union decline. The logic of the structural-compositional explanation relies on the assumption that the characteristics of those who were unionized in the past are good predictors of who can be unionized. For example, women historically have had lower rates of unionization than males, so when the labor force shifts to include more women, the structural explanation depicts this change as adverse to union organizing. Yet among unorganized workers, higher percentages of women than men report that they would be willing to vote for a union, and so the underlying assumption may be false. Thus, present or past union characteristics may provide an unsound basis for extrapolation.

Although conflicting findings remain, recent research suggests that structural and compositional factors played an important role during the early years of the unions' decline but a much more limited role beginning in the mid-1970s. Richard Freeman and James Medoff, for example, studied the period 1954–79 and found that structural and compositional factors accounted for more than 72 percent of the union decline. Although, for reasons that they note, this estimate is surely on the high side, it seems likely that these factors did have considerable impact. After the 1970s, however, structural and compositional shifts accounted for far less of the union decline. MIT's [Massachusetts Institute of Technology] Henry Farber, in perhaps the most persuasive study, finds that only about 20 percent of the decline between 1977 and 1984 can be traced to structural and compositional factors.

A Host of Explanations

Among the host of other possible explanations for the unions' declining success at new organizing, four causes in particular have gotten substantial empirical support. First, unions seem to be putting fewer resources into organizing. Paula Voos found that unions' expenditures to organize nonunion workers within their jurisdictions fell dramatically during the period she studied, 1953 to 1977. Richard Freeman and James Medoff suggest that as much as one-third of the decline in new members attracted through organizing may be due to this factor. When unions do invest in organizing campaigns, their return in terms of new members is less than in the past, so some have argued that the unions' shrinking investment in organizing is simply a rational response.

Second, it is clear that the legal environment has become increasingly hostile to union organizing. For example, it has become much more difficult for a union, after it obtains sufficient worker signatures to trigger an NLRB election, to get the Labor Board to hold an election; the opportunities for employers to challenge, delay, and disrupt the election process have substantially expanded. So too, adverse labor-law rulings have greatly strengthened the employers' role in elections and weakened the unions' hand. All efforts to achieve major reforms, such as amending the NLRA [National Labor Relations Act] to tip the balance in favor of unions, have failed. Indeed, AFL-CIO [American Federation of Labor–Congress of Industrial Organizations] president Lane Kirkland, reflecting the deep antipathy of unionism to the current legal situation, has termed labor law a "dead letter" and occasionally called for its repeal, saying at one point that

110

workers may be "better off with the law of the jungle. . . . Let us go mano a mano. I think we could organize very rapidly."

Third, many investigators have documented the explosive growth of employer opposition to union organizing. Assisted by burgeoning numbers of "union-avoidance" consultants, employers have developed sophisticated defenses against organizing campaigns, and many observers have suggested that management resistance plays a central role in the unions' lack of organizing success. Richard Freeman and James Medoff assign between a quarter and a half of the decline in union organizing success through NLRB elections to rising management opposition. Henry Farber also finds significant evidence of increased employer resistance to unionization. Indeed, this employer offensive has been so powerful that "decertification" efforts—attempts to dislodge existing unions—have become increasingly successful. In 1989 there were 622 decertification elections, with the antiunion side winning 70.9 percent of them and the unions losing the right to represent 14,809 workers. Although this figure represents a tiny fraction of a private labor force totaling more than 90 million, it looms large when compared to the unions' yield (96,771 in 1989) from organizing: for every 6.5 new members the unions manage to attract, 1 existing member is lost through decertification.

Worker Disinterest in Unionization

Finally, and perhaps most disturbingly for the union cause, there is growing evidence to support the conclusion that nonunion workers do not see unions as effective agents on their behalf and that growing numbers of them do not want union representation. Although workers' perceptions of unions are not formed independently of, for example, employers' efforts to oppose unions or the unions' ability to achieve real gains for workers, the unions' task is made immeasurably more difficult if their organizing efforts are not only stymied by law and resisted by employers but also spurned by the unorganized. Yet that conclusion is indicated by the downward trends, already noted, in pro-union votes in NLRB elections. One might expect that workers voting in these elections would be more strongly pro-union than other unorganized workers, because an election typically is triggered only when an organizing team is convinced that it has sufficient support to win. Yet among the limited and presumably more pro-union set of workers who get a chance to vote in these elections, fewer than half (49.0 percent in 1989) cast ballots for unionization. The high rate of antiunion votes in NLRB decertification elections would reinforce this point, although in these elections the voters are workers who already are represented by a union. In the same vein, Henry Farber reports that between 1977 and 1984 the percentage of nonunion workers who said they would vote for a union if given the chance fell from 38.6 percent to 32.4 percent; Farber concludes that the reduction in the demand for unionization played a crucial part in the union decline. Finally, these results parallel the public's increasingly unfavorable image of union leaders: as late as the early 1970s, 20 percent of the public as surveyed by the Harris Poll had "a great deal of confidence" in union leaders, but by the end of the 1980s this figure had slumped to 10 percent.

To summarize, the severe decline in the unionized share of private-sector workers has resulted from the unions' loss of previously organized members and inability to attract new ones. The NLRB elections for union certification engage a declining percentage of the economy's unorganized work force, and voters in these elections are less likely to vote union. Structural or compositional changes in jobs and workers may account for part of the unions' troubles, but more crucial are diminishing union resources devoted to organizing drives, adverse legal changes, a powerful antiunion offensive by employers, and declining interest in unionization among nonunion workers.

"The labor movement . . . is slowly beginning to awake."

The Influence of Labor Unions May Be Increasing

John B. Judis

At the end of the 1970s membership in labor unions began to decline steadily. In the following viewpoint, John B. Judis maintains that union membership is now beginning to increase. Unions are attracting new members, he argues, by starting new organizing efforts, electing new leaders, and changing strategies to soften their often-adversarial relationship with management. Judis is a contributing editor for the *New Republic*, a weekly journal of opinion.

As you read, consider the following questions:

1. Why are labor unions increasing in popularity among workers, according to Judis?
2. According to the author, what are some of the tactics labor's new leaders are using to increase union popularity?
3. How would the revival of unions benefit society, according to Judis?

From John B. Judis, "Can Labor Come Back?" *The New Republic*, May 23, 1994. Reprinted by permission of *The New Republic*, ©1994, The New Republic, Inc.

The 1994 Teamsters strike, the *Los Angeles Times* declared, "has served as a reminder of how much the union's influence has waned." The outcome, the *New York Times* wrote, showed how the union's "power has shrunk." There is some truth in these statements, but they reveal more about the national press's attitude toward labor than about the Teamsters union. During the twenty-four-day strike, the longest in Teamster history and the first since 1979, the union achieved almost 100 percent support from its rank and file, in spite of violent dissension in its upper ranks. In the provisional settlement the union made concessions on the use of rail to replace trucks, but it won wage and benefit increases and halted the replacement of full-time union workers with part-time nonunion help. The deal was not a spectacular union victory, but the strike itself was a sign that the labor movement, which has slumbered for the past fifteen years, is slowly beginning to awake.

Union Gains

There are other signs of stirring. Although union membership steadily declined from 22 million in 1975 to 16.4 million in 1992, it actually grew in 1993, to 16.6 million—the first gain since 1980. Unions are winning strikes they would have lost a decade ago; in late 1993 both the American Airlines flight attendants and the United Mine Workers (UMW) concluded successful actions. Workers are more receptive to joining unions. "We're walking into situations where workers are begging us to organize," says Richard Bensinger, the director of the AFL-CIO's [American Federation of Labor–Congress of Industrial Organizations] Organizing Institute, which trains union organizers. "There is a new anger when we go into the field." And a new, militant leadership has emerged atop many of the major unions.

After the AFL-CIO's lobbying failed to block the North American Free Trade Agreement (NAFTA), there were also pronouncements that labor had lost its clout in Washington. But while the AFL-CIO couldn't buck Clinton on a treaty that may have little impact on its members—American firms were already moving to Mexico without NAFTA's encouragement—labor has gotten Clinton to cooperate on appointments and legislation that matter more.

What accounts for labor's new stirring? Workers across the spectrum have grown restive. Frustrated by two decades of falling wages, they're angered by runaway shops and corporate downsizing at companies like Zenith and Sears. Truckers' and dock workers' real wages, for instance, declined by 20 percent from 1977 to 1992. Unions, for their part, are discovering that they can organize workers they formerly ignored or gave up on. Once, union leaders assumed it was much more difficult to recruit nurses or waitresses than machinists or assembly-line workers, because service-sector workers were either professionals who disdained unions or part-time minimum wage workers who didn't stay in one job long enough to be organized. Union leaders have discovered it is quite possible to organize such workers, because the owners of hotels, hospitals or grocery stores can't respond to organizing drives by threatening to move their businesses elsewhere.

A New Era of Union Growth

AFL-CIO President Lane Kirkland applauded President Bill Clinton for lifting the lifetime ban on permanent hiring of air traffic controllers imposed by former President Ronald Reagan.

This, along with a string of recent labor-organizing victories and union mergers, suggests that the trade union movement may be on the brink of a new era of growth. No development would do more to raise the living standards of the entire labor force, including unorganized workers, who have also benefited by organized labor's pioneering of such reforms as the minimum wage, workmen's compensation and health and safety requirements.

Coretta Scott King, *Liberal Opinion Week*, September 13, 1993.

Unions are having their greatest success among white-collar, service and government workers. At the same time that blue-collar manufacturing unions have lost members, the Service Employees International Union (SEIU), the United Food and Commercial Workers (UFCW), the National Education Association, the American Federation of Teachers and the American Federation of State, County and Municipal Employees (AFSCME) have each continued to grow. SEIU has gained 400,000 members since 1980. Since 1988 the UFCW has increased the number of unionized workers in retail grocery stores from 67 percent to 72 percent and in meat packing from 50 percent to 65 percent. The UFCW, which added 100,000 workers during the entire 1980s, added the same amount in 1993 alone. Also in 1993 AFSCME upped its membership by 22,000; it is now on the verge of displacing the Teamsters as the nation's largest union. Though some dismiss public workers as a valid group, there are now more people employed in government than in private manufacturing.

Unions themselves have developed new organizing strategies. Consider the success of Justice for Janitors, an SEIU organizing project. Two decades ago buildings began contracting out their janitorial work to nonunion businesses with work forces made up of minorities and recent immigrants, many of whom had been hired on a part-time basis. By the start of the '80s the old janitorial unions were decimated—for instance, none of Washington, D.C.'s and only 30 percent of Los Angeles's janitors were organized.

Justice for Janitors, founded in 1987, has reversed that trend. The union introduced a strategy, borrowed from the industrial unions of the '30s, of seeking area-wide contracts with building owners regardless of which janitorial service they hired to do their cleaning. Instead of seeking supervised elections through the National Labor Relations Board [NLRB], which employers can thwart through court appeals, Justice for Janitors forced the building owners to negotiate directly with the unions. And they used '60s-style sit-downs and demonstrations to embarrass building owners, many of whom were prominent in local politics. "What we are doing is sort of back to the future," says Justice for Janitors cofounder Steve Lerner. Today, 40 percent of D.C.'s janitors and 90 percent of L.A.'s janitors are organized— thanks to Justice for Janitors.

Labor Leaders

Some of labor's revival has to do with new leaders who have emerged since 1980. In contrast to the generation that reigned after World War II, these leaders are more focused on organizing new members rather than simply meeting the needs of the old. In 1982 Richard Trumka was elected president of the UMW against a slate that threatened to take the union back to the dark days of W.A. "Tony" Boyle, when dues were squandered and dissidents were murdered. Trumka, a coal miner with a law degree, has since been twice re-elected. In 1993 he led a successful seven-month strike against the large companies of the Bituminous Coal Operators Association. The strategy that Trumka followed may set a trend for future labor actions: it combined old-style militancy with a willingness to set up a joint labor-management program in the coal fields. The miners call it a "get along" program.

Then there are the Teamsters. In 1992, in a government-supervised vote, former UPS driver Ron Carey took over the 1.4-million-member union, which was controlled by organized crime. During the strike the press made much of Carey's personal real estate holdings—a common way in which better-paid blue-collar workers invest their earnings and inheritance—but failed to uncover any evidence of corruption. Indeed, Carey appears to have struggled valiantly to reform the Teamsters, which are still plagued by fierce factionalism and by the remnants of the old regime. It was remarkable that he was able to lead a nationwide strike—the largest in the United States since 1986—in the face of vocal rebellion.

Other unions have also undergone dramatic changes. In 1991 delegates from the Transportation Communications International Union (TCU), which organizes railroad and airline workers, threw out their longtime leaders, whom they charged with paying more attention to their own needs than to their members' needs. The union's new president, Bob Scardelletti, shuns the Washington luncheon circuit for meetings with the union's rank and file. In 1994 the UFCW ousted its president, William Wynn, who faced charges of union fund misuse, and elected Doug Dority, a former grocery clerk, who headed the union's highly successful organizing drives during the '80s.

Unions also have found unexpected support from a group of liberal and left-wing intellectuals—many of them associated with the Economic Policy Institute (EPI), a Washington think tank. These economists and sociologists represent a dissenting current within the broader left. Since the '60s, most left-wing academics have gravitated toward more fashionable concerns with racial and sexual inequality or Third World underdevelopment. Those who have professed an interest in labor generally have seen the movement as an instrument of revolution, weakened by a cadre of industrial quislings.

The dissenters concern themselves with the actual function of unions and with the evolving relations between business and labor. Some of them, such as Barry Bluestone of the University of Massachusetts or Brian Turner of Washington's Institute for Work and Technology, are children of union officials; others, such as the University of California's Harley Shaiken, are veterans of the assembly line. They include Richard Freeman of Harvard (co-author of the landmark *What Do Unions Do?*), Bennett Harrison of Carnegie-Mellon, Paula Voos, the chair of the University of Wisconsin's department of industrial relations, and several Clinton administration officials, among them Labor Department Chief Economist Lawrence Katz, Labor Secretary Robert Reich and Council of Economic Advisers Chair Laura Tyson.

Increasing Competitiveness

These intellectuals generally recognize that unions can't content themselves simply with getting the best deal for their members; unions also have to worry about helping companies compete effectively. Freeman, Bluestone, Turner and others argue that new forms of labor/management cooperation can protect worker rights and raise firms' productivity, as has already happened in Japan and Western Europe and is happening now at Corning Glass, General Motors's Saturn division and U.S. West's Home and Personal Services division. Within the labor movement they promote a subtle interplay between militance and cooperation. And their vision of America bears far more resemblance to progressive era industrial democracy than to Marxian socialism.

This strategy of fostering higher productivity through labor/management cooperation is still opposed by some union leaders, including the Teamsters' Carey and Moe Biller of the Postal Workers. But since 1984 leaders of several major unions, including the United Auto Workers, United Steel Workers and the Communications Workers of America, have embraced it and the intellectuals who have espoused it.

Labor is also getting a boost from the Clinton administration. Clinton, the former governor of a right-to-work state, has never expressed the same kind of affection for the labor movement that he has for the civil rights or women's movements, but he knows that labor is an important part of his political coalition. Clinton has made pro-labor appointments to government agencies, and his administration has consulted closely with unions on relevant legislation (welfare reform, national service, health care). "Our experience has been the absolute opposite of [what it was with] Reagan and Bush," says AFSCME President Gerald McEntee. "With these people, we have input and influence.". . .

A Pro-Labor Administration

On the legislative front, Clinton has endorsed a bill that would end the use of replacement workers during strikes and another that would strengthen worker health and safety rules. . . . Clinton and Reich have sent several other pro-labor signals as well: removing Reagan's ban on hiring the air-traffic controllers fired during the 1981 PATCO [Professional Air Traffic Controllers Organization] strike; rescinding Bush administration strictures on construction unions; limiting government enforcement of the court decision allowing union workers to demand back money spent for union political activity; intervening personally and forcefully to settle the American Airlines flight attendants' strike; and playing a quiet role in helping conclude the mine workers' strike.

The rise of new leadership and a new intelligentsia, a sympathetic administration, growing anger in the workplace—all these suggest that labor may be on the verge of the kind of breakthrough that took place in the '30s, when union membership doubled in four years. Yet some of the same factors that contributed to labor's subsequent decline still exist.

Problems to Overcome

One major problem is business hostility to unions. Labor's seventeen-year decline in membership was caused primarily by a concerted business offensive that began in the early '70s and still has not abated. Threatened by competition from abroad and by overcapacity in many industries, corporate managers have aggressively fought unionization and have even attempted to de-certify existing unions. They have used the threat of moving jobs overseas to intimidate workers who want to form unions; they have hired anti-union consultants to contest representation elections; and they have sometimes refused to sign contracts with unions—even when they have lost union elections.

Many of their tactics violate existing labor law. In 1957 the NLRB ordered the reinstatement of 922 workers fired illegally for organizing a union; in 1980 more than 10,000 workers were reinstated. Yet the penalties for breaking the law are minimal. If the board finds a company guilty, the company has to reinstate the worker and pay his or her back wages—minus whatever the worker has earned from another job. . . .

Leadership Problems

A second problem for the movement is a national leadership vacuum that holds back its growth. Like his predecessor, George Meany, AFL-CIO President Lane Kirkland conceives of the fed-eration as a kind of city-state—a labor Vatican rather than the center of a social movement. While Kirkland deserves credit for bringing the UAW, the UMW and the Teamsters back into the federation, he has devoted his attention primarily to establishing the AFL-CIO as a player in Washington politics, while leaving the task of organizing the unorganized to the federation's affili-ates. Incredibly, the federation continues to spend more money on foreign policy ventures than on organizing. . . .

Under Kirkland the AFL CIO also has kept its distance from new experiments in labor relations and collective bargaining. "I describe the platform of the AFL-CIO in high performance workplace issues as having its head stuck in the sand and its hand over its crotch hoping for the best," says a union official who pushed for such cooperation.

Some union leaders argue that what the federation does is far less important than what the individual unions do—that it's not the federation's job to push organizing. That's partly true. Yet Kirkland's approach has filtered down through the movement it-self. Many unions and their locals still put far more emphasis on conventional political lobbying and campaigning than on or-ganizing new members. One labor organizer tells of speaking at a recent meeting of 150 local union leaders in Chicago. When he asked how many of them had worked on a Democratic party campaign, almost every hand went up. When he asked how many of them had participated in an organizing drive, not one hand went up.

119

What would be the consequences of labor's revival? I would suggest that many of the social and economic ills Americans now blame on technology, television and drug trafficking—from the decline in living standards to the loss of community—are traceable to labor's decline and could be partly remedied by its rejuvenation.

Beginning in the mid-1930s unions raised workers' wages well above what they otherwise would have been; the result has been a fairer distribution of the nation's wealth and greater purchasing power for the country's goods. Nonunionized workers also benefited, as employers raised their wages and gave them benefits to discourage them from joining unions. Conversely, when unions declined in the 1970s, so did the real wages of union and nonunion workers alike.

At the same time, in many towns and cities, thriving union halls replaced churches and pubs as the center of social and political life, holding together neighborhoods that would have been divided bitterly along racial and ethnic lines. The labor movement had an especially profound effect on black Americans, contributing a generation of black leaders—including A. Philip Randolph, Bayard Rustin, Coleman Young and Charles Hayes—who pursued the ideal of racial integration rather than separation. As the labor movement has receded, this broader sense of community has disappeared in favor of polarizing visions based on racial or ethnic animosity. The left itself has become an apostle of division and divisiveness.

The success of unions also forged some balance between business and labor in the market and in politics. The postwar American pluralism celebrated by political scientists David Truman, Robert Dahl and V. O. Key had its defects, but it was far more representative than the system that preceded and succeeded it. When labor faltered, a disproportionate amount of power was placed in the hands not only of business but of special interest groups—from NARAL [National Abortion Rights Action League] to the NRA [National Rifle Association]. The shift in power didn't enhance direct democracy; it led to greater manipulation by unaccountable elites.

Competition and Rights

Of course, there is another side to this story. Freeman and other labor economists acknowledge that the high wages and elaborate work rules won by labor unions contributed to the failure of American firms to keep pace with their competitors in the '70s. Labor's revival could similarly cripple American firms and leave workers worse off in the long run. And while the leadership of the United Auto Workers, the Communications Workers of America and other major unions have learned over the last two decades that it is not in their interest to reach agreements that will make it harder for companies to compete, other unions still adhere to a 1930s, us-vs.-them model of industrial unionism. The intransigence of these unions is reinforced by the hostility that many employers display toward any union, whatever its objectives.

The question for the '90s will be whether labor and business can meet each other halfway—exchanging, in effect, union recognition of business's need to compete with business's recognition of unions' right to represent workers. If labor and business do come together, we'll all benefit, whether we belong to a union or not.

"The need for the protection and support of trade unionism in a variety of U.S. industries has perhaps never been greater."

Unions Are Still Necessary

Kevin Clarke

In the following viewpoint, Kevin Clarke argues that unions are vital to women, minorities, immigrants, and some industries well known for abusing their workers. Without unions and the power they wield through collective bargaining and the threat of strikes, Clarke argues, these groups will continue to suffer from abusive supervisors, dangerous working conditions, and artificially low wages. Clarke is a freelance writer and an assistant editor for *Salt*, a Christian magazine dedicated to social justice.

As you read, consider the following questions:

1. What stereotypes have organizers had to overcome about unions, according to Clarke?
2. What techniques have business owners and managers adopted to thwart union organizing, according to the author?
3. According to Clarke, in what industries have unions succeeded in improving working conditions for their members?

Kevin Clarke, "Four Places Where Unions Still Have a Job to Do," *Salt*, February 1994. Reprinted with permission of the author.

Carmen Ivarra worked sewing together blue jeans for 23 years in El Paso, Texas. She doesn't even know what brand of jeans they were. That's not too surprising, though. She didn't work for a brand name, just a Texas subcontractor. That makes things easier for the client company when an inevitable round of layoffs begin.

She never made much more than whatever the minimum wage of the era happened to be.

"And they tell you, 'If you don't like that pay, you can leave.' "

She never got paid holidays, vacation, benefits. One thing she did get was a bit of a surprise one day a few years ago when she went to work and discovered her job had shipped out to Mexico.

Ivarra is currently the director of El Paso's Mujer Obrera, an educational and advocacy agency for the Hispanic women who work in the city's garment industry.

Tough Conditions

During her working life in the industry, she remembers laboring under tough conditions and under male supervisors who didn't speak her language, who daily treated her and her coworkers with contempt.

"They would be always patting you, touching you—especially the pretty [women], the young ones. They would say, 'If you want to work here, you have to go out with me,' and do, you know, what they asked. But what could you do? These women had two or three children at home to support. You don't want to lose your job."

Throughout the hot Texas summers she worked in warehouses without air conditioning or proper ventilation; in the winter without heat. She worked long hours on unannounced overtime shifts that left her worrying about her children but unable to leave to check on them under the familiar threat of losing her job.

Her supervisors rained abuse on the workers. "That was harder on the ones who spoke English because they could understand all the nasty things they were saying," she says.

While some like to argue that unionism has outlived its usefulness in the United States, Ivarra's experience is depressing evidence that as the nation approaches the 21st century, the need for the protection and support of trade unionism in a variety of U.S. industries has perhaps never been greater. As unions are dislocated from good-paying, heavy industrial jobs finding homes in other nations, they have begun to reach out to the low-paying, semi- or low-skilled, often minority work force that Ivarra and her coworkers represent. . . .

The nonunion women workers of El Paso are not alone. Of the nation's approximately 52 million working women, only about 12 percent—or a little over 6 million—are organized. But that percentage has been increasing; two out of every three new union members are women.

Many working women in the U.S. earn their paychecks in clerical, office, and other low-level white-collar jobs—the kind of work that Rondy Murray, president of the Clerical-Technical Union of Michigan State University in East Lansing, Michigan, believes could easily go union.

"When organizing clerical workers you have to have a different language than when you're talking to autoworkers.

"Clerical workers don't necessarily think of themselves as being part of a culture of unionism—they see it as a male, factory [experience].

"Clerical workers develop a loyalty to their immediate boss. The intimacy of the relationship works against unionizing," Murray says. "You hear things like: 'I really like my professor; I don't want him to be mad at me if I ask for a raise.'"

She says it took five years for most women workers at her university to finally call their organization a union instead of an "association.". . .

Coming Clean on Immigrant Workers

The federal Bureau of Labor Statistics doesn't regularly track the number of people who have come from other nations to work in the United States, whether documented or undocumented. But a 1989 report projected that just under 10 million of the nation's 109 million workers are immigrants.

One labor advocate says, because of their "newness," immigrants entering the U.S. labor force are "wide open for exploitation." Many don't speak English and, as a result, don't understand the work agreements they're signing. That can mean, for instance, that they end up accepting overtime agreements that would make even the most cold-blooded capitalist blush. Many immigrant workers don't know or understand their civil and labor rights under U.S. law and don't know where to turn when those rights have been abused. Many are working in the United States without the proper documentation and unwilling to get involved with anything official-looking like union paperwork.

They can be easily intimidated by employers who threaten them with the Immigration and Naturalization Service (INS). One union organizer tells the story of a meat-packing plant about to "go union." When the plant's workers, most of them Mexican, voted to join the United Food and Commercial Workers (UFCW), managers contacted the INS and organized a raid on their own factory.

Often a particularly abhorrent tactic is to pit the latest immigrant group against another ethnic labor population that may have itself been used to displace a previous group. For example,

Mexican workers who may have been hired to bust a union in a meat-packing plant find their own jobs jeopardized by Southeast Asian workers being recruited for even less money than they accepted.

"That [strategy has] been used in a lot of places," says Joan Suarez, Southwest regional director of organizing for the Amalgamated Clothing and Textile Workers Union (ACTWU).

"What you have to do then is make clear to [both groups of workers] their common interests and make them understand that they are not enemies."

Suarez interrupts herself with a related thought: "That goes for workers across the border [in Mexico] as well."

Cultural Sensitivity

To combat those kinds of strategies, unions are hiring organizers right out of the ethnic communities they are attempting to organize. Vietnamese organizers go after Vietnamese laborers; Spanish-speaking organizers reach out to Mexican and Central American workers.

"Having people who look like you, who understand your culture, organizing for you—and finding them on your shop floor best of all—this whole emphasis on understanding culture and language can't be diminished," says Jim Benn of Chicago's Federation for Industrial Retention and Renewal.

That sensitivity to culture and ethnicity means that whether they intend it or not, many unions focusing on immigrant workers have found themselves at the forefront of the fight for racial tolerance in some communities.

"You can't say [to immigrant workers] you're going to be union without embracing their cause," says Benn.

That has been part of the strategy at the heart of the nationwide Justice for Janitors campaign. Stephen Lerner is working on that effort as an organizer for the Service Employees International Union (SEIU). Lerner says his union has found itself battling on such nonwork issues as affordable housing and police brutality. . . .

New Corporate Strategies

The industry that Lerner is attempting to organize has undergone a drastic transformation in only a few short years. Not only has the work force shifted to primarily immigrant labor, but maintenance employees have become pawns in a perplexing new corporate strategy.

While in the past janitors may have worked directly for specific building owners, they now find themselves working for "maintenance contractors," businesses that bid among each other for cleaning contracts.

Often the competitive edge contractors seek is sharpened on the salaries of their employees.

"Workers will go to the contractor and say they need to be paid more money, and he'll say, 'I'm sorry, I haven't got any more; that's what we bid for. Go talk to the building owner,'" Lerner says.

"When they talk to the building owner they're told, 'It's not my problem; I don't have any employees.'"

Membership Gains

[Some] unions are actually posting membership gains because of their organizing focus. The Service Employees International Union has grown from 817,000 members in 1985 to more than 1 million today. That makes the SEIU one of the fastest-growing unions in the U.S. Andrew Stern, the head of organizing at SEIU, estimates that only 20% of his union's expansion is attributable to the service sector's growth. The vast majority of the growth comes from organizing.

Granted, the SEIU is lucky to have a constituency largely comprised of women and minorities, two of the best groups to target these days, according to Edward Cohen-Rosenthal of Cornell University's School of Industrial and Labor Relations. "The union member of the future is increasingly professional, increasingly female, increasingly minority," he says.

Nanette Byrnes, *Financial World*, November 23, 1993.

"A big real-estate corporation would never admit that it's operating under these conditions . . . contracting out to skip the responsibility of paying the workers. Some people call it competitiveness and some people say it is increasing productivity, but all it is is passing the buck.

"There's been a dramatic decline in wage rates, and the working conditions just get worse and worse."

Jobs that had been well-paying now are falling to minimum-wage levels. And sometimes even below that, Lerner says.

"There's a number of scams to get around the minimum wage," he says, such as keeping workers on an extended "apprentice" status or informing them that they are no longer employees but "entrepreneurs" who aren't on a clock but contracting as individual "businesses" for work.

Under that scheme, cleaning companies subcontract a job they've received to a specific maintenance worker, offering him or her a predetermined, unadjustable rate for cleaning a building, say $400 a week or a flat annual fee.

Desperate to get the job, workers cornered in this manner often enlist their families to help with the cleaning job (often violating child-labor laws in the process) so that when the total worker hours are factored in, a maintenance "subcontractor" can be earning significantly less than minimum wage.

The Invisible Workforce

"I call janitors the invisible work force," says Lerner, trying to explain why his workers have endured such a rough ride.

"They come in at night, and they do their work when nobody's around. In one sense, it's easy to pay them poorly."

But that's not the only reason for the downturn in building workers' real income. Lerner says it would be hard to prove, but he thinks in the late 1980s there was a deliberate attempt to hire immigrant labor in an effort to break janitors' unions.

In 1984, says Lerner, maintenance workers in San Francisco—most commonly African American—were earning on average $7.49 an hour with full health and other union benefits.

In just three years the work force had shifted to immigrant workers earning minimum wage, and the union was totally broken.

"Just as [companies] had searched out African Americans because they thought they would be more vulnerable, they looked for workers they could exploit."

In SEIU's efforts to rebuild the union, however, Lerner is discovering their supposed vulnerability is only one of many possible misperceptions regarding immigrant workers. Lerner and other organizers are finding that immigrant workers are not only interested in unionizing, but that many of them had been leaders of far more dangerous trade-unionist fights back in their native lands.

"When I come into a room full of El Salvadoran workers and I . . . try to warn them, 'This is going to be a tough fight and some of you may lose your jobs and some of you may get harassed somehow,' they look at me and say, 'Is that all? You mean they don't shoot you for joining a union here?'" . . .

The Meat of the Matter

Another U.S. industry employing increasing numbers of immigrants—most frequently Mexican and Southeast Asian—is meat packing and processing. And it's in attempts to organize those workers that activists are encountering some of the nakedly anti-union tactics perhaps most associated in the public mind with the great and sometimes violent union struggles of the late 19th and early 20th centuries.

Unfortunately, that kind of resistance to trade unionism by management is hardly limited to the meat-packing industry.

Most organizers can tell tales similar to the horror stories the United Food and Commercial Workers' [UFCW] Greg Dineer recounts.

Anti-Union Tactics

A well-worn tactic employed by one of the largest meat-packing companies in the country is simply to close down a plant when its workers vote in a union—opening another plant in another city with nonunion workers or simply waiting awhile and reopening the same plant with newly recruited workers.

"The conditions in a meat-processing plant in the late 20th century are not terribly different from those of the late 19th century—both in terms of the way workers are treated and in terms of the sanitary conditions.

"We have to fight the same kinds of battles," Dineer says. "In fact, the sanitary conditions in the plants are part of the health and safety [concerns the workers have]. If you have unsanitary conditions in a plant, then it's generally not a safe place for workers, and it's generally not good for producing safe food."

Upton Sinclair would have little problem producing a sequel to *The Jungle* [a 1906 exposé of abuses in the meat-packing industry], according to Dineer, if he were around to tour the meat-packing industry today.

Conditions in poultry-processing facilities can be among the worst.

"If you went to a poultry plant, you might never eat chicken again," Dineer says with a short laugh. At one Tyson facility, he adds, workers had to bring in their own drinking water because the plant's system had become so contaminated. Workers at a hog-processing facility have contracted brucellosis, a bacterial infection leading to fever and chills usually limited to livestock. It can be hard to treat in humans.

Beyond issues of health and safety, Dineer says meat packers face an almost constant barrage of threats and intimidation when they raise the issue of organizing. Creating tension between one ethnic group and another is only part of the union-busting tactics he has encountered. The shutdown of a union plant is frequently used as an example—and thinly veiled threat—when workers at other plants seek a wage hike. . . .

The UFCW currently represents 180,000 food- and meat-packing industry workers—over 60 percent of the nation's beef-processing workers and lower percentages of hog and poultry workers. Increasing these percentages is important, Dineer says, because "the nonunion plants will set the wage rates if they are the dominant force in the industry. " Almost 400,000 people are currently employed in the meat-packing industry.

"Electronic sweatshops": offices where men and women labor

before buzzing computer terminals—not blasting furnaces—engaged in data processing, accepting airplane and hotel reservations, taking telephone sales orders, or otherwise moving information along. Equipped with trusty headset and keyboard, these workers represent what may become a large part of the nation's future employment profile.

They will join the 18 million people now working in the nation's administrative and clerical jobs. Only about 2.3 million of those workers are organized, which is unfortunate by at least one standard. According to the Bureau of Labor Statistics, union administrative and clerical workers earn a median weekly income of $493; nonunion counterparts take home $363.

The number of organized office workers has to go up, says Debbie Schneider [president of District 925, a national, predominately female union of clerical workers]. "More and more people are working in these office factories," Schneider says.

Her use of "factories" is no slip of the tongue.

In her view, union representation will be critical to the office workers of the future as they begin to face the same treatment previously unheard of outside of manufacturing industries. . . .

But unions have another, more positive role to play in the workplace of the future, according to U.S. Steelworkers Union President Lynn Williams. Team management and a gamut of other worker-participation and empowerment programs have been part of the manufacturing mantra since the 1980s.

"Having a say in how work is performed is an absolutely essential element in producing in a high-quality, highly competitive enterprise," Williams says. He cites the successes of Saturn automobiles and a recently resurgent Xerox Corporation as two instances where union-worker participation made the difference in putting out a high-quality, technologically sophisticated product.

But, Williams argues, it's only in a union environment that significant worker participation can be achieved.

"A lot of employers say they want to hear your opinion. They want to hear you speak up. Well . . . maybe you can and maybe you can't," he says.

Unions provide workers not only with an assurance that they can participate—that they can speak their minds without retribution—but also with the infrastructure, the platform, to do it upon. "You can't create a democracy without a constitution," Williams says.

"People need to feel confident and able to be candid and open in that process." And, last but certainly not least, unions help workers define through collective bargaining what their share in their industry's success will be.

═══════════════════════════════════════

"The majority—as many as two thirds—of nonunion workers oppose unionism."

═══════════════════════════════════════

Unions Are Outdated

Leo Troy

Leo Troy is a professor of economics at Rutgers University in Newark, New Jersey. In the following viewpoint, he maintains that the decline in union membership that began in the 1950s will continue into the twenty-first century. Unions, Troy argues, will represent a few industries, but international competition will continue to weaken their influence. Although the Clinton administration in 1993 professed an alliance with organized labor, government attempts to revive unionism will fail because they run counter to the increasing acceptance and expansion of market forces worldwide.

As you read, consider the following questions:

1. How has international competition affected unions all over the world, according to the author?
2. According to Troy, why has labor law weakened?
3. Why do most nonunion workers oppose unionism, according to the Harris poll cited by the author?

From Leo Troy, "Big Labor's Big Problems," *Business & Society Review*, Fall 1993. Reprinted with permission of the author.

Private sector unionism, what may be termed the Old Unionism, has shrunk so drastically in membership and market share, and its future looks so bleak, that its condition begs the question, "Are we witnessing the end of the Old Unionism?" In short, my answer is no. However, in the future, the Old Unionism will be limited to a few industries, and its impact on the economy and society in general will be substantially reduced.

Trends in the Old Unionism's market share and membership support this forecast. The peak of the Old Unionism in market share, 36 percent, was scaled in 1953. It has continued to skid without a single year's interruption ever since. Currently it is approaching 10 percent of the labor market, a rate of penetration less than in 1929. Membership, which in 1970 numbered 17 million at its all-time high, has shrunk to less than 10 million over the last two decades. And by the turn of the new century, I estimate that the Old Unionism will represent only 7 percent of the labor market, or a share about the same as at the beginning of the twentieth century.

A much different record and future describe the other branch of unionism—public sector, or the New Unionism—which is one of growth or at least stability. An analysis of its different future is beyond the scope of this account, except to point out that the New Unionism's different prospects arise from its virtual immunity to market forces.

Secretary of Labor Robert B. Reich told the AFL-CIO [American Federation of Labor–Congress of Industrial Organizations] at its 1993 convention that the Clinton Administration identified itself completely with the interests of organized labor: "We understand that our agenda is exactly the same." Clearly, one shared goal would be to rebuild the Old Unionism. But can the Clinton Administration deliver?

To restore the Old Unionism to its record market penetration, unions would have to recruit over 22 million new members while holding on to all those they now enroll—an impossible task. This implies a total membership in excess of 32 million, a population which the Old Unionism never had. Consider a more modest goal. Could Clinton-Reich help the Old Unionism to recapture the 7 million members that unions lost over the last two decades? It appears not.

Markets Yes—Unionism No

The decline of the Old Unionism can be understood by examining what happened to membership and by what happened to labor markets. Global competition has been a major factor explaining the downsizing of the Old Unionism over the last two decades. The North American Free Trade Agreement (NAFTA) will reinforce international competition, and thereby further undermine union ranks.

The Administration and organized labor were at odds on NAFTA, so Reich's proclaimed solidarity with labor was breached on a matter of major concern to the AFL-CIO.

Global competition also explains why the decline of the Old Unionism is not unique to the United States. Its impact has been registered in Canada, Britain, Germany, France, other continental countries, and Japan. As in the United States, the Old Unionism in these nations has also declined both in membership and market share.

Choosing Union-Free Workplaces

Collective bargaining no longer provides a useful framework for a generalized system of workers' rights. Put simply, this is because unions today represent far too few workers to serve as the centerpiece for workers' rights. In the private sector, union members now account for only about one out of every eight workers. The overwhelming majority of workers do not have or do not choose to have unions to represent them.

Richard Edwards, *Rights at Work*, 1993.

While competition (domestic as well as international) reduced membership, structural changes in labor markets have shrunk the Old Unionism's market share. The structural change involves not only the overall shift of employment from goods to services, but also detailed changes within industries, most notably the increasing proportion of white-collar jobs that accompanied the switch to high-technology output. These are the types of jobs that the Old Unionism has historically been conspicuously unsuccessful in organizing. This structural change, even if the Old Unionism lost no members, reduced the Old Unionism's market share.

Competition and structural change led to the extensive deunionization of manufacturing, the core of union strength. Once over 40 percent unionized, manufacturing is now less than half [that] organized. Instead of deindustrialization, the claim that the U.S. was losing its manufacturing base, America experienced widespread deunionization. Not only was the charge of deindustrialization wrong on employment trends, but more important, in output: Manufacturing's share of real gross domestic product over the past several decades has remained stable. Because of increased productivity, fewer workers, especially blue-collar workers, were required for production. And since these were predominantly unionized blue-collar workers, union membership naturally declined.

Unions and their supporters attribute the decline of organized labor to employer opposition. Although this is a factor, it is a marginal one. In addition, unions and their supporters ascribe the growing ineffectiveness of the law to the Reagan-Bush presidencies. They personalize the effects of competitive markets, which are impersonal forces.

Markets have been the catalyst common to union decline and weakening of labor law because competition, the natural nemesis of monopoly, attacked both the monopoly power of unionism and the monopoly power of labor law. Thus, what is termed "labor law reform" by the Clinton-Reich team is, in economic terms, an effort to resuscitate the monopoly power of the Old Unionism and of labor law. However, the Clinton-Reich plans to revive monopoly power will be swimming against the tide. As market forces gain ever-widening acceptance worldwide (paradoxically, including the Administration's support of NAFTA), the Administration's anticipated labor policies are monopolistic, or what I term neomercantilist.

The Administration's program divides into two parts: The first, according to Labor Secretary Reich, is "to help close the chapter on the last twelve years." The second is "to outline a new, more productive chapter in the history of worker-management relations."

The Dirty Dozen Years

Secretary Reich's rationale for closing the Reagan-Bush chapter can only be described as Orwellian Newspeak. During those dozen years, the economy and the labor market experienced the longest peacetime expansion in the history of the country—ninety-two months. Second in duration was that under the first George, that is, George Washington, when the economy grew seventy-two months during the years of his two administrations, 1790 to 1798. In the period from 1980 to 1992, the labor market generated over 18 million jobs, more than three times the number of jobs (about 5 million) generated by the major countries of Western Europe—Germany, France, Italy, and the United Kingdom. Moreover, most of the new jobs generated in Europe were apparently in the public sector; few were private. The opposite was true in the United States.

In addition, the employment ratio in the United States reached new record highs in the 1980s. (The employment ratio is the proportion of employed to the potential working age population.) The rising ratio enabled new job entrants and the unemployed to find jobs, and thus pushed unemployment rates down. Meanwhile, Europe's employment ratio stagnated, limiting the number of new labor market entrants and the unemployed who could find jobs, and kept unemployment rates high.

Real domestic product in the United States increased nearly 28 percent over the "dirty dozen" Reagan-Bush years. Inflation and interest rates, which had run rampant in the Carter years, both dropped precipitously.

Secretary Reich also described the Reagan-Bush years as a period of "polarized distrust" and as a "conflict-ridden era" between workers and employers. How such a description can be reconciled with historic lows in strikes is a mystery. In addition, there were numerous instances of labor-management cooperation during those years: Employee stock ownership plans (ESOPs) that brought about the transfer of ownership from businessmen to workers and agreements such as the one between the United Auto Workers and General Motors regarding the Saturn automobile are but two examples.

The New Chapter in Worker-Management Relations

We are told that the Administration's new chapter in labor relations will contain a new "structure that furthers constant experimentation, development, and the flexibility to respond quickly to new ideas and needs by providing incrementally better products." To this end, the secretaries of labor and commerce jointly appointed a Commission on the Future of Worker-Management Relations. The euphemism "worker-management" relations should be read as "union-management" relations. Most of the American private work force—the nonunion work force that is nearly 90 percent of the total—was left out, as was small business. One needs to recall, too, that the Clinton inaugural festivities forced the cancellation of a parade float when it was learned that it was built and manned by nonunion workers. For an Administration that wants diversity, the principle evidently did not apply to even a minority representation for the majority of the work force.

In another example of Newspeak, Reich identified the commission as "a balanced group of experts from business, labor, and academia." If there is one certainty about the makeup of the commission it is its bias in favor of unions and collective bargaining. Indeed, the known positions of leading commission members facilitates the anticipation of the commission's recommendations.

The Administration intends to begin its plans for labor law reform with a ban on the permanent replacement of strikers. . . . The proposed ban has been an item on the unions' political wish list for a long time. However, the Carter Administration, as sympathetic as it was to organized labor, refused to include it in its proposed revision of the National Labor Relations Act in 1977.

If enacted, the ban will incite employer resistance to union organizing to a higher pitch because it will shackle employers' ability to resist bargaining demands. Denying employers the ability to produce during an economic siege (the strike) is one-sided, as the Roosevelt Supreme Court pointed out in upholding an employer's right to replace strikers in 1938. For unions, a ban on replacement would remove all economic risks to settle. If employers are denied the right to permanently replace strikers, the market will supply alternatives—increased substitution of capital for labor, contracting out, and outsourcing. Higher labor costs make capital substitution and technological changes relatively cheaper. Increased costs will give impetus to employers to move production offshore. Another incentive is NAFTA. Since the Administration supported NAFTA, and still claims to share solidarity with labor, which commitment is the public and organized labor to believe?

Backdoor Organizing

Among proposals that the commission of the Future of Worker-Management Relations is likely to introduce are "innovative forms of employee participation" or "alternative vehicles of representation." In essence, these would be tantamount to establishing mandatory works councils. One of its intellectual sponsors wrote that "it is necessary to take away from the employees (and also the employer) the choice about whether such a participatory mechanism will be present" with the right "of internal participation in a specified range of decisions in all enterprises." Not only would workers and employers have no voice in the matter, but the "range of decisions" must necessarily cover investment and locational decisions. Ultimately, the goal is union organization through the back door.

Other measures that might be anticipated from the commission are extending bargaining rights to supervisory employees; restoring the secondary boycott; quickie elections; card checks as a substitute for an election; banning state right-to-work laws; binding arbitration on first contract impasses; and the right of union representation even when the union represents only a minority of the work force.

Also expect other proposals that would increase the political power of unions. These would overturn the Supreme Court's decisions that hamper union expenditures of represented workers' dues and fees for political purposes. Meanwhile, Secretary Reich has already suspended plans to change unions' reporting requirements under the Labor-Management Reporting and Disclosure Act of 1958, which would compel them to show funds allocated to political purposes.

Finally, the National Labor Relations Board (NLRB) and the Office of the General Counsel will be reconstituted by new appointees, appointees whose views are indeed consonant with the Old Unionism.

But will all this government intervention—industrial policy in the labor market—revive the Old Unionism? No, it won't. Increased competition in the marketplace and changes in the labor market, which have undermined the membership and market share of the Old Unionism, have been under way for a generation, and more of the same is on the way. Despite more interventionist labor law, labor markets will continue to move in a direction away from the Old Unionism's historical base—blue-collar workers in goods industries (here and abroad)—and toward jobs and industries in which unions have never had much success in organizing.

Nonunion Labor Relations

Meanwhile, the extensive deunionization of industry has been accompanied by fundamental changes in nonunion labor relations. These innovations have strengthened the ability of nonunion employers to hold union organization at arm's length.

More important than employer opposition is employee opposition to the Old Unionism. Contrary to the conventional beliefs, polls have shown that the majority—as many as two thirds—of nonunion workers oppose unionism. They oppose joining unions, as a Harris poll showed, because they regard collective bargaining as basically irrelevant to their working lives. Fear of the employer ranked near the bottom of nonunion workers' reasons for opposing organization. Pragmatic, not ideological, reasons explain their attitudes. These attitudes have been reflected in the unions' losses in NLRB representation elections since President Carter's time.

Conceptually, the Old Unionism is essentially a twentieth-century phenomenon and, except in a few industries (auto, aerospace, steel), it will not be a significant general institution in the general labor market of the twenty-first century.

"Companies heeding the call for a dose of economic democracy have significantly improved their performance and competitive posture."

Labor-Management Partnerships Are Beneficial

Barry Bluestone and Irving Bluestone

Irving Bluestone is a professor of labor studies at Wayne State University in Detroit. He retired in 1980 as vice president of the United Auto Workers and director of its General Motors division. Barry Bluestone is a professor of political economy at the University of Massachusetts at Boston and a senior fellow at the university's Institute of Public Affairs. In the following viewpoint, adapted from their book *Negotiating the Future: A Labor Perspective on American Business*, the Bluestones contend that in order to become more competitive in the international economy, companies need to change the way their workplaces operate. They argue that management and labor must stop viewing each other as adversaries and find creative new ways, especially partnerships between labor unions and management, to make their industries succeed.

As you read, consider the following questions:

1. According to the authors, what may be "a dominant reason for the collapse in U.S. productivity growth"?
2. What benefits has the Donnelly Corporation received from its employee-management partnership, according to the Bluestones?

Life in the American workplace is changing. Industries are caught up in a whirlwind of experiments with "employee involvement," "problem-solving teams," "autonomous work groups," and "participative management." Along the way, "worker empowerment" has become part of the lexicon of some of America's toughest CEOs. Company leaders are ordering line supervisors to show greater respect for employees who not so long ago were treated merely as expendable cogs in a vast production machine. Teamwork, cooperation, and mutual trust are in; adversarialism is out.

These are refreshing trends. And companies heeding the call for a dose of economic democracy have significantly improved their performance and competitive posture. But the transformation of U.S. business is not spreading anywhere near fast enough or penetrating deep enough to meet the doggedly persistent challenge of global competition. Too few companies have taken industrial relations much beyond the archaic model of boss as "order giver" and employee as "order taker." And when times get tough, even the most progressive firms respond by getting lean and mean—that is, they lay off their workers.

An American economic renaissance requires not merely improvement but a revolution in the nation's work culture and in the structure of labor-management relations. Instead of limiting workers' input to the factory floor or outer office, management must bring labor into the inner circle where strategic decisions about the enterprise are made. And instead of viewing the company as its mortal enemy, labor must be willing to focus its energy on improving the competitiveness of the enterprise.

End of the Glory Days

The pressure for a labor-management revolution is of recent vintage. During America's economic "glory days"—roughly from 1947 through 1973—conflicts in authoritarian workplaces did not prevent stockholders from enjoying buoyant profits and workers from enjoying a modicum of employment security and a steadily rising standard of living. If workers stood around while engineers and supervisors tried to solve a machining problem because line employees were not expected to solve it on their own, or even allowed to try, there was enough slack in the system to permit such inefficiency. Hardly anyone was losing sales or jobs to the Japanese or the Germans, let alone the South Koreans or the Taiwanese.

But by the mid-1970s, the effortless economic superiority that America had come to know in the aftermath of World War II—measured in terms of productivity, product quality, and product innovation—evaporated in one industry after another. Productivity growth in the 1970s and 1980s fell well below previous post-war levels and continues to trail the growth rates achieved by our trading partners. With wages and profits outstripping efficiency growth during the 1970s, U.S. production costs increased relative to the competition with the result that many American goods were priced out of the market.

Product quality also lagged. By the mid 1980s, Americans were buying Hondas instead of Chevys not because they were cheaper—in fact they were not—but because their performance was better, their fuel efficiency superior, and their frequency of repair lower.

And in terms of new-product development and innovation, American firms were falling rapidly behind. VCRs and Nintendo games have perennially dominated Christmas sales, yet not a single one is designed or built by a U.S. firm. We can now add the laptop computer, the fax machine, and the video camcorder to the list of products for which the U.S. market share is essentially zero.

Why, after so much success in the early post-war years, has the United States fallen behind in these areas? The best economic statisticians have been able to explain only a fraction of the sharp decline. The oft-mentioned culprits of unsatisfactory savings rates and anemic capital investment, the shift from manufacturing to services, rising energy prices, and government "over-regulation" are apparently responsible for much less than half of the loss. After dozens of attempts, the consensus is that the remainder of the decline is due to "unmeasured factors."

But what is unmeasured? An intriguing factor, by economists' reckoning, is the failure of corporate managers to manage resources effectively. That productivity growth has been lowest in the labor-intensive service sector—indeed, negative in some nonmanufacturing industries including finance, insurance, real estate, and construction—suggests that how labor is used in the firm may well be a dominant reason for the collapse in U.S. productivity growth.

One revealing bit of data can be found in a major study of corporate efficiency conducted during the late 1970s by Theodore H. Barry Associates, a management consulting firm. The study found that only 4.4 hours of a typical employee's work day are used productively; some 1.2 hours are lost because of personal and other unavoidable delays while 2.4 hours are "just wasted." Such inefficiency is not anywhere near as common in Europe and Japan. This research does not necessarily imply that labor is lazy in America; it suggests that workers are poorly managed, that their intelligence, skill, and motivation go underused.

Employee Empowerment

As international competition began to squeeze profits, firms concluded correctly that they needed to get more than 4.4 hours of work out of an 8-hour day. To their discredit, however, and for many firms their demise, corporate leaders often went about improving efficiency in precisely the wrong way. They rolled up their sleeves, took a deep breath, and proceeded to imitate a management style pioneered by the Prussian military.

Because of its now infamous CEO, the most publicized case is Eastern Airlines. Aaron Bernstein, a journalist who followed the airline during its turbulent flight to bankruptcy, writes that Frank Lorenzo "represented the get-tough approach to management that Ronald Reagan had revived when the president fired striking air-traffic controllers in 1981." Instead of maintaining the high level of labor-management cooperation that had been forged in the company before his arrival, Lorenzo swerved 180 degrees. Intimidating employees into working harder and enacting unprecedented wage and benefit cuts, he so alienated them that they were ultimately willing to sacrifice their jobs to get rid of him. In fact, in April 1990, in the wake of one of the most bitter strikes in recent U.S. history and only four years after Lorenzo took over Eastern and the management of its 38,000 employees, a New York bankruptcy court declared him unfit to run the company. Eastern's logo disappeared from the sky and all employees lost their jobs.

Fortunately, a growing number of companies are much closer to the opposite end of the labor-management continuum. In their 1984 nationwide compendium *The 100 Best Companies to Work for in America*, Robert Levering and his colleagues identified the "best" companies as those that had transcended the manipulative framework of traditional management and achieved a sense of "we are all in it together." According to their criteria, a "good" company makes people feel that they are part of a team or, in some cases, a family. It encourages open communication, informing people of new developments, and encouraging them to offer suggestions and complaints. It stresses quality, enabling people to feel pride in the products or services they are providing. It reduces the distinctions of rank between top management and those in entry-level jobs. And, as a result, it enjoys a high level of success.

Worker Self-Management

Donnelly Corp., a Holland, Michigan–based manufacturer of mirrors, windows, and glass products for the auto industry, ranked as one of the 100 best. The goal at Donnelly is worker self-management. The firm has removed time clocks from its factory floor and put everyone on salary. Employees work in teams of eight or nine, with each team responsible for its own production goals. No one can be displaced by technological improvement. All grievances are reviewed and employee policies

140

set by a plant-wide committee with two-thirds of the membership composed of production workers. And all Donnelly employees share in profits through a bonus system.

Between 1975 and 1984, productivity at Donnelly rose 110 percent—a compounded rate of better than 7 percent per year, or five times greater than the national average. Despite the grave recession that struck the auto industry in the early 1990s, the company continued to expand and remain profitable. Employment has more than doubled since 1985, partially as a result of successfully increasing sales volume to the 10 major Japanese auto plants operating in the United States. The company openly credits its success to employee empowerment.

Workers and Management Reconciling Interests

Introduction of a new technology often requires a more highly and generally skilled workforce. . . .

Employers who have invested substantially in [such a] workforce can ill afford to lose these workers. The employer must, therefore, provide mechanisms for the expression and resolution of grievances and for consultation and participation.

Here, then, is the bridge between the interests of workers and employers. The enlightened self-interest of managers counsels the need for worker participation. Furthermore, the presence of strong unions leads to more careful and rational decision making by management—another necessity when making decisions about new technologies. The differing, but partially reconcilable, interests of workers and management allow for industrial relations where cooperation and participation and conflict and adversarial mechanisms of dispute resolution are interdependent.

Lawrence E. Rothstein, *Society*, May/June 1993.

Dozens of other firms and organizations have reaped similar rewards from greater worker participation. At Corning Glass, for example, management and the union jointly established teams of hourly employees to redesign their factories and decide who should work which jobs. A total of forty-seven job classifications were folded into one. Employees rotate through jobs and earn higher pay for each new skill they learn in a "pay-for-knowledge" system.

Those who have studied the Corning Glass case conclude that the company's improved labor-management relations contributed significantly to improved quality and profitability. Since the program was implemented in 1983, defects in the ceramics plant have been cut from 10,000 parts per million to 3 parts per million. And return on equity rose from 7.3 percent to 16.3 percent.

Such union-management team efforts have not been limited to the private sector. The New York City Sanitation Department's Bureau of Motor Equipment (BME) has made extensive use of joint action. Working with the 20 trade unions representing the facility's repair workers, the deputy commissioner of BME began establishing joint problem-solving teams throughout the facility in the late 1970s. As a result, vehicle downtime declined markedly, work that was being assigned to private contractors was brought back in-house, and skilled workers were hired to staff a preventive-maintenance unit. One of the teams was even credited with designing a robot for repainting sanitation equipment. In the first year of service operation, the work teams increased productivity by 24 percent and saved the city $2.4 million.

A Critical Element: Unions

A study by William Seidman, the former chairman of the Federal Deposit Insurance Corp., and his colleague Steven Skanche found one thing in common among U.S. companies that maintained their competitive edge: virtually all had implemented substantial labor-management innovations aimed at empowering workers. Other researchers have found two additional factors that substantially increase the odds of success. One is a system of financial reward for employees through profit or gain sharing. When workers as a group share the rewards of improved productivity, quality, or company profitability, their motivation pays off more handsomely.

Study after study shows that the other factor contributing to higher productivity and quality is the presence of a labor union. Participation turns out to work best when it is organized jointly between union and management and when workers have a voice independent from management that cannot be unilaterally stifled. Mixing adversarial and cooperative relations—negotiated within a context where employees are represented by legally recognized unions—proves to be the most successful form of employee involvement for all participants.

Suggesting that unions might be a critical missing element in a national campaign for global competitiveness may seem far-fetched. In some circles, deep resentment of unions remains. Union leaders have traditionally received ratings in opinion polls right down there with politicians and used-car dealers. As late as 1981 only half of Americans had a favorable view of labor leaders and fully two out of five Americans viewed them with hostility.

In some cases, unions have brought this on themselves. In the incessant struggle to maintain job security for members, unions face enormous pressure to retain outdated work rules. The most flagrant examples receive great attention: after the diesel locomotive replaced the steam-driven railroad engine, the engineers' union insisted on maintaining a fireman on board to stoke a non-existent coal-burning furnace. In other situations, electricians have refused to change light bulbs because that task was not explicitly written into the job description. And at the start of the school year in the fall of 1991, the school bus drivers in Boston exasperated parents and school board members by striking for the third time in six years in a bid to gain another pay raise—at a time when teachers were being laid off.

Although this type of behavior demeans the union movement, the instances in which unions cross the boundary of unjustified behavior are relatively isolated. In fact, more than 99 percent of all contract negotiations between companies and unions are concluded without a work stoppage. Most unions today recognize the fact that if the companies they bargain with are not profitable, their members' job security will be severely jeopardized.

But even more important, there are good reasons for the widespread findings of positive effects of unions. One is that unionized employers normally have a lower rate of turnover and thus spend fewer resources on training new workers. Another is that the presence of a union keeps managers on their toes, forcing them to strive harder to improve productivity in the face of union demands for higher wages.

Furthermore, since the mid-1970s, unions within key industries have widened the traditional workplace contract—which represents the standard adversarial positions between labor and management over wages, benefits, and working conditions—to include employee involvement in workplace decisions.

Mutual Concerns

Indeed, an examination of unfolding developments points to what may be termed the creation of a three-track system of labor-management relations. Track I is represented by the traditional labor contract with a carefully spelled-out grievance procedure. Track II provides for employee involvement in the decision-making process, empowering individual employees to help determine workplace issues, such as the methods, means, and processes of manufacturing or providing services. Track III is characterized by the establishment of joint union-management committees empowered to deal with specific issues of mutual concern—problems of quality, efficiency, health and safety, alcoholism and drug-addiction rehabilitation, child care, and a host of other issues that previously fell within the sole domain of management.

143

Such expanded workplace contracts have helped to change the culture of production, whether of goods or services, in the direction of improved employee satisfaction, thereby markedly boosting the efficiency of each individual job.

In practice, however, employee participation in the workplace has a mixed record in boosting productivity and output quality. Survey research and more formal economic analyses indicate that three underlying conditions are absolutely indispensable to the success of participatory programs: full commitment to the concept of involvement throughout the business organization, attainment of mutual trust and respect between labor and management, and a genuine opportunity for broad-based direct employee involvement in decision making. This amounts to, in short, democratization of the workplace. Merely setting up work teams or paying lip service to participation can be downright counterproductive.

Even where participation seems to be working, most efforts are limited to the problems of the factory floor or the office setting. They do not address the "strategic" decisions of the firm. The crucial factors that determine whether an enterprise flourishes or flounders—including pricing and accounting, design and engineering, advertising and marketing, investment and subcontracting—remain firmly within the purview of top management. Yet given the track record of American industry, it is abundantly clear that management does not have all the answers. . . .

Retooling the Workforce

The mere suggestion of such extensive empowerment of labor inevitably sets off alarms. Even those who do not automatically dismiss the idea raise two general questions. One concerns the degree of worker and union expertise necessary to handle complex issues such as pricing, finance, and the introduction of new technology. To deal with this issue, companies and unions can create jointly administered training programs. The union can also hire consultants—specialists in finance, occupational safety and health, time-and-motion study, or law—to represent its interests, much as they do today when negotiating collective bargaining agreements.

The second and far more challenging question concerns who makes the final decision when consensus cannot be reached between management and labor. One solution is to decide that labor will be fully consulted, but will ultimately defer to management. An alternative is to submit both positions to a jointly selected mediator who will attempt to forge consensus. Still a third possibility is to submit the case to a neutral arbitrator or panel, which will make a binding decision.

Giving participatory management a government imprimatur

could also help management and labor move toward adopting the spirit and perhaps the provisions of the enterprise compact. But the federal government has so far been a serious roadblock. . . .

An economic renaissance can only come about with much more attention to labor-management relations and human resource management. Such a renaissance will require a profound change in attitude on the part of corporate executives and the government toward organized labor. And it will require a broader vision among union leaders of labor's role in advancing the nation's economy and the welfare of the workers they represent. Transforming labor relations from the adversarial system of the workplace contract to an all-encompassing joint-action system . . . will be no easy task. But it is precisely the metamorphosis the U.S. production system needs.

"Management has mapped a clear road to a union-free economic world where most of us have poor jobs and no job security."

Labor-Management Partnerships Are Harmful

Mike Parker and Jane Slaughter

The business sector has recently begun promoting new methods to involve workers in making industries more competitive. In the following viewpoint, Mike Parker and Jane Slaughter contend that many of these "new" ideas have been around for many years under different names. The "new" labor-management partnerships are really attempts to eliminate unions and reduce the workforce while increasing productivity, the authors maintain. According to the authors, the partnerships are not well-meant attempts to involve workers in the success of the company, and labor unions should oppose them. Parker reports on the QWL (Quality of Work Life) Task Force for, and Slaughter is the director of, *Labor Notes*, the monthly publication of the Labor Education and Research Project, a pro-labor organization in Detroit, Michigan.

As you read, consider the following questions:

1. What are some of the work reorganization programs that preceded recent labor-management partnerships, according to the authors?
2. According to Parker and Slaughter, what are the three assumptions underlying reengineering?

Mike Parker and Jane Slaughter, "From 'QWL' to 'Reengineering': Management Takes Off the Gloves," *Labor Notes*, April 1994. Reprinted with permission.

"Reengineering," "Reinventing," "Agile Institutions," and "virtual corporations" lead the crop of management buzzwords that have blossomed this season. From the vantage of the shop floor or the union hall, these have a lot in common with the work reorganization programs that preceded them. But they also reflect a continuing shift, since the late 1970s, in management's attitudes toward its workforce and toward unions.

A look at the history of work reorganization programs reveals that management has mapped a clear road to a union-free economic world where most of us have poor jobs and no job security.

In order to make the claim that both workers and management will benefit, every reorganization scheme contains a list of positive results for the workforce. But the promised benefits rarely show up in the workplace or last longer than the sugar coating on a bitter pill.

Some union advocates of labor-management participation argue this is simply a matter of poor implementation: management doesn't "walk the talk." But mistakes in implementation are not the problem. It is management's goals, behind their adoption of work reorganization, that make it impossible to deliver the promised benefits for working people. Experience has supported this view, as one program after the next has discredited itself and burned the union.

However, even false promises are revealing. They reflect management's view of the power of the labor movement at the time they were made, and the kinds of pledges management must make to keep that power in check.

Blue Collar Blues

Quality of Work Life programs came on the scene late in the 1970s. They claimed to be a response to worker alienation, the "blue collar blues."

The idea was that if you improved the conditions of work, absentee problems would decline, quality would improve, and companies would be more profitable. But the focus was to be on improving work life. Productivity and profits were by-products. Indeed, both company and union proponents warned that any attempt to organize around productivity would doom the programs.

With the recession of the early 1980s, there was a shift toward the term Employee Involvement or Employee Participation, to get away from the expectation that the focus should be on improving working conditions. We were encouraged to get beyond the belittling "creature comfort" issues (fans, water fountains), and move on to the more challenging questions of improving productivity and quality.

Management renamed workers "associates" and declared them to be "our most important asset."

Later in the 1980s, Team Concept carried this notion further: we were all said to be in this competitiveness rat-race together. "We want your brain as well as your muscles," management stroked us. "We want you to work smarter—not harder." We all had to take responsibility for productivity increases, and apply peer pressure if our fellow workers were not pulling their load.

©1993 Huck/Konopacki Labor Cartoons. Reprinted with permission.

However, the concept of "teamwork" was usually attached to Lean Production, a system more accurately called Management-by-Stress. Lean Production included just-in-time delivery, elimination of classifications, and "constant improvement," or constant speed-up. The bible for this phase, a book called *The Machine That Changed the World* from the Massachusetts Institute of Technology, treated unions as either an obstacle or irrelevant.

Decisions "Cascade Down"

None of these 1980s management fads did workers much good. But at least they claimed to believe in the value of employees and their ideas. Management said that their programs were the road to job security. There was even talk—by the gurus, not by management—that the programs should include

Japanese-style lifetime employment.

But then, in the 1990s, Total Quality Management placed the emphasis on top management's setting the course and organizing the workplace so that decisions would "cascade down." The main role for employees was to bring their activities into alignment with the organization's overall goal and eliminate any variation (judgment) they might introduce into the process. Employee ideas to management were welcome, but management had to control all change decisions.

Management viewed TQM as a matter of management method, and therefore tended to install TQM programs unilaterally. Unions that agreed to cooperate might get a few crumbs.

Looking forward, perhaps unions might have taken consolation in the fact that TQM was an incremental approach; it claimed to take the organization as it was and improve it. Some strains of TQM (notably those of the late W.E. Deming) also talked about "driving out fear" from the workplace, with the implication that management should offer job security.

Upheaval

Now we have Reengineering and Reinventing. Management is applying these with a vengeance to white-collar and service jobs—areas that were often bypassed when the focus was on lean production.

The *Wall Street Journal* warned in March 1994, "Much of the huge U.S. service sector seems on the verge of an upheaval similar to that which hit farming and manufacturing, where employment plunged for years while production increased steadily."

Since it is hard to measure the direct impact of a work reorganization program on quality or even profitability, the bench mark for reengineering is: how many jobs did you erase?

Take the U.S. Department of Health and Human Services, for example. You might think that this agency's mission should be responding to the crises in medical care, AIDS, homelessness, etc. But the Department's "streamlining" plan for the end of the century offers only the vaguest ideas of how the department will be reorganized or the services it will offer. There is only one specific: reduce the staff by 12%.

We have only to look at the notions of Agile Institutions and Virtual Corporations to see where all of this is leading.

Agile Production is promoted by the Iacocca Institute at Lehigh University. This system, we are told, puts human decisions at the center of the production system, rather than dumb machines. Thus production can respond rapidly to changes in the market, new customer requirements, and business opportunities. The Agile Corporation is able to shift quickly from one task or process to another.

149

To do this the company has to be freed from commitments to particular factories, processes, or machines, and therefore freed of commitment to the workers whose jobs depend on these expendable elements of profit making.

The Virtual Corporation provides maximum agility. It keeps only that which is central to the corporation: its profit center. For continuity, the corporation maintains its top management, the key idea people, the organizers, and the brokers. As much as possible everything else—manufacturing, service, clerical work, communications work—is sourced out. Every project is temporary.

Robert Reich, now Secretary of Labor, explained the concept in his 1991 book, *The Work of Nations:*

> In the high-value enterprise . . . all that really counts is rapid problem-identifying and problem-solving, the marriage of technical insight with marketing know-how, blessed by strategic and financial acumen. Everything else—all of the more standardized pieces—can be obtained as needed.
>
> Office space, factories, and warehouses can be rented; standard equipment can be leased; standard components can be bought wholesale from cheap producers (many of them overseas); secretaries, routine data processors, bookkeepers, and routine production workers can be hired temporarily.
>
> In fact, relatively few people actually work for the high-value enterprise in the traditional sense of having steady jobs with fixed salaries.

The model is a Hollywood production. The producers raise the money, hire the writers, actors, and technicians. When the movie is in the can, everyone returns to the marketplace, waiting to be called for the next project.

Another image that comes to mind is the day-labor markets on the street corners of Los Angeles, where contractors bring their pick-up trucks and Mexican immigrants line up to compete for a day's work.

Down the Food Chain

Frightening? Yes. On the agenda? In most cases, not in full form. Big manufacturing can't achieve the full virtual model, but companies can aim to reduce their built-in capability as much as possible to "fast assembly" operations. At the same time the labor content of assembly is reduced by new modular processes and "design for manufacturing" [products designed with the method of manufacturing in mind, not just the end product].

The same logic applies at each level of the economy. Second-tier suppliers find that they too must be more agile to meet the needs of their customers, so they look to minimizing their own commitment to buildings, machinery and workers. The pressures move down the food chain.

Reengineering and Agile Institutions mean that long-term commitments to employees ("our most important asset") and "lifetime jobs" hit the trash bin, along with decent jobs and strong unions. Contractual and moral commitments are collapsing around the world—in Japan and Europe as well as in North America.

Who benefits from this increased speed and efficiency? Clearly the corporations do. In many cases, the gains show up only in the profit column and never get translated into gains for the customer. And as workers we have lost a lot already, with no end in sight.

Efficiency, or the idea of redesigning jobs or products or processes so that they're easily done, is not a bad concept. In fact it is vital to recognize that the system is broke and needs fixing. The problem is, what are the assumptions that are the basis of Reengineering?

Management's assumptions are:
- that the primary goal is to obliterate jobs;
- that management has no responsibility;
- that the marketplace, or society, or your family, or someone else will absorb the consequences.

The union starting point has to be the right to work at a decent job. Doing our work in less time would be fine—if it means a shorter work week and not a smaller workforce.

It All Adds Up

The nub of the problem is that all the work reorganization programs add up. Each company or government agency, each pursuing its own competitive ends—together they add up to a prescription for the society as a whole.

Their underlying assumption is that there are too many good jobs. The solution is to reduce the number of people working and to extract more work for less cost from those who remain. This assumption continues our march to a have and have-not society, where a few live very well and an increasing portion is considered disposable.

That is the management agenda for the 1990s. Now more than ever the labor movement must put forward its own vision. The problem with our economy is not too many decent jobs but too few. The solution is to increase the number of people working at decent wages and hours, and to see that what they do is of value to society rather than a waste.

What makes the management scenario even more disastrous is that so many unions have embraced management's agenda as their own, in the futile hope that they can salvage a piece of the action. The worse things get, the more some union leaders lay down our remaining weapons in exchange for the promise of "partnership."

151

In 1992 AT&T and the Communications Workers signed a Workplace of the Future agreement to, the union says, "give CWA a voice in the redesign of our jobs." Union members are on Reengineering teams, contributing their knowledge to the job-cutting process. At the same time, AT&T is transferring work to its anti-union subsidiary, NCR. In March 1994 AT&T announced it was cutting 15,000 jobs, without even so much as a prior discussion with its union partner (to the "shock and disgust" of the CWA vice president in charge of AT&T).

Union Label Pink Slips

Bill Clinton has made cutting government jobs both a priority for his administration and the model for private enterprise and state and local government to follow. Despite this, lured by the possibility of an agency shop [a variation of a union shop where employees are not required to join a union, but if they choose not to, they must pay a fee equal to union dues for union services], the federal employee unions have announced a new management/labor "partnership."

A video distributed by the American Federation of Government Employees gives us one example of what this will mean in practice.

AFGE President John Sturdivant cites Local 2302 in Kentucky as the example of "successful experiences" with partnership. Instead of management's doing the cuts, the union did them. In fact, the union did so well, says Local 2302 President Butch Henry, that "we reduced our payroll budget 16% in 14 months—4% more [than required over five years in the Clinton plan]."

The Labor Department's point man for labor-management cooperation, Chuck Richards, endorsed this outlook at a union conference in Iowa on March 4, 1994. "Two hundred fifty thousand [jobs] will be gone from the government by attrition," Richards said, "as a result of an agreement by [Vice President] Gore and Sturdivant through the National Partnership Council." Although the AFGE members present called this "putting the AFGE label on your pink slip," Richards said it was positive that the agreement was a joint one. . . .

Despite the gloomy prognosis, it's not the end of the world for the union:

- Never underestimate the incompetence of management in executing its plans.
- Often management is caught between conflicting pressures, from both above and below. Smart unions look for the cracks, and for unanticipated events.

The big danger to the labor movement is that union after union—each acting alone and trying to make the best of its own situation—will sap labor's strength by endorsing the doctrine that the workforce must be reduced.

The multinational corporations are powerful, but they are not all-powerful. The companies' programs to expand their profits also make them potentially more vulnerable.

- A tight just-in-time system is very easily disrupted by concerted action—by even a relatively small number of employees, or contractors.
- Sourcing-out can stimulate solidarity actions between newly linked workplaces.

The future won't be easy. Unions will have to take all kinds of tactical turns—including retreats and side-stepping.

But only if we stop the wishful thinking about "win-win" solutions can we rebuild our only source of power—a committed union membership.

"The permanent replacement of strikers exemplifies practices and attitudes that make real cooperation between labor and management impossible."

Business Should Not Be Allowed to Permanently Replace Striking Workers

Robert B. Reich

Robert B. Reich is secretary of labor for the Clinton administration. In the following viewpoint, Reich argues in favor of legislation that would prevent business owners from permanently replacing striking workers. He maintains that the legal option to permanently replace striking workers—which became common after 11,400 striking air traffic controllers were fired by the federal government in 1981—eliminates workers' viable right to strike and therefore weakens labor's position in relation to management. Preventing business owners from replacing striking workers, Reich maintains, will foster cooperation between workers and management.

As you read, consider the following questions:

1. What kind of workforce does Reich advocate for the United States in the twenty-first century?
2. According to the author, what position did the federal government take on the replacement of striking workers from 1981 to 1992?
3. How will banning the permanent replacement of strikers foster the kind of workforce the author advocates?

From Robert B. Reich's testimony before the U.S. Senate Committee on Labor and Human Resources, Subcommittee on Labor, March 30, 1993, regarding S.R. 55, the Workplace Fairness Act.

As our national economy becomes, increasingly, a global and technological economy, America's ability to be competitive will depend on how well we have invested in developing a skilled and motivated workforce. To succeed in this new economy, we cannot afford to waste any of our resources, especially the resource most firmly rooted within our borders: our people, their ideas, their education, and their skills.

But to compete effectively on a world-class level, we need even more than a high-skill, high-wage workforce. We also need a new framework for labor relations—one that stimulates employee productivity and enables management to get the most out of its employees' skills, brainpower, and effort.

An Invaluable Asset

Workers on the front line have unique perspectives on production and immediate access to information that smart businesses depend on for quick response and high quality. So it is not surprising that an increasing number of companies are finding that they profit when they treat their workforce not as just another cost to be cut—but as an invaluable asset to be developed.

The Clinton Administration is committed to fostering practices that improve productivity. I have seen many illustrations that both productivity and profitability increase when workers have a voice—whether through collective bargaining or other means of promoting cooperation between workers and management and fostering employee involvement and participation in workplace decision-making. We cannot afford to limit American competitiveness by any practices that inspire workers and managers to work at cross purposes. What will make us most competitive is a dedicated and innovative workforce—and this requires a partnership between workers and employers, predicated on teamwork and mutual respect.

In short, good labor-management relations make good business—and a healthy economy. But in the most recent chapter of American labor history, productive relations between some companies and their unions have been thwarted by increasing distrust, hostility, and litigation. The permanent replacement of strikers exemplifies practices and attitudes that make real cooperation between labor and management impossible, by undermining the basic foundations of the collective bargaining system. As an editorial pointed out, labor cannot approach negotiations with trust and a sense of shared purpose when management has a gun pointed at the union's head. Management that has the option of simply eliminating the other side has little commitment to finding a mutually satisfactory resolution of differences.

The practice of permanent striker replacement became a prominent feature of American labor relations only since 1981. I be-

155

lieve many employers were emboldened when, in 1981, 11,400 PATCO [Professional Air Traffic Controllers Organization] strikers were fired and permanently barred from reinstatement. Although PATCO was considered an illegal strike involving public sector employees—which differentiates it from the work stoppages addressed by proposed legislation [called the Workplace Fairness Act, designed to prevent employers from firing striking workers]—the action taken in 1981 sent a loud signal to the business community that the hiring of permanent replacement workers was an acceptable way of doing business. This, coupled with a distorted focus on short-term performance at the expense of long-term interests, began a decade characterized by a wave of labor disputes in which thousands of employees lost their jobs after they engaged in completely lawful economic strikes.

Contrary to the National Interest

The *Mackay* doctrine [*Labor Board v. Mackay Co.* is the Supreme Court case that upheld employers' ability to permanently replace striking workers] is contrary to the national interest in long-term labor and management relationships, and in investment in our human resources. Permanent replacement is not a means of building a quality workforce, of investing in workers' skills, or of developing relationships built on mutual respect. It betrays a management approach whose premise is that workers are a disposable resource, to be exploited for short-term profit, and then, if the worker questions the employer's unilateral authority, discarded.

Thomas R. Donahue, testimony given before the Labor Subcommittee of the Senate Labor and Human Resources Committee on March 30, 1993.

Strikes are usually an act of desperation, a last resort which employees undertake at great economic and often personal risk to themselves and their families. When workers enter negotiations, the last thing they want to do is strike. But the availability of that option is a crucial counter-weight to the economic powers that business owners and managers bring to the fundamental premise of American labor law.

At its best, collective bargaining is a win-win process. But without a viable right to strike, employers have less incentive to engage in serious bargaining with their unions, to hammer out mutually satisfactory solutions. And unions see no point in trying to work cooperatively with management when there is no real avenue for dialogue.

In the changed climate of labor relations, more employers have been willing to choose intimidation over serious negotia-

tion. Some companies even advertise for permanent replacement workers before they begin negotiations—stockpiling them
just like raw materials.

Successful bargaining is made even less likely if the workers
do take on this added risk and strike—and are permanently replaced. The rehiring of the strikers, and the fate of their replacements, add highly charged, problematic issues that replace and
obscure the original dispute.

A study conducted in 1989 indicated that the use of permanent
replacements not only complicates the dispute, but also prolongs
the strike. Productivity is reduced by prolonged strikes—as well
as by the permanent displacement of skilled and experienced
workers.

Although permanent replacements have been used only by a
minority of employers, the practice affects even those employers
who would never use, or even threaten to use, this weapon. All
employees receive the message that they are disposable, each
time a workforce is permanently replaced or threatened with
permanent replacement. This undermines, throughout the economy, the trust necessary for true cooperation between workers
and managers.

The Workplace Fairness Act would enable us to close the book
on this counterproductive recent chapter in American labor law.
The legislation would restore balance in collective bargaining,
allowing management to operate during a strike through alter-
nate means, but not destroying fundamental union rights. The
Clinton Administration supports this legislation, because it
would foster the equilibrium and stability in industrial relations
which are critical to the health of our economy. The sooner that
we can conclude this chapter, the sooner we can turn our attention from the past and begin, together, to write the next chapter.

But we risk failing to meet the challenges that await us if—as
Louis Brandeis said nearly 90 years ago—we "assume that the
interests of employer and employee are necessarily hostile—that
what is good for one is necessarily bad for the other. The opposite is more likely to be the case. While they have different interests, they are likely to prosper or suffer together." We need to
remember that management doesn't "win" when labor "loses,"
just as workers don't triumph when businesses fail. Maintaining
a balance of power that promotes labor-management cooperation promotes our long-term economic strength; undermining
that balance puts us all at risk.

"Denying employers the ability to continue operations during a strike would foster more labor-management strife."

Business Must Be Allowed to Permanently Replace Striking Workers

David Warner

The Wagner Act, governing collective bargaining and union organizing, was passed in 1935 and upheld by the U.S. Supreme Court in 1938. That law gives businesses the right to permanently replace workers striking for economic reasons, primarily wages and benefits. David Warner, in the following viewpoint, contends that this right is vital to businesses that find themselves the victims of bitter, unreasonable strikes. If they were not permitted to hire replacements for striking workers, he suggests, many companies would be forced out of business due to lost productivity or, if they acquiesced to the strikers' demands, impossible labor costs. David Warner is an associate editor of *Nation's Business*, published by the United States Chamber of Commerce, a federation of businesses, trade organizations, local and state chambers, and American chambers of commerce abroad.

As you read, consider the following questions:

1. How does the Wagner Act provide striking workers protection from unfair dismissal, according to Warner?
2. Why do labor unions support striker-replacement legislation, according to John Irving and the author?

William A. Stone was on the shop floor of his business, Louisville Plate Glass Co., along with 3 salesmen and 2 supervisors, cutting glass to fill customers' orders. Outside the Louisville, Kentucky, plant, 15 of his 25 employees—members of Local 1529 of the Glass Glazers and Painters International Union—were on strike for higher wages and benefits. The union was seeking an increase that would double Stone's labor costs over three years, he says.

The strike occurred in June 1977, in the midst of double-digit inflation and high interest rates. Stone and the 5 management employees continued to run the company's normally 15-man shop floor operation for almost a month, hoping the striking workers would back off from their position. "But they hardly gave," Stone says.

After six months on the picket line, the union was still seeking an 80 percent increase in wages and benefits.

The company started losing orders—it lost 50 percent of its volume in the first month of the strike. "It became apparent that either we replaced our [striking] employees or we would be out of business," says Stone.

So the firm hired 7 new employees as permanent replacements for strikers. Eventually, 8 of the strikers crossed the picket line to return to work. Because only seven of the 15 workers who went on strike were replaced, the 8 who returned were given back their jobs.

Stone's company survived that labor unrest, primarily because he was able to replace the strikers. And the company has since expanded to three plants—two were added in Georgia—and 100 employees.

[But proposed] legislation would bar employers from permanently replacing employees who walk off the job for economic reasons, such as wages and benefits.

The Wagner Act

Employers have been able to hire permanent replacements for economic strikers since 1935, when Congress passed the Wagner Act—also known as the National Labor Relations Act—which governs union organizing and collective bargaining.

The U.S. Supreme Court affirmed that ability as a "right" in a 1938 case, *NLRB [National Labor Relations Board] vs. Mackay Radio & Telegraph Co.* The high court also ruled in that case that permanent replacements were prohibited if the employer had committed an unfair labor practice, such as provoking a strike to "bust" the union.

The Workplace Fairness Act, or striker-replacement bill—it's one of the top priorities of organized labor—would reverse the Supreme Court ruling dealing with economic strikes.

The Clinton administration supports the legislation.

The AFL-CIO [American Federation of Labor–Congress of Industrial Organizations] and Labor Secretary Robert Reich maintain the legislation is needed to level the playing field between management and labor during contract negotiations. And Reich states that banning permanent replacements is a step toward ending what he and the unions assert has been years of growing distrust between labor and management.

At House and Senate hearings on the striker-replacement bill, the labor secretary told lawmakers that "employees suffer as a result of strikes; they are putting their jobs and their livelihoods on the line."

A Core Principle

The Strike Bill [the Workplace Fairness Act] . . . would prohibit employers from defending their businesses by offering permanent jobs to replacement workers during a strike over economic issues such as pay raises and benefits.

Proponents of the Strike Bill claim that employers' use of permanent replacement workers during an economic strike is a recent phenomenon. This simply is not true. The National Labor Relations Act, enacted in 1935, provided a delicate balance that allows unions to strike over wage demands and allows employers to defend their businesses by hiring permanent replacement workers.

The striker-replacement legislation would destroy this core principle of United States labor law, which has been consistently supported by Democratic and Republican presidents and federal courts for over half a century.

Howard Jenkins and John A. Penello, *The Christian Science Monitor*, July 11, 1994.

Many labor-law experts, however, believe barring permanent replacements would have grave effects on the collective-bargaining process.

Daniel Yeager, a labor lawyer with the Labor Policy Association, a business-supported Washington, D.C., group focusing on human-resources issues, says the ability of the union to strike and the capability of management to hire permanent replacements are weapons whose "mere presence has the effect of bringing the parties to agreement at the bargaining table." If management lost its weapon, "unions would be able to call virtually risk-free strikes over any issue," says Yeager.

Republican Sen. Nancy Landon Kassebaum of Kansas says that denying employers the ability to continue operations during a strike would foster more labor-management strife.

The legislation "will turn the clock back to the era of bitter, prolonged, and divisive strikes, where everyone loses—not only the workers but the economy as well," she says. Kassebaum is the ranking minority member of the Senate Labor and Human Resources Committee.

The Harm of No-Risk Strikes

Management would have to accede to the union's demands or try to weather a strike, says John Irving, a partner in the Washington, D.C., law firm of Kirkland & Ellis and general counsel to the National Labor Relations Board from 1975 to 1979. Irving also believes that in the absence of any risk that their members would be replaced, unions would be likely to strike more often and for longer periods.

Some industries can afford to take a strike for a while, says Irving. "But there are many, many others that . . . simply can't afford to do that; they must continue to operate, or their competitors will be all too happy to permanently take their customers."

Reich and the unions argue that employers have other means, such as hiring temporary replacements, to continue operations during a strike.

While employers in some businesses—mostly those requiring low-skilled workers—can use temporary replacements as long as there's no violence by strikers on the picket line, says Irving, many others cannot. "If they can't," he says, "and they need to hire permanent replacements, . . . they should have that right. Otherwise, the union just sits out there [on the picket line], and employees dictate when they're going to come back.

"Employers permanently replace their workers only as a last resort. No employer in his right mind wants to get rid of his skilled workers and have to train a bunch of 'green' people."

In addition to the costs of training temporary replacements, under state and federal laws employers could owe these workers unemployment and health benefits once a strike is resolved and they are let go.

Health care is one industry in which hiring temporaries often is not a viable option and where the ability to replace striking workers can literally be a matter of life or death.

For the 110 residents of the Jewish Home for the Aged, in Cincinnati, that certainly was the case in early 1993 when 80 of the nursing home's 95 employees, members of District 1199 of the Service Employees International Union, went on strike for, among other things, higher wages.

The nonprofit health-care facility was able to use temporary replacements for the first three weeks of the strike. But because it had to hire some high-priced temporary-agency workers and because of certain state-mandated staffing and training requirements, permanent replacements were later hired.

"The union recognizes how vulnerable health-care institutions are," says Alan Lips, a partner with Taft, Stettinius & Hollister, a Cincinnati law firm representing the Jewish Home. "If [union members] can hold the residents hostage to the boycott of their labor . . . and they can prevent the hiring of replacement labor, then the employer has to capitulate quickly [to union demands] because he's got an overriding, moral imperative to take care of the residents."

The Replacement Workers

Stone, who is president and CEO of Louisville Plate Glass, points out that replacement workers take physical and emotional risks when they agree to work for a company being struck. "They're going to be insulted and called 'scabs'; they're going to be threatened and intimidated. You couldn't get most people to cross a picket line in any kind of intense negotiation situation unless the carrot of permanent replacement were available."

Under current law, even "permanent" replacements aren't necessarily permanent. Striking unions often file charges of unfair labor practices with the NLRB against a company that hires such replacements. If the labor board agrees with the charges, the employer would be prohibited from hiring permanent replacements.

Strike settlement agreements often provide for reinstatement of all strikers at the expense of the replacement workers' jobs.

A March 1992 survey by the Bureau of National Affairs, a private research and publishing company in Washington, D.C., found that 75 percent of replaced strikers return to their jobs after a strike.

Under current law, striking workers cannot be fired; they can return to their jobs even during a strike; and, at the end of a strike, they must be given first priority when job vacancies occur.

The striker-replacement measure would require employers to favor returning strikers over nonstrikers—both replacements and those who did not strike—for jobs and to ensure that the strikers' seniority remained unaffected by their absence. . . .

Nonunion and union small companies that supply goods and services to companies could also suffer financially if their customers are unable to continue operations during a strike, say several business organizations.

"The little guy can really be hurt by having his customer shut down," says Irving.

Labor unions are looking to the striker-replacement bill not only as a way to help secure higher wages and benefits but also as an organizing tool, says Irving. If a union can guarantee workers' jobs even when they strike for unreasonably high wages and benefits, chances are good the union's organizing efforts will be successful, he says.

And the unions are eager to achieve such success. Union membership has been declining steadily since it reached its peak of 35.5 percent of the work force in 1945. In 1994, organized workers make up just 11.5 percent of the nation's work force.

Kassebaum sums up the stakes involved in the striker bill this way: "At a time when we should be enhancing our competitiveness, we ought to be looking for ways not to destroy but to encourage labor and management cooperation."

Says Stone of the striker-replacement measure: "Had there not been the right to hire permanent replacements [during the 1977 strike], I would be doing something else, somewhere else." And 100 more Americans might be without jobs.

Periodical Bibliography

The following articles have been selected to supplement the diverse views presented in this chapter.

Charles W. Baird
"Strikers and Scabs," *The Freeman*, March 1994. Available from the Foundation for Economic Education, Irvington-on-Hudson, NY 10533.

Doug Bandow
"Workers Already Have the Right to Strike," *Conservative Chronicle*, July 13, 1994. Available from PO Box 11297, Des Moines, IA 50340-1297.

Aaron Bernstein
"Why America Needs Unions, but Not the Kind It Has Now," *Business Week*, May 23, 1994.

Nanette Byrnes
"Blue Collar Blues," *Financial World*, November 23, 1993. Available from 1328 Broadway, New York, NY 10001-2116.

Stephen Chapman
"A Favor to Unions Is No Help to Everyone Else," *Conservative Chronicle*, June 2, 1993.

George J. Church
"Unions Arise—with New Tricks," *Time*, June 13, 1994.

Dan Cornfield
"Making a Meaningful Labor Movement," *Tikkun*, July/August 1994.

Susan Dentzer
"Hijacking 'High Performance,'" *U.S. News & World Report*, August 2, 1993.

Dollars & Sense
"The Changing Face of Labor," September/October 1993. Special issue on labor unions.

Peter Downs
"UAW: Death of a Union?" *Against the Current*, July/August 1994.

Michael Eisenscher
"High-Performance Cooptation," *Crossroads*, March 1994.

Tom Geoghegan
"West of Eden," *The New Republic*, May 23, 1994.

Dave Hage, Robin Knight, and Steven Butler
"Unions Feel the Heat: Organized Labor Around the World Scrambles to Save Jobs," *U.S. News & World Report*, January 24, 1994.

Kevin Kelly and Aaron Bernstein
"Labor Deals That Offer a Break from 'Us vs. Them,'" *Business Week*, August 2, 1993.

Joe Klein
"Labor's Leverage Lost," *Newsweek*, December 6, 1993.

Robert Kuttner — "So You Thought Unions Were Obsolete?" *The Washington Post National Weekly Edition*, December 6-12, 1993.

George C. Leef — "Workers and Unions—How About Freedom of Contract?" *The Freeman*, December 1992.

Denis MacShane — "Do Europeans Do It Better? Foreign Lessons for U.S. Labor," *The American Prospect*, Summer 1993.

Denis MacShane — "Lessons for Bosses and the Bossed," *The New York Times*, July 19, 1993.

David Moberg — "Prairie Fires," *In These Times*, July 25, 1994.

Peter Nulty — "Look What the Unions Want Now," *Fortune*, February 8, 1993.

Gehan Perara — "Labor: Take the Responsibility," *Crossroads*, May 1994.

Lawrence E. Rothstein — "Labor-Management Relations," *Society*, May/June 1993.

Agis Salpukas — "Labor's Showdown at Federal Express," *The New York Times*, February 7, 1993.

Jack Sheinkman — "We Need Labor Law Reform," *Democratic Left*, May/June 1993.

Tony Snow — "Organized Labor Continues to Lose Power," *Conservative Chronicle*, May 18, 1994.

William Tucker — "Unions Work Toward a Comeback," *Insight on the News*, January 10, 1994. Available from 3600 New York Ave. NE, Washington, DC 20002.

Michael Zweig — "In Defense of Unions," *Tikkun*, March/April 1994.

How Should Equality
in the Workplace
Be Achieved?

Work

Chapter Preface

In its 1987 report *Workforce 2000*, the Hudson Institute, a public policy research center, noted that white males were already a minority in the workplace and predicted that by the year 2000, 85 percent of new entrants to the workforce would be women, nonwhites, and immigrants. Faced with these demographic shifts, business leaders have begun to reassess their management practices, and many now endorse "diversity management"—a management philosophy that seeks to accommodate and benefit from the increasing diversity of the workforce. Diversity management refers to a wide range of practices, including audits to determine the extent of institutional racism in the workplace, policies to reduce discrimination, and sensitivity training in culture, race, and gender differences.

Many analysts contend that because of the changes in the workforce highlighted by *Workforce 2000*, diversity management is essential for business success. To proponents, diversity management is a strategy to extract as much productivity as possible from an increasingly diverse labor pool. According to Sharon Nelton of *Nation's Business* magazine, "Managing diversity . . . [means] fostering an environment in which workers of all kinds . . . can flourish and . . . give top performance to a company." R. Roosevelt Thomas Jr., author of *Beyond Race and Gender*, agrees: "The goal is to manage diversity in such a way as to get from a diverse work force the same productivity we once got from a homogeneous work force."

Others criticize diversity management for causing discord between workers. For example, writer Heather MacDonald contends that in their overly zealous attempts to expose racism among employees, diversity consultants hired by businesses often stir up conflict rather than ease tensions between different groups. Others argue that diversity management is often simply an attack on white men. Steven Yates, author of *Civil Wrongs: What Went Wrong with Affirmative Action*, writes that "today's 'sensitivity training' seems intended to inculcate in the white male who is turned down for a job or a promotion in favor of a less qualified woman or minority that, as a member of the oppressor group, he had it coming!" MacDonald and others argue that this perception has led to resistance to diversity training on the part of many white men, adding to the stresses already present in the workplace.

Whether diversity management fosters productivity or conflict, its growing presence evinces a changing conception of the American workforce. Diversity management is one issue discussed in the following chapter on equality in the workplace.

"[Affirmative action] is an instrument for ending occupational segregation of blacks, a legacy of their enslavement."

Affirmative Action Promotes Equality

Gertrude Ezorsky

Gertrude Ezorsky argues that affirmative action programs that give preferential treatment in employment to blacks are justified for two reasons: They compensate blacks for their past treatment under slavery and racism, and they will reduce institutional racism in the future by integrating blacks into the occupational mainstream. Ezorsky disputes several common oppositions to affirmative action, including the charge that it gives black job candidates an unfair advantage over more meritorious whites. Ezorsky is the author of *Racism and Justice: The Case for Affirmative Action*, from which the following viewpoint is excerpted.

As you read, consider the following questions:

1. Why is the analogy between the freedom to marry and the freedom to hire unacceptable, according to Ezorsky?
2. The author concedes that denying preference to "basically qualified" blacks might produce some gains in efficiency. On what basis does she nevertheless support preferential treatment?
3. Why does Ezorsky believe that blacks who receive preferential treatment in employment have no reason to feel unworthy?

AA's [affirmative action's] benefits to blacks can be viewed from both a forward-looking and a backward-looking moral perspective. From a forward-looking perspective, the purpose of AA is to reduce institutional racism, thereby moving blacks toward the goal of occupational integration. When that goal is achieved, millions of blacks will no longer be unfairly barred by the effects of their racist history from employment benefits. Moreover, such integration will significantly dissipate invidious racist attitudes. Individuals socialized in a world where blacks are assimilated throughout the hierarchy of employment will no longer readily assume that they belong at the bottom.

From a backward-looking perspective, blacks have a moral claim to compensation for past injury. The paramount injustice perpetrated against blacks—enslavement—requires such compensation. If the effects of that murderous institution had been dissipated over time, the claim to compensation now would certainly be weaker. From the post-Reconstruction period to the present, however, racist practices have continued to transmit and reinforce the consequences of slavery. Today blacks still predominate in those occupations that in a slave society would be reserved for slaves.

Racism as Official Public Policy

Such ongoing racism has not been the work only of private parties. The racism of government practices encouraged race discrimination by landlords who blocked the escape of blacks from ghettos, and by employers and unions who refused to hire, promote, or train them, as well as widespread communication of an insulting stereotype of blacks, derogatory to their ability and character. During the first two-thirds of this century, racism was in many respects official public policy. That policy included: legally compulsory segregation into inferior private and publicly owned facilities such as schools, which—as recognized in *Brown* v. *Board of Education of Topeka* (1954)—violated the constitutional rights of black children; court-upheld racially restrictive covenants in the transfer of private residences; antimiscegenation laws that resembled the prohibition of marriage by persons with venereal diseases; race discrimination in government practices such as public employment, voting registration procedures, federal assistance to business persons and farmers, and allocation of state and municipal services to black neighborhoods (e.g., police protection, sanitation, and educational resources); manifest racial bias in the courts; and pervasive police brutality against black people.

The practices of the Federal Housing Authority exemplified governmental racism. For decades after its inception in 1934, the FHA, which insured mortgage loans, enshrined racial segregation as public policy. The agency set itself up as the protector of all-white neighborhoods, especially in the suburbs. According to urban planner Charles Abrams, the FHA's racial policies could "well have been culled from the Nuremberg Laws." Today white suburban youths continue to benefit from the past racist practices of this government agency. Not only will they inherit homes purchased with the FHA assistance, denied to blacks; they also enjoy racially privileged access to the expanding employment opportunities in all-white suburbs. In 1973, legal scholar Boris I. Bittker summed up governmental misconduct against blacks: "More than any other form of official misconduct, racial discrimination against blacks was systematic, unrelenting, authorized at the highest governmental levels, and practiced by large segments of the population." The role of government in practicing, protecting, and providing sanction for racism by private parties suffices to demonstrate the moral legitimacy of legally required compensation to blacks.

This past of pervasive racism—public and private—follows blacks into the labor market. They are also especially vulnerable to recessionary layoffs because they possess far smaller reserves of money and property to sustain them during periods of joblessness. Such vulnerability also affects many newly middle-class blacks who, lacking inherited or accumulated assets, are—as the saying goes—two paychecks away from poverty.

Preferential Treatment Is Appropriate

Are AA measures, such as preferential treatment in employment, an appropriate method of compensation for blacks? In fact, federal and state governments recognized the appropriateness of employment preference as an instrument of compensation to veterans long before the adoption of AA measures. This court-sanctioned policy has affected the employment of millions of workers, and in some states where veteran preference is practiced, nonveterans have practically no chance to obtain the best positions. . . .

Shelby Steele, a professor of English, criticizes the compensatory claim for AA, according to which AA is "something 'owed,' as reparation": "Suffering can be endured and overcome, it cannot be repaid. To think otherwise is to prolong the suffering." But if compensation should be withheld from blacks because suffering cannot be repaid, then for the same reason compensation should also be withheld from veterans, Holocaust survivors, and victims of industrial accidents. Members of these groups do not complain that compensation prolongs their "suffering"; on the contrary, they have often insisted on their right to such benefits. I see no reason for assuming that compensation per se injures its recipients.

The philosopher William Blackstone criticizes the compensatory rationale for preferential treatment for affluent blacks:

> There is no invariable connection between a person's being black . . . and suffering from past invidious discrimination. . . . There are many blacks and other minority group members who are highly advantaged, who are sons and daughters of well-educated, affluent lawyers, doctors and industrialists. A policy of reverse discrimination would mean that such highly advantaged individuals would receive preferential treatment over the sons and daughters of disadvantaged whites or disadvantaged members of other minorities. I submit that such a situation is not social justice.

Blackstone offers two arguments: (1) Black persons born into better-off black families have not suffered discrimination; hence, he suggests, they do not deserve compensation. (2) Preference that benefits these blacks at the expense of disadvantaged nonblacks is unjust.

Blacks Deserve Compensation

First, it is false that blacks born into better-off families have not been injured by discrimination. Because racist treatment of blacks in business and professions reduced family income, it hurt their sons and daughters. Among the racist injuries these black parents suffered were the racially discriminatory policies of federal agencies in allocation of business loans, low-interest mortgages, agrarian price supports, and government contracts. They also were victimized by racist exclusion from practice in white law firms and hospitals and by legally imposed or encouraged residential and school segregation that impaired their education and isolated them from white business contacts. Because of such invidious discrimination, black professionals and entrepreneurs could do far less for their children than their white counterparts. Moreover, the sons and daughters of black lawyers, doctors, and business persons have themselves suffered the experience of living in a segregated, pervasively racist society. . . .

Even if one assumes that the economically better-off blacks are less deserving of compensation, it hardly follows that they do not deserve any compensation. As Bernard Boxill observes in *Blacks and Social Justice:* "Because I have lost only one leg, I may be less deserving of compensation than another who has lost two legs, but it does not follow that I deserve no compensation."

It is true that where preference has been extended to blacks—as with craft workers, professionals, blue- and white-collar employees, teachers, police, and firefighters—some excluded whites may be financially less well off than the blacks who gained. This shift fails to show that these blacks were not victimized by invidious discrimination for which they should be compensated. Also, compensatory employment preference is sometimes given to veterans who are more affluent than the nonveterans who are thereby excluded from jobs. Indeed, some veterans gained, on the whole, from military life: placed in non-combat units, they often learned a valuable skill. Yet no one proposes that for this reason veteran preference be abandoned.

Unqualified Blacks as Unaffected by AA

Thomas Nagel, a philosopher who endorses preferential treatment, nevertheless faults the compensatory justification for such preference, claiming that blacks who benefit from it are probably not the ones who suffered most from discrimination; "those who don't have the qualifications even to be considered" do not gain from preferential policies.

Of course, AA preference does not help blacks obtain very desirable employment if they lack the qualifications even to be considered for such positions. But preferential treatment in diverse areas of the public and private sector has benefited not only highly skilled persons but also poorly educated workers. It is also true that blacks who lack the qualifications even to be considered for *any* employment will not gain from AA preference. AA cannot help those so destroyed as to be incapable of any work or on-the-job training, who require other compensatory race-specific rehabilitation programs. But AA employment programs should not perform the function of these programs. The claim that unemployable blacks are most deserving does not imply that employable blacks fail to deserve any—or even a great deal of—compensation.

Granted, we do not know whether the particular blacks who benefit from preference at each level in the hierarchy of employment are the very same individuals who, absent a racist past, would have qualified at that level by customary standards. Justified group compensation, however, does not require satisfaction of such rigid criteria. Veterans who enjoy hiring, promotion, and seniority preference are surely not the very same individuals who, absent their military service, would have qualified for the positions they gained by such preference.

Unlike job preference for veterans, AA racial preference in employment contributes to eradication of a future evil. It is an instrument for ending occupational segregation of blacks, a legacy of their enslavement.

The Rights of Employers

According to libertarian philosophers, laws that require any type of AA in the workplace—indeed, those merely requiring passive nondiscrimination—violate the rights of private employers. The philosopher Robert Nozick suggests that the right of employers to hire is relevantly similar to the right of individuals to marry. Just as individuals should be free to marry whomever they please, so private entrepreneurs should be free to employ whomever they please, and government should not interfere with employers in their hiring decisions.

©1991, Kirk Anderson. Reprinted with permission.

But surely the freedom to choose one's spouse and the freedom to select one's employees are relevantly different. Individuals denied such freedom of choice in marriage are forced to give their bodies to their spouses. They are subject to rape—a destructive, brutal, and degrading intrusion. Marital choices belong to the deeply personal sphere where indeed government should keep out. State intervention in employment is another matter. To require that an auto plant hire some black machinists falls outside the sphere of the deeply personal; it is not, like rape, a destructive, brutal, and degrading personal intrusion. I conclude that the analogy between freedom to marry and freedom to hire fails. . . .

Meritocratic Critics

Some AA critics, whom I shall call meritocrats, believe that justice in the workplace is exemplified by selection according to merit standards. Hence they claim that racial preference violates the rights of more qualified white candidates. . . .

Whatever the effect of AA measures in their entirety, it is true that racial preference for a less qualified black can, in specific situations, reduce effective job performance. According to meritocrats, such selection violates the rights of adversely affected white candidates. Thus the philosopher Alan Goldman states:

> Unless reverse discrimination violates some *presently accepted rule for hiring* it will not be seriously unjust in the current social context. . . . The *currently accepted* rule which I believe to be just is that of *hiring by competence*. . . . In addition to its vast utility, competence is some barometer of prior effort. Thus society, it seems, does have a right in the name of welfare and equal opportunity to impose a rule for hiring, and the general rule ought to be hiring the most competent. This means that those individuals who attain maximal competence for various positions acquire rights through their efforts to those positions. [emphases added by Ezorsky]

Let us assume that insofar as maximally qualified candidates have exerted effort to attain positions under an accepted and just rule, they have a prima facie right to such positions. But the fact is that, contrary to Goldman, hiring the most competent candidate is not the "currently accepted" rule in employment. Being the most qualified candidate is indeed one way to get the job, but employers' ignoring of merit standards and their explicit preference for specific groups are widespread. Merit criteria are either ignored or undermined in several ways.

Employment "At Will"

In accordance with a traditional legal principle—employment "at will"—private U.S. employers have had the right to discharge their workers without a reasonable cause based on work performance. This principle gives employers the legal right to dismiss qualified employees merely for refusing to support political candidates of the employer's choice or for expressing unpopular views on the job or even in the privacy of their own homes. An employer's right to arbitrary discharge without reasonable cause is hardly compatible with a merit system. Although the employer's right to discharge is now restricted by specific exceptions identified in union contracts and in federal and state laws (e.g., prohibiting race and sex discrimination), employment at will is still a significant legal principle in U.S. courts.

Competent job performance has also been undermined by the widespread use of unvalidated employment tests and irrelevant subjective standards for hiring and promotion.

Federal and state governments have continuously given employment preference to veterans, thereby excluding large numbers of more qualified nonveterans.

Many employees obtain their vocational qualifications in colleges and professional schools. In some such institutions preference for admission has been extended to children of alumni.

After Allan Bakke sued the University of California medical school, it was revealed that the dean had been permitted to select some admittees without reference to the usual screening process. As one writer [Allan P. Sindler] noted, "The dean's 'special admissions program' was evidently devoted to the *realpolitik* of sustaining influential support for the school." (This practice was ended in 1977.)

Seniority-based selection for training, promotion, and retention in layoff is commonly practiced in both the private and public sector of the economy. Such selection is based on years of service, not evaluation of job performance. Adherence to meritocratic principles would in some situations require the abolition of seniority criteria for reward.

Personal Connections

Reliance on personal connections is probably the most widely used recruitment method in American employment, a practice that often works against a merit system. An incumbent's graduate-school friend, the boss's nephew, or a political-patronage appointee is frequently not the most qualified person available for the job.

Note too that gaining promotion through social networks within the firm may have a corrupting effect on job performance as well as on moral character. The employee may see pandering to the right people as the best route to success.

Because traditionally accepted preference is so widespread, some blacks selected by AA preference may in fact replace less-qualified whites who would have been chosen by such traditional preference.

I conclude that merit selection is not, as Goldman claims, the currently accepted rule. Goldman states, however, that unless preferential treatment violates a currently accepted rule it is not "seriously unjust." In that case, preferential treatment is not seriously unjust.

A different version of the meritocratic claim might be that although hiring the best candidate is not the currently accepted rule and because (as Goldman says) merit selection has social utility, such selection *ought* to be the rule, and thus preferential treatment should not be extended to blacks. According to this meritocratic claim, all practices that often conflict with merit standards, such as selection by seniority ranking, veteran status, and powerful personal connections, should be eliminated. In that case, why not begin the struggle for merit in American employment by calling for an end to these practices? Why start by excluding members of a largely poor and powerless group, such as black people?

Let us focus on the consequences simply of denying preference to basically qualified blacks. Let us assume that this denial would produce some gain in social utility, that is, efficiency. That benefit would, I suggest, weigh very little in the moral balance against the double accomplishment of preferential treatment: compensation to blacks for past wrongs against them and achieving what this nation has never known—occupational integration, racial justice in the workplace.

Preferential Treatment and Black Self-Respect

Some commentators suggest that preferential treatment may be morally injurious to black persons. Thus Midge Decter and the economist Thomas Sowell worry that preference damages the self-respect of blacks.

Does preference really injure the self-respect of those it benefits? Traditional preference extended to personal connections has occasioned no such visible injury to self-respect. Career counselors who advise job seekers to develop influential contacts exhibit no fear that their clients will think less well of themselves; indeed, job candidates who secure powerful connections count themselves *fortunate*.

It might be objected that blacks (or any persons) who gain their positions through preferential treatment ought to respect themselves less. But this claim assumes that these blacks do not deserve such treatment. I believe that, because the overwhelming majority of blacks has been grievously wronged by racism, they deserve to be compensated for such injury and that black beneficiaries of employment preference—like veterans compensated by employment preference—have no good reason to feel unworthy.

Moreover, telling blacks—the descendants of slaves—that they ought to feel unworthy of their preferential positions can become self-fulfilling prophecy. Where are the black persons whose spirit and self-confidence have not already suffered because of the palpable barriers to attending white schools, living in white neighborhoods, and enjoying relations of friendship and intimacy with white people? Those blacks who, despite all the obstacles of overt and institutional racism, have become basically qualified for their positions should be respected for that achievement. Justice Marshall reminds us that the history of blacks differs from that of other ethnic groups. It includes not only slavery but also its aftermath, in which as a people they were marked inferior by our laws, a mark that has endured. Opportunities created by preferential treatment should symbolize an acknowledgment of such injustice and a commitment to create a future free of racism.

"The affirmative action strategy of using racial criteria to eliminate racial discrimination is inherently contradictory and futile."

Affirmative Action Does Not Promote Equality

Herman Belz

The purpose of affirmative action laws and policies is to eliminate discrimination in the workplace by increasing employment opportunities for minorities and women. Herman Belz argues that affirmative action's emphasis on group rights—specifically preferential treatment for blacks—contradicts and undermines the idea underlying the Declaration of Independence and the right guaranteed by the Civil Rights Act of 1964: equality of opportunity for all individuals regardless of race. Belz is a professor of American constitutional history at the University of Maryland in College Park and the author of *Equality Transformed: A Quarter Century of Affirmative Action*, from which the following viewpoint is excerpted.

As you read, consider the following questions:

1. According to Belz, what are the two basic elements of affirmative action that have remained constant?
2. Why does preferential treatment fail to provide a remedy for discrimination, according to the author?
3. What does Belz see as "the chief historical significance of affirmative action"?

Published by permission of Transaction Publishers from pp. 235-37, 242-49, 264-65 of *Equality Transformed: A Quarter Century of Affirmative Action* by Herman Belz. Copyright ©1991 by the Social Philosophy and Policy Center.

Analysis of the affirmative action debate begins with the idea of equality of opportunity on which traditional anti-discrimination law rests. Based on the natural rights principles of the Declaration of Independence, equal opportunity rejects distinctions of legal status and privilege defined by race, religion, ethnicity, language, sex, and family inheritance that formed the basis of premodern societies. Defined by the guarantee of equal treatment regardless of superficial differences such as race, it is a means by which individuals, through talent, ability and other personal attributes, take responsibility for themselves and pursue their interests. The rule of equal opportunity does not guarantee equal results. Because it values liberty and gives scope to differences among individuals with respect to interest and ability, it recognizes the impossibility of achieving perfect equality in the distribution of social and economic goods.

In comparative historical terms, the promise of equal opportunity inherent in the American Revolution was broadly realized in nineteenth-century America. Even in a country like the United States, however, where feudal or aristocratic institutions were never firmly established, equal opportunity was seriously restricted by the existence of slavery. Nevertheless the idea of equality of opportunity possessed unquestioned political legitimacy, even among groups that were excluded from its full benefits. This fact explains why equal opportunity was the aim of democratic political reformers, abolitionists, and women's rights advocates in the nineteenth century as well as progressive reformers in the early twentieth century.

From Equal Opportunity to Group-Based Equality

In race relations, equal opportunity—long denied by the system of legalized segregation—was guaranteed in the Civil Rights Act of 1964. The law commanded indifference to race in private employment in order to reinforce the government's own constitutionally required indifference to race under the equal protection clause of the Fourteenth and (by judicial construction) Fifth Amendments. In a political sense, Title VII [of the Civil Rights Act] reflected an interest-group outlook, insofar as the right of individuals not to be discriminated against because of race was intended to improve economic conditions for blacks in general. Under the law, however, the rights of individuals were the basis for any group concern. The Civil Rights Act recognized that individuals are morally prior to rather than dependent upon groups.

The civil rights establishment and the equal employment opportunity bureaucracy in the 1960s rejected equal opportunity because it did not lead to equality of condition. In their view, the legal capacity to participate and the right to equal treatment in a procedural sense—the central meaning of equal opportunity—were insignificant compared to the socially determined meaning of opportunity. The social and cultural deprivation suffered by blacks and other minority groups was seen as constituting an inseparable obstacle to the advancement of their interests and socioeconomic status. Civil rights policymakers therefore infused the equal opportunity law with the new meaning of group-based equality of result.

Disparate Impact Discrimination

The theory of disparate impact discrimination [that the unintentional exclusion of blacks from jobs constituted discrimination] provided the means for this transformation. Under pre–Title VII fair employment practice legislation, an inference—though not a conclusive finding—of intentional discrimination could be drawn from statistics of racial imbalance or exclusion. In enforcing Title VII, civil rights strategists persuaded the courts to accept statistical racial disparity, completely apart from an employer's intent, as *prima facie* evidence of unlawful discrimination. The *prima facie* evidence became a conclusive finding of discrimination if the employer could not prove that the employment practice that caused the disparate impact was a business necessity. Accordingly, in order to avoid discrimination charges under the disparate impact theory of liability, employers were forced to have a sufficient number of blacks in their work force. This method of enforcing or complying with Title VII focused attention on the results of the employment process, or on the 'bottom line,' rather than on equality of opportunity defined as the removal of procedural barriers to the equal treatment of individuals. The civil rights lobby argued that focusing on bottom-line results was a way of monitoring the extent to which an employer was providing equal opportunity in employment. In reality, employers were forced to guarantee equal or racially proportionate results in disregard of equal opportunity for individuals irrespective of race—as was required by Title VII.

Under disparate impact theory routine business practices could be found unlawful. The theory served the liberal purpose of expanding government regulation of business and forcing private employers and white workers to bear the cost and responsibility of compensating blacks for societal discrimination. Liberals were able to pursue the goal of restricting the operation of the labor market for social redistributive purposes while justifying it simply as a means of securing equal opportunity.

Disparate impact theory also provided a rationalization for preferential treatment, whether voluntary or coerced, as a remedy for unlawful discrimination. Preferential treatment as public policy was adopted in the absence of informed national discussion of the remedial concept [of providing a remedy for discrimination to people not directly victimized by discrimination] or of the theory of disparate impact discrimination on which it rested. No one in Congress supported quotas in the Title VII debate; when affirmative action preferences were introduced, policymakers deliberately obscured their coercive, race-conscious character. Objections had been raised against compensatory preference since the idea was first proposed in the early 1960s; not until the early 1970s, however, when defenders of the new civil rights ideology undertook to justify race-conscious measures, did the affirmative action debate really take shape.

Affirmative action preferences were initially justified as a legal remedy for past discrimination. . . . Courts proceeded to exercise broad remedial authority and elaborate the remedial rationale as an instrument of social reform. From the standpoint of public opinion, remedying past unlawful discrimination remains the principal justification of preferential treatment. . . .

Race as Merit

Two basic elements of affirmative action have remained constant. The first is the idea that individual merit should be defined in social terms, in relation to the principle of racial group equality of result. The second is the idea that reverse discrimination differs from traditional racial discrimination in being non-stigmatic. . . .

The affirmative action vision identifies race as a major component of the concept of merit. According to sociologist Benjamin Ringer, in a true merit society each group will be represented at each occupational level according to its numbers in the total work force. Most defenders of affirmative action reject the traditional idea of individual merit as culturally biased and redefine it in terms of racial and ethnic diversity. Psychologist Craig Haney contends that test-based selection should be supplemented by "recognition of the special merit that racial minorities bring to the work place by virtue of their unique perspectives and experiences." Linda S. Greene views individual merit as "a visionary ideal" that should not be embodied in legal doctrine before it is actually realized in social practice. Asserting that the concept of merit is political, Randall Kennedy reasons that since the elevation of blacks is a response to pressing social needs, race is rightly to be considered one of the primary traits that constitutes merit. Jeffrey Prager explains that under affirmative action, race *per se* is a merit deserving of reward, expressed in the rhetoric of diversity and representation rather than intelligence and achievement. Affirmative action rejects the idea of a hierarchy of merit: instead, it argues for the concept of a pool of candidates who are equally qualified—that is, who are all equally likely to succeed on the job. Prager contends

180

that companies operating under affirmative action plans should be permitted to set an absolute minimum standard of merit, rather than in effect be forced to accept the higher standards set by the abilities of candidates competing under a rank-ordered free-market concept of qualifications. Affirmative action merit is thus collectivistic, sociological, and relativistic.

Enforcing Discrimination

Ironically, just as socialism has collapsed across the globe, the leading capitalist power has adopted a peculiarly American neosocialism, putting politics (and lawyers) in command of its workplace, albeit on the pretext of equity rather than efficiency. . . .

Quotas are not the law of the land, exactly. They are explicitly banned in both the 1964 and 1991 Civil Rights Acts. Nevertheless, corporate America has been terrorized by the legal legerdemain whereby any statistical disparity between work force and population is equated with intentional discrimination. Throughout American business, newly entrenched affirmative action bureaucrats are enforcing discrimination by race and sex—in favor of the "protected classes" (women, minorities and, most recently, the disabled)—as decreed by Washington.

Peter Brimelow and Leslie Spencer, *Forbes*, February 15, 1993.

The non-stigmatic nature of affirmative action preferences is a second feature of the policy that is consistently asserted. This argument rests on the presumption that in a democratic political system governed by a white majority, it is not possible for policy outcomes to be antagonistic to the interests of members of the dominant group. Because of this fact, racial classifications may be used in relation to whites without the suspicion of unconstitutionality that ordinarily attaches to racial criteria. . . .

Basic Rights

Analyzing the quota controversy, a defender of affirmative action in a judicious moment said there were two major reasons for opposing preferential treatment: it denied basic rights, and it might not serve the good of the community. This comment aptly summarizes the position of critics of preferential treatment through two decades of controversy.

Opponents of preferential treatment argued, to begin with, that the Constitution guarantees equal protection of the laws to all persons, and that Title VII prohibits discrimination against any individual on account of race, color, religion, national origin, or sex. In their view, the anti-discrimination principle of the

Civil Rights Act was effective in eliminating racial barriers to equal opportunity, enabling blacks to achieve social and economic gains. Urging that the policy of individual rights and equal opportunity be continued, critics held that preferential treatment did not address the problem of unlawful discrimination and economic deprivation. On the contrary, they contended, it exacerbated racial tension, impeded the formulation of sound social policy, and undermined equality of opportunity. . . .

A more systematic argument against affirmative action developed in the later 1970s. Its fundamental premise is that the constitutional equal protection principle prohibits the distribution of benefits and costs by government on racial and ethnic grounds. Richard A. Posner states that to use race for constructive social purposes in non-stigmatizing or non-invidious ways, as affirmative action policy professes to do, requires courts to decide whether race-conscious measures harm a group. This involves weighing competing claims of racial groups on a subjective political scale that deprives the equal protection principle of its precision and objectivity. According to William Van Alstyne, determining that racial classification favoring certain groups can be justified under the Fourteenth Amendment by a compelling governmental interest rests on questionable judgments about motive and purpose. "That is not . . . a constitutional standard at all," Van Alstyne declares. "It is, rather a sieve . . . that encourages renewed race-based laws, racial discrimination, racial competition, racial spoils systems, and mere judicial sport.". . .

An Over-Inclusive Remedy

Opponents contend that preferential treatment is not only wrong in principle, it is also ineffective for achieving its intended purpose. It does not provide a remedy for discrimination, as its legal justification asserts. Anglo-American jurisprudence holds that where the law creates an injury, the law must afford a remedy. The corollary, reflecting the principle of individual moral autonomy, is that no one can be made part of the remedy who is not part of the injury. Under quota orders, however, those who receive preferential treatment often are not victims of discrimination, and those who are victims receive no benefit. In addition, members of excluded non-minority groups are unlikely to have perpetrated or benefited from the discrimination, while the employer guilty of discrimination bears none of the burden. The idea of group discrimination implies that individual members of the group suffer injury because of their race. Yet compensation to the group as a whole in the form of preferential hiring is directed at the wrong target. If past discrimination is the reason for giving compensatory preference, the recipients are deserving because they are victims of discrimination, not because of their race. And assuming that personal qualifications count even minimally in affirmative action, the beneficiaries of racial preference are those who suffer the least discrimination and are most qualified. Race-conscious affirmative action is thus over-inclusive. Any reason given for group preference, Alan Goldman points out, such as compensating for injury or giving opportunity to persons in need, provides grounds for defining the preference more narrowly than race.

Contradicting Social Science and History

Critics further aver that insofar as preferential remedies are aimed at attaining racial balance or proportional representation, affirmative action rests on erroneous social science. Disparate impact theory holds that racial group differences in income, occupation, educational achievement, test scores, and other indicators are the result of discrimination. Opponents of preference contend, on the contrary, that to a considerable extent group differences are based on aptitude, ability, taste, and opportunity. Questioning the notion that members of minority groups can actually be placed in the position they would have occupied but for discrimination, critics claim that education, cultural values, age, geographical location, and the character of the labor market are causes of racial group disparities. Moreover, it is false to assume that without discrimination, one can expect a nearly random distribution of women and minorities in all jobs. Economist Walter Williams says there is no known theory indicating the "correct" number of minorities that should be found in an activity or organization.

Affirmative action not only contradicts social science, it disregards the lesson of history that race and ethnicity as principles of social organization result in hostility and repression. If discrimination along racial lines divides societies into oppressors and oppressed, observes Barry Gross, "it is scarcely reasonable to hope to heal the split and redress the wrongs by further reference to those things." In his view, the main argument against preferential treatment is the historical fact that racial, religious, and ethnic discrimination have led to social disorder, war, and mass slaughter. Alan Goldman notes that whereas the historic achievement of liberalism was to eliminate native differences like race as determinants of social roles and benefits, affirmative action reversed this trend. According to critics, the affirmative action strategy of using racial criteria to eliminate racial discrimination is inherently contradictory and futile. "We shall not now see racism disappear by employing its own ways of classifying people and of measuring their rights," declares William Van Alstyne. Douglas Rae expresses the fallacy of affirmative action thus: "The trouble with compensatory inequality—'inequality in the name of equality'—is that it is akin to 'killing for peace' or 'lying in the name of the truth.' "

Achievement Obscured

Still another argument against affirmative action is that it obscures the genuine achievement of those who receive preferential treatment. In 1973, business writer Daniel Seligman reported the observation of a black corporate equal employment opportunity officer that all minorities are stigmatized when less qualified applicants are hired. Reverse discrimination denies minorities the satisfaction of having their ability validated if they otherwise would have made it on their own. Criticism of this feature of affirmative action gained force as the policy spread. According to Charles Murray, under affirmative action a market premium attaches to race, with the result that every black professional, no matter how able, is tainted. Some black supporters of preferential treatment concede its stigmatizing effect, but believe it is less than the stigma associated with exclusion. Other blacks insist on standards that judge individuals by ability and achievement. If the worst feature of slavery was the dishonor it imposed on blacks, Glenn C. Loury asserts, then affirmative action preferences will not resolve but only prolong this destructive legacy. Neither white guilt, special favors, nor racial proportionalism decreed by government can secure the freely conveyed respect of one's peers that signifies real equality, Loury concludes. . . .

According to Harvey C. Mansfield, Jr., the most obvious meaning of affirmative action is that certain groups of people are not sufficiently capable of helping themselves and so require assistance. In order not to hurt the pride of the minority groups, however, this fact cannot be publicly admitted. It is not the injustice of preferential treatment that is its worst feature, Mansfield contends, but its evil and underhanded means. In essence, affirmative action categorically accuses the American people of racial discrimination in order to avoid telling the truth that minorities, in the eyes of the civil rights bureaucracy, are incapable of competing in society. By focusing on equality of result instead of equal opportunity, Mansfield charges, preferential treatment encourages indifference to means as long as the end is achieved. The consequence is indifference to morality. This is seen in the "immoral moralism" of the consent decree, wherein a defendant employer who does not admit he is guilty agrees under compulsion to act as if he were. Mansfield warns that under the rule of affirmative action, government by consent decree threatens to replace government by consent.

The ultimate criticism of race-conscious affirmative action, therefore, is that it lacks political legitimacy. While it purports to enforce civil rights and remedy discriminatory injury, it is in reality a policy of resource allocation and social redistribution that in a substantial sense has not been approved by democratic decision-making. Although most Americans supported the goal of bringing minority groups into the economic mainstream, they were divided on the problem of means. The question of whether measures going beyond the anti-discrimination principle were needed, the identification of alternative principles on which preferential treatment rested, and the reconciliation of conflicting values and interests provoked by affirmative action proposals were political questions that should have been decided by representative institutions. It is true that some preferential programs were adopted by legislative bodies, but these were by far the exception rather than the rule and occurred long after the courts and administrative agencies had fundamentally installed a new policy in place of the Civil Rights Act. . . .

Affirmative action is often viewed as simply a strong means of enforcing traditional equal opportunity that can be used temporarily without weakening the principle of individual rights. Even so persistent a critic as Nathan Glazer says that preferential treatment has helped institutionalize nondiscrimination laws. The longer racial criteria are employed, however, the more likely they are to become permanent. This result can only be at the expense of genuine equality of opportunity.

The chief historical significance of affirmative action has therefore been to promote statist intervention into the free market and weaken political and social institutions based on individual rights. In an era when proposals of social reform based on the rationale of class conflict have generally been rejected by the electorate, affirmative action attempts to achieve the redistributive and anti-capitalist purposes of contemporary liberalism by other means. Instead of promising liberty through social welfare and security, it promises substantial racial equality. To carry out its promise, it attacks individual liberty. Describing the obstacles to a policy of more far-reaching equality of result, Judge Damon J. Keith expresses the essential spirit of affirmative action when he critically observes: "Despite the progress of the past two decades, an entrenched belief in the sanctity of individual rights remains. Our courts have time and again explicitly or implicitly shied away from 'intruding' too far into the rights of private individuals."

Affirmative action requires ever-expanding government regulation if the new American dilemma perceived by radical egalitarians—the unwillingness of democratic majorities to adopt measures necessary to achieve equality of condition for racial minorities—is to be resolved. Ultimately, then, the struggle to define American equality will determine whether the United States will remain a free society.

"Comparable worth is a worthy policy."

Comparable Worth Policies Can Be Effective

Elaine Sorensen

Comparable worth policies are intended to eliminate the under-payment of women in jobs equal in worth to, but requiring different skills than, positions predominately held by men. To achieve pay equity, jobs are evaluated and assigned fixed wages; then current wages are adjusted in accordance with the new standards. Elaine Sorensen maintains that the potential effectiveness of the comparable worth approach is illustrated by the successful implementation of such a policy in Minnesota. She argues that the U.S. federal government should enact a comparable worth policy, but that further observations should be made before mandating such policies in the private sector. Sorensen is the author of *Comparable Worth: Is It a Worthy Policy?*, from which the following viewpoint is excerpted.

As you read, consider the following questions:

1. What two models of economic discrimination against women are described by the author?
2. According to Sorensen, why is the "Minnesota-type" approach to comparable worth superior to the "pay for points" approach?
3. How did the comparable worth policy affect the pay of male and female state employees in Minnesota, according to the author?

Although the gender pay gap [the underpayment of women relative to men] declined in the 1980s, women working full-time still earned 70 percent less than men in 1991. A significant portion of this pay gap is the result of occupational segregation in the labor market. In 1991, over half of female workers were concentrated in three traditionally female fields—clerical, sales, and service work; only one in five worked in blue-collar jobs or managerial positions, the occupations in which most men worked. A broad range of empirical research almost universally shows that occupational segregation in the labor market results in lower pay for "women's work." This kind of pay inequity is responsible for approximately 27 percent of the total pay gap between women and men.

After reviewing the economic literature on pay differentials and conducting original research on this topic, I conclude that this underpayment of "women's work" results from economic discrimination against women. This does not imply intent on the part of employers. Economic discrimination exists when workers of one sex are denied economic opportunities available to workers of another sex for reasons that have little or nothing to do with their individual abilities.

I find that the crowding model of discrimination provides the best explanation of the discrimination process in the private sector. According to this theory, employers discriminate against women by excluding them from occupations considered "men's work," which in turn increases their supply and reduces their salaries in other occupations, typically referred to as "women's work." Hence, the lower pay in "women's work" reflects discrimination. A specific employer may not engage in these discriminatory practices, but she or he takes advantage of a discriminatory outcome by paying prevailing wages for "women's work."

In contrast, the discrimination process in the public sector is better characterized by the institutional model of discrimination. Here, the underpayment of "women's work" does not solely reflect the use of prevailing wages from the external labor market. On the contrary, even after prevailing wages are taken into account, I find that "women's work" is significantly underpaid in the public sector. This suggests that institutional factors specific to the public sector contribute to the underpayment of "women's work."

Potential Weaknesses

The purpose of comparable worth policies is to eliminate intrafirm pay discrepancies between male- and female-dominated jobs that are not accounted for by differences in job requirements. Policy implementation consists of three basic steps: conducting a job evaluation plan, assessing wages, and making the

187

necessary comparable worth wage adjustments.

Many have voiced concern over the central role of job evaluations in comparable worth policies. They note that job evaluation plans are inherently subjective and arbitrary. But steps can be taken to reduce the negative aspects of job evaluation plans.

Two basic approaches to enacting comparable worth have emerged: the "pay for points" approach and the Minnesota-type approach. The "pay for points" approach asserts that all jobs should be paid according to their job evaluation score. Thus, jobs currently overpaid according to the job evaluation plan are targeted for pay cuts; those underpaid are expected to receive pay increases. A *pure* "pay for points" approach, however, has never been implemented because the workers who are employed in the jobs destined for pay cuts, or their representatives, strongly object to it. Instead, a compromise is implemented where smaller pay increases are given to underpaid jobs, but no pay cuts are administered.

1992 Median Annual Earnings of Full-Time Workers by Gender, Race, and Education

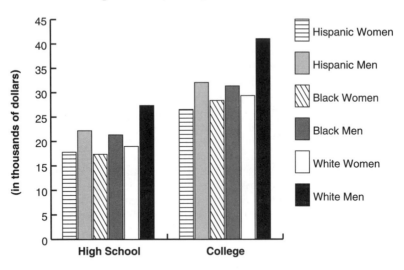

Source: U.S. Census Bureau, Current Population Reports, Series P-60, No. 180.

This compromise "pay for points" approach has three serious weaknesses: (1) it does not achieve the basic purpose of comparable worth—to eliminate the underpayment of "women's work"; (2) it does not target pay adjustments to female-dominated jobs;

and (3) it is overly dependent on the job evaluation system. This approach cannot achieve equal pay for comparable worth because it relies on pay cuts to achieve this aim, but these cuts are never enacted. By targeting all underpaid jobs for pay adjustments, this approach increases the cost of comparable worth and undercuts the gains to female workers. Finally, it relies primarily on the job evaluation system to determine salaries, a system that is known to be subjective and arbitrary. A comparable worth policy only needs to eliminate the variation in wages that is negatively correlated with the "femaleness" of a job once job requirements are taken into account. This approach tries to eliminate *all* wage variation once job requirements are accounted for.

In contrast, the Minnesota-type approach avoids these weaknesses. It achieves the basic goal of comparable worth by targeting female-dominated jobs for wage adjustments, which eliminate the underpayment of "women's work." It only needs a job evaluation plan to assess the size of this underpayment. It does not rely on the job evaluation plan to determine the salaries of all jobs.

Wage and Employment Effects

The primary effect of comparable worth is on the pay structure of the employer enacting the policy. The basic aim of comparable worth is to eliminate the pay discrepancy between predominantly male and female jobs that have comparable job requirements. Hence, the first question is: To what extent has implementation achieved this goal? A broader goal of comparable worth policies is to reduce the earnings disparity between women and men. Thus, progress on this front also measures the effectiveness of the policy. The salaries of jobs not targeted for comparable worth should also be examined to determine whether these salaries have been altered to offset the cost of comparable worth.

Secondary consequences of this policy may include alteration of the employment opportunities in the jurisdiction enacting comparable worth. Neoclassical theory predicts that an employer will decrease employment in those jobs that receive comparable worth pay adjustments. Other secondary effects of comparable worth include its impact on taxpayers and private sector employers.

In the case of Minnesota [where a comparable worth policy was implemented for state employees], I find that the comparable worth policy was quite successful. It practically eliminated the entire pay disparity between male- and female-dominated jobs that is unaccounted for by differences in job requirements. The wage penalty associated with female-dominated jobs declined from 21 to 3 percent during the implementation of comparable worth. This policy was also quite successful in increasing the female-to-male pay from 72 to 80.5 percent, representing a 12 percent increase in women's relative pay. Furthermore, the state of Minnesota did not offset the cost of comparable worth by reducing the wage growth of its male work force. On the contrary, comparable worth resulted in a 3 percent increase in men's pay and a 15 percent increase in women's pay. Finally, comparable worth had negligible effects on state government employment. Women's and men's employment continued to grow during the enactment of comparable worth, but this policy reduced their employment growth by 2.6 and 0.9 percent, respectively, reducing women's relative employment by 1.7 percent.

The Minnesota case, however, represents only one successful implementation of a comparable worth policy. Many other states that implemented comparable worth do not appear to have had this kind of success. Success depends, in part, on the method of implementation and the economic conditions at the time of enactment. Furthermore, I did not examine the effect of comparable worth on taxpayers or private sector employers, who also may be negatively affected by comparable worth. Future research should examine these effects as well as the wage and employment effects of comparable worth. . . .

Comparable Worth Legislation

The Congress has been relatively supportive of comparable worth policies. Legislation to conduct a comparable worth study of the federal job classification system passed the House of Representatives several times during the 1980s, but similar bills introduced in the Senate were never formally voted on. At the request of the Congress, the General Accounting Office (GAO) has begun a study of the federal government's pay and classification systems to determine whether gender bias exists in these systems.

There are several reasons why the federal government should enact a comparable worth policy. First, original research shows that governments pay "women's work" significantly less than "men's work" even after controlling for productivity differences and market forces. This strongly suggests that the federal government's current pay and classification systems treat "women's work" and "men's work" differently.

The second reason the federal government should enact a comparable worth policy is that the gains to female employees do not have to be offset by serious negative effects. The state of Minnesota has implemented this policy with negligible negative effects. Public sector employers are not forced to minimize costs to the extent that private sector firms are. Although it is true that taxpayers ultimately determine the size of government, providing a constraint to government costs, governments do not face the kind of competitive pressure from other suppliers as do private firms. Hence, governments can more easily absorb a one-time increase in payroll costs, which is how comparable worth policies are generally implemented.

Median Weekly Earnings for Full-Time Workers

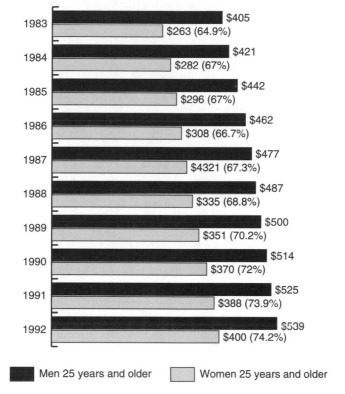

Year	Men 25 years and older	Women 25 years and older
1983	$405	$263 (64.9%)
1984	$421	$282 (67%)
1985	$442	$296 (67%)
1986	$462	$308 (66.7%)
1987	$477	$4321 (67.3%)
1988	$487	$335 (68.8%)
1989	$500	$351 (70.2%)
1990	$514	$370 (72%)
1991	$525	$388 (73.9%)
1992	$539	$400 (74.2%)

■ Men 25 years and older   □ Women 25 years and older

Note: The numbers are for men and women 25 and older working full-time. The median is the point at which half are above and half below.

Source: Bureau of Labor Statistics.

Finally, a comparable worth policy is quite compatible with the federal government's existing salary administration. The federal government has a highly structured salary system made up of grades and steps that each employee must follow. This system is quite isolated from the external labor market. Salary surveys of the private sector may be conducted for a small portion of its jobs, but many government jobs have no private sector counterparts. Hence, internal equity and job requirements already play a large role in wage determination in the federal government.

Comparable Worth in the Private Sector

In the United States a comparable worth policy in the private sector could be implemented by extending Executive Order 11246. This executive order requires that federal contractors take affirmative action in hiring and promoting members of protected classes. In late 1980, the Carter administration's Office for Federal Contract Compliance, the federal agency that enforces the executive order, proposed revisions that would have contained comparable worth language. The revisions stated: "The contractor's wage schedules must not be related to or based on the sex of the employees." These proposed revisions were dropped shortly after President Reagan took office. However, the proposed regulations remain open to a future administration with a different orientation.

Extending Executive Order 11246 to require enactment of comparable worth by federal contractors would result in partial coverage of the private sector by a comparable worth mandate. Several economists have noted that partial coverage of the private sector by a comparable worth policy may have negative wage and employment effects on workers in the uncovered sector. Fewer workers may be hired in the covered sector due to higher wages required by a comparable worth policy. These displaced workers could then end up in the sector of the economy not covered by comparable worth. This increase in the supply of workers could result in higher unemployment and lower wages in the uncovered sector. Such results depend, in part, on the labor demand elasticities within and between the covered and uncovered sectors, elasticities that are currently unknown. Hence, extension of comparable worth to the private sector should depend, in part, on further research into the possible negative effects of a policy's partial coverage of the private sector.

Federal legislation requiring all private sector employers to implement comparable worth is not likely in the United States. Nonetheless, our neighbor to the north, the Province of Ontario, has already implemented such a policy. . . . Policymakers in the United States can learn a great deal from Ontario's experience with comparable worth. Evidence of its economic effects can shed light on the likely effects of extending comparable worth to the private sector in the United States.

In conclusion, a serious problem exists in the U.S. labor market in that women are paid less than men for comparable work. In the public sector, comparable worth policies have been implemented successfully—they have improved the relative economic position of women without causing significant employment loss—suggesting comparable worth is a worthy policy. But these implementations have been the exception rather than the rule. Certain procedures should be followed to reduce the weaknesses of this policy. Extending it to other public jurisdictions, such as the federal government, could be beneficial if implemented appropriately. Any federally mandated extension of comparable worth to the private sector should first examine the outcomes of the Ontario Province comparable worth policy that covers both the private and public sectors. When extending comparable worth to the private sector, other issues related to the partial coverage of the private sector under a comparable worth policy should also be considered.

"Comparable worth . . . is bad public policy."

Comparable Worth Policies Are Ineffective

Steven E. Rhoads

By evaluating the worth of jobs and attaching fixed wages to them, comparable worth policies are intended to eliminate the inequities in pay for women and men doing work of equal value that requires different skills. Steven E. Rhoads argues that comparable worth programs in Minnesota, the United Kingdom, and Australia reveal that such policies are ineffective. Rhoads contends that evaluations to determine the worth of jobs cause ill will among workers and produce inconsistent and unfair results. Moreover, according to Rhoads, such pay requirements disrupt the free market process by which rising and falling wages ameliorate shortages and surpluses of labor. Rhoads is a professor of government at the University of Virginia in Charlottesville and the author of *Incomparable Worth: Pay Equity Meets the Market*.

As you read, consider the following questions:

1. How much money do women earn for every dollar earned by men, according to Rhoads?
2. According to the author, why would an equitable worth system in the United States inevitably become centralized.

From Steven E. Rhoads, "Pay Equity Won't Go Away." Reprinted with permission from the July/August 1993 *Across the Board*, the magazine of the Conference Board, New York, NY.

A single number fuels the comparable-worth movement: 75 cents. This is the amount, based on median weekly earnings as of 1992, that women working full time earn for every dollar earned by men working full time. Proponents of comparable worth point to studies suggesting that at least half of the wage gap may result from discrimination and that women in many predominantly female occupations are paid substantially less than their work is actually worth. Opponents note other studies claiming that variables such as education, job experience, and women's tendency to rank pay as less important than flexible scheduling and good working conditions explain almost all of the wage gap.

The role that discrimination plays in producing the wage gap remains unclear. I am convinced, however, that comparable worth, just one of a number of possible remedies for workplace discrimination, is bad public policy even if wage discrimination were as pervasive as proponents believe.

My conviction is based on five years of studying pay equity in three places where proponents believe it has been implemented successfully—the United Kingdom, Australia, and Minnesota. In none of these has comparable worth proven to be a reliable method of spotting and overcoming discrimination. Moreover, the costs of the policies are extremely high. Most of these costs will be absorbed by businesses, and business leaders should be aware of them before mandatory comparable worth gets a toehold in the private sector. The U.K. and Australian experiences show how measures intended to have limited scope and impact can grow to cause economy-wide turmoil.

Jealousy, Discontent, Ill Will, and Bitterness

Comparable worth requires some form of job-evaluation system. U.S. supporters of comparable worth often say that the concept relies on objective criteria to assess the comparative value of historically "male" and "female" jobs. Opponents believe no such thing as objective job evaluation exists; surprisingly, comparable-worth proponents readily acknowledge as much when talking privately.

In the absence of objective criteria, an arbitrary, political process determines wage levels. In Minnesota, where the practice applies throughout the public sector, results often depend heavily on employee skill in filling out questionnaires describing their job duties, and on having articulate, forceful representatives on evaluation committees, which study questionnaire responses and debate job importance to decide wage levels.

In Australia, where government has been involved deeply in setting occupational wages for most of this century, the politicking takes the form of frequent union strikes, threats, and occasionally sabotage (such as welding Melbourne's trains to their rails) to get the attention of the Industrial Relations Commission, which sets pay rates. In the United Kingdom's judicial system, the arbitrariness is best seen in the conflicting decisions of different industrial-relations tribunals confronting essentially identical cases.

Wreaking Economic Havoc

Overall, the many regulations that control banking, trucking, the airlines, mergers, workplace safety, and the like are industry-specific or activity-specific, and are intended, rightly or wrongly, to preserve the free market against its own excesses. Wage and price controls, when imposed, are usually justified as temporary measures to curb inflation. Even socialism itself was originally conceived as a more efficient way of harnessing the productive capacity generated by capitalism. And because New Deal–type regulations purport to secure specific results, they contain built-in standards against which they may be assessed.

But comparable worth, like affirmative action, contains none of these self-limitations. Its scope includes every job in the work force; since most jobs are sex-segregated, most pay scales would be open to challenge. Nor does comparable worth pretend to facilitate the best tendencies of the free market; it explicitly seeks to bypass the market. It does this, moreover, without clearly specifying what positive goal is to be achieved beyond "justice"; under this loose mantle, the pursuit of comparable worth can ignore any economic havoc it wreaks as irrelevant to its "success" as long as the wage gap is closed.

Michael Levin, *Feminism and Freedom*, 1987.

The wrangling about job-evaluation scores and the resulting pay rates has led to bad employee relations in every place I studied. In 1990 the Minneapolis/St. Paul *Star Tribune Newspaper of the Twin Cities* reported that some Minnesota city and county representatives "say pay equity has bred so much jealousy and discontent that small-town city halls and county courthouses have become almost impossible to work in." Whether speaking with proponents or opponents in Minnesota, I found wide agreement that the process of reaching decisions was disruptive. It produced ill will and bitterness.

Over some 12 to 18 months, the largest Minnesota county, Hennepin, tallied more than 3,500 individual appeals of preliminary job values (out of 10,201 employees) in addition to departmental appeals. One personnel chief reflecting on the ill will caused by the "comparing you and me business" seemed to long wistfully for the days when "the market decided." When I thanked another personnel expert for the interview, he said: "My pleasure. I am glad to talk about this in a setting where I am not getting yelled at."

The U.K. experience is of even more interest: Unlike Minnesota, its system reaches the private sector and is like that envisioned by U.S. proponents—decentralized, company-centered, and complaint-based. Since nothing happens unless a complaint is filed, complaints are a rewarding way for U.K. women to raise their pay. As would happen in the United States, lawyers jump in and participate in an adversarial system characterized by company representatives' trying to belittle the responsibility and effort involved in the complainant's job, while her representatives in turn run down the importance of the male jobs chosen for comparison. The effect on employee morale of these cases, which can drag on for years through several layers of appeal, is predictably bad.

Wage Fixing Harms Industrial Relations

In Australia, with the most deeply embedded comparable-worth system of the three, evidence shows that industrial relations are unusually poor, with strikes much more frequent than in most industrial countries. Moreover, one study of the 24 Organization for Economic Cooperation and Development countries ranks Australia 15th on labor flexibility and on employee productivity, 17th on worker motivation, and 20th on absenteeism and on the impact of job turnover on enterprises.

Many observers place much of the blame for this situation on Australia's wage-fixing system. Under the tribunal system, industrial relations have been centralized: Instead of talking seriously with each other, business and labor first stage ritual confrontations—with one-day strikes and blustery threats—and then, at hearings, speak in legal jargon to less-knowledgeable third parties who decide their fates.

From labor's point of view, disputes become a no-lose proposition. If the tribunal sides with workers, they get more money; if it does not, they retain their old wages. Also, as noted by U.S. labor-relations expert George Strauss, wage awards are *imposed*, not reached through negotiation, and thus Australian unionists lack any sense of moral obligation to live up to an agreement they have helped make.

From management's point of view, competence in industrial relations is equated with skill in negotiating the rules and procedures of the tribunals. Industrial-relations departments in companies develop a remedial rather than a preventive orientation.

Comparable-worth job evaluation produces bizarre and indefensible results in all three of the areas studied. The United Kingdom makes a serious attempt to keep things decentralized and simple: If a woman feels her job is equal to that of one or more better-paid male employees in the company, she files a complaint. A tribunal, guided by the report of an "independent expert," either agrees with the complaint, granting the female a wage equivalent to the male comparator, or disagrees, and all remains as it was before.

But it is not as simple as it sounds: If a worker successfully files a complaint in the United Kingdom, it often results in raises for other workers at a company, too. For example, in one celebrated U.K. case a cafeteria cook in a shipyard was found to deserve a pay raise so as to reach the salary level of male carpenters and other male-dominated trades. The raise left the cook earning more than her supervisor—whose salary then had to be raised above the cook's.

Other indefensible outcomes flow from the arbitrary nature of comparable-worth job evaluation. Independent U.K. experts disagree about evaluation factors that should be included and about how they should be weighed and measured. One consequence has been that experts assigned to different companies in the same industry have been unable to agree whether, say, female sewing machinists are as valuable as male upholsterers. Because one unlucky company drew an expert who believed sewers should be paid as much as upholsterers, that business now is required legally to pay its machinists more than its competitors pay theirs. Similar inequities among companies also have arisen in the fish-packing industry because of conflicting decisions by different experts confronting similar cases.

In Minnesota, several of the evaluation systems award high points and thus high pay for decision-making. Some department heads soon discovered that they would be paid more if they delegated less, and thus comparable worth unintentionally has encouraged a more authoritarian management style. What the systems count as a decision also is controversial. One sign-language interpreter told a legislative committee that she had to make four decisions at the same time in her work, but under her jurisdiction's evaluation system these decisions did not count.

Abandoning the Market Standard

Proponents of comparable worth defend job-evaluation systems by noting that private-sector companies commissioned in-house evaluations comparing their workers' wages for decades before the birth of the comparable-worth movement. They wonder why the systems suddenly became controversial when used to spot long-standing inequities. This line of argument ignores the fact that comparable-worth job evaluation revolutionizes private-sector job evaluation even as it preserves its name. As industrial-relations specialist Donald Schwab has noted, "The actual criterion of job evaluation [in the private sector] is not worth in a job-content sense, but market wages." Samples of jobs and job factors are juggled until there is a satisfactory fit between evaluations and actual wages.

Despite attempts to let actual market wages guide evaluation results, sometimes market data are at odds with evaluation results for a particular job. When this conflict occurs in the private sector, the market nearly always takes precedence over job evaluation. For example, pay is raised for jobs with high turnover rates.

Comparable-worth job evaluation abandons the market standard for validity and offers no alternative to replace it. As a result, the inequitable and inefficient differences among experts, committees, and tribunals are inevitable, and the wrangling that surrounds the standardless process produces the ill will catalogued earlier.

This type of job evaluation also differs from the market-based variant because it often is mandatory. When job evaluation is imposed on all companies, we are unable to see if companies that use it do better or worse than those that do not. Some think that job evaluation harms companies' efficiency because it makes response to market signals more difficult and encourages workers to adopt rigid views of their jobs' duties.

Comparable worth coerces many companies into paying according to rigid job-evaluation criteria at a time when job evaluation is frequently called into question: "Employers are increasingly seeking to avoid sharp job definitions to enable the contribution of individuals to develop as their potential is realized," read a 1987 Confederation of British Industry report. "Such an approach is often associated with multi skilling arrangements consequent on the introduction of new technology, greater flexibility in working arrangements and increasing interest in performance-related pay."

Labor Shortages and Surpluses

Even if comparable worth could produce agreed-upon wage rates without heightening societal tensions, implementation of the new administered wage levels would be accompanied by huge economic costs. Well-functioning market economies use rising wages to ameliorate shortages of labor in an occupation or at a particular location, and use static or falling wages to reduce surpluses by encouraging worker exit and discouraging entry. Comparable worth does not allow this flexibility.

Ironically, one of the better recent examples of how market-driven wages can help overcome shortages is provided by the female-dominated nursing profession. For years, comparable-worth proponents have said that markets treat nurses unfairly because people link the profession with women's unpaid and underappreciated nurturing role in the family. Yet during the 1980s this supposed market bias against female-dominated nurturing professions was nowhere in evidence. In response to shortages, U.S. registered-nurses' salaries *after inflation* rose 27.7 percent from 1981 to 1990, while the average inflation-adjusted male salary declined 2.8 percent over the decade. These rapidly rising wages helped dramatically reverse a decline in the number of women in nursing programs.

The Minnesota experience shows how comparable worth can make such efficient labor-supply responses much more difficult. Although comparable-worth supporters were certain that job-evaluation results would lead to large raises for nurses, the results in many parts of the state showed nurses to be overpaid at new prevailing market rates. Many public-health directors complained to me about their vacancies and about their inability to meet the private-sector competition with comparable-worth-established pay rates. One related her frustration by noting that her nursing program had begun losing nurses to a nearby locality paying more than $2 an hour more. "Two nurses left for the money," she said, and "we could find no one for three to four months."

Despite the problems in their public-health nursing departments, localities felt they could not make an exception for nurses and pay them more than their comparable-worth pay plan dictated. The ill will caused by the job-evaluation process led to lawsuits challenging the final results in a number of localities. The last thing local officials wanted to do was open themselves up to the charge that their new comparable-worth pay plans were being implemented discriminatorily as well.

Librarians v. Foresters

Although nurses in Minnesota were hurt by comparable worth, librarians made out like bandits. Far from being in short supply, there is a great surplus of librarians in Minnesota as elsewhere in the United States. The head librarians I spoke with said that even in pre-comparable-worth days, libraries rarely had an opening and would have 40 to 60 applicants when one occurred. Librarians eager to get an edge on their competitors for jobs often get a master's degree in library science, and the resulting pool of highly educated applicants enables libraries to make a master's a requirement for many jobs. And finally, under comparable-worth policies, one can complain that librarians are paid far less than people with other jobs for which an M.A. is required.

Actually, in Minnesota state government the male-dominated

foresters and wildlife managers are paid at least as poorly as librarians, even though many hold master's degrees. Like librarians, these natural-resource specialists are dedicated and highly educated. Also like librarians, they are convinced that society undervalues the importance of what they do. And, like librarians, people are lined up to get their jobs. This excess supply holds their salaries down just as it does for librarians, but Minnesota assumed that discrimination was the culprit when it came to librarians. Librarians, paid less than their comparable-worth points dictated, have received large comparable-worth raises; the foresters and wildlife managers—as state workers in male-dominated professions—remain ineligible for this type of increase.

The Minnesota experience suggests that a national comparable-worth policy would make it much harder for flexible wages to coax labor toward areas of shortage and away from areas of surplus. In this regard, the Australian experience also is relevant. In that country, small wage premiums for skills are driving workers away from the skilled trades and toward easier unskilled jobs—or skilled jobs elsewhere. For years Qantas Airways Ltd.'s mechanics serviced other airlines' aircraft, but recently the airline has been unable to service even its own because the wage-setting authorities require a mechanics' wage $100 a week below the market wages paid by other nations' carriers. Many Qantas mechanics have moved to other airlines in and out of Australia.

Centralization Is Inevitable

Comparable-worth proponents in the United States argue that a mandated system would not require a more centralized means of fixing wages. They submit that employers will be free to use any nondiscriminatory pay system, with the courts resolving the issue if complainants believe they are paid unfairly because of their sex. But as we have seen, the United Kingdom's decentralized system leads to paying workers more than their bosses and to inconsistent decisions among similar jobs in different companies. The pressure to resolve such inequities by centralizing and establishing a consistent system eventually will be overwhelming.

In Australia a simple dispute-resolution procedure to avoid strikes grew into a wage-fixing monster because of concern about consistent treatment of similar workers in different companies. But centralization has not ended Australian inconsistency. The Industrial Relations Commission, which itself determines most pay rates throughout the country, recently noted that the results of its handiwork included "widespread examples of the prescription of different rates of pay for employees performing the same work.". . .

The stakes here are not small. Salaries total 73.3 percent of national income—and comparable-worth studies often charge that the market gets salaries very wrong indeed. For example, a study of state workers in Washington gave clerical supervisors more points than chemists, though the market paid the chemists 41 percent more, and gave retail clerks higher points than truck drivers, though drivers got 30 percent more in the market.

The economic costs of comparable worth are likely to be enormous. Since Australia began its centralized wage-fixing system in 1913, its per-capita income has fallen from highest in the world to 13th, 30 percent behind the United States. Many economists think Australia's inflexible wage system explains much of this deterioration, and all the major Australian political parties now favor more decentralized, market-driven wages as a way to improve efficiency and growth.

Normal market processes (including a decrease in the percentage of female workers who are inexperienced) and existing anti-discrimination laws cut the U.S. full-time weekly pay gap [the ratio of women's to men's income] from 64.6 percent in 1981 to 75 percent in 1992. This rate of progress in the United States is far better than that of Australia (no change) or the United Kingdom (a closing of the wage gap from 65.1 percent to 69.7 percent) over this approximate time frame.

This doesn't mean we should do nothing to help close the wage gap further. For example, state laws could be changed so that legal secretaries could help clients with routine legal documents, and nurses could perform more medical procedures without a doctor's supervision. Such measures would increase demand for secretaries and nurses, and thus raise their salaries. Progress might be faster still if enforcement of anti-discrimination laws pertaining to hiring and promotion were strengthened. In addition, public policy might continue to oppose, through education in the schools, stereotypes that could limit artificially the range of young women's occupational choices. We also could help working women in ways costing far less than comparable worth by granting a fuller tax deduction for child-care costs, restoring the two-earner tax deduction, or punishing more severely non-custodial parents who ignore their legal obligations.

Whether or not such measures are adopted, comparable worth should not be. Predictable and insurmountable problems have occurred wherever it has been tried. To adopt it as public policy would bring us more acrimonious politics and a much weaker economy. Women—and men—would both be losers.

"Diversity efforts have the potential to play a significant role in solving the problems that plague organizations and society at large."

Diversity Management Is Beneficial

Ann M. Morrison

In 1987, the Hudson Institute report *Workforce 2000* predicted that in the 1990s, the number of minorities and women entering the workforce would vastly exceed that of white men. In response, many corporations have instituted "diversity management" programs designed to ensure equitable and effective business operations in the face of these demographic shifts. Ann M. Morrison argues that diversity management enables companies to increase their market shares, increase productivity, improve management, and promote fairness. Morrison is the author of *Breaking the Glass Ceiling* and *The New Leaders: Guidelines on Leadership Diversity in America*, from which the following viewpoint is excerpted.

As you read, consider the following questions:

1. According to James Preston, cited by the author, why was Avon able to turn around its unprofitable inner-city markets?
2. Why does diversity management lead to reduced legal costs, according to Morrison?
3. According to the author, why is the performance of all managers improved when nontraditional workers are included in the competition for management positions?

Workforce 2000, a report by the Hudson Institute, created quite a stir in the business community when it was published in 1987, but it has not been the compelling force for change that some people thought it would be. The report's figures documenting the demographic shifts taking place in the U.S. workforce are certainly dramatic. For anyone not already familiar with them, the most striking figures relate to the composition of the net new workforce through the year 2000: only about 15 percent will be native white men, while the rest will be native white women (42 percent), native nonwhite women (13 percent) and men (7 percent), and immigrant men (13 percent) and women (9 percent). In other words, nearly all the growth in the workforce in the 1990s will come from people who are not white and male. . . .

The Benefits of Diversity

The hard realities of competition and the marketplace are convincing many executives that diversity is a necessary part of their business strategy. They promote diversity for four business reasons: to keep and gain market share, to reduce costs, to increase productivity, and to improve the quality of management in their organizations. Many executives also support diversity for other reasons, not the least of which is a sense that bringing business practices more in line with personal values of fairness is the right thing to do.

The five reasons noted here are similar to the benefits described by researchers Taylor Cox and Stacy Blake, who assert that diversity increases organizational competitiveness. These authors present evidence that sound management of diversity affects cost savings, creativity, problem solving, flexibility, marketing, and resource acquisition, in addition to social responsibility. There is considerable overlap between the benefits cited by Cox and Blake and those reported by the managers in our study [Guidelines on Leadership Diversity (GOLD) Project, conducted to identify tools and techniques for fostering workforce diversity].

Keeping and Gaining Market Share

As markets grow increasingly diverse and competition for market share escalates, managers who have an understanding of their customers' preferences become more important. In many organizations, managers are encouraged to learn to think like their customers. While it doesn't necessarily take a woman to understand what female consumers will buy or a Latino to penetrate the rapidly growing Latino market, the experiences and perspectives that nontraditional [other than white male] managers bring to their work can certainly be valuable in building sales. That value is increasingly recognized by executives.

The responsibility to reflect market reality goes beyond creating a representative personnel profile for its own sake. Many managers argue that diversity among the organization's decision makers is the best way to ensure that the organization has the flexibility to capture diverse markets and provide adequate customer service. The understanding and shared experience of marketing managers with other Cuban-Americans or Asian-American women, for example, may motivate them to respond to growing market niches. According to CEO James Preston, Avon was able to turn around its unprofitable inner-city markets, making them its most productive U.S. markets, by handing them over to Hispanic and black sales managers.

A Competitive Edge

Many employers are concluding that there are significant, long-term reasons for encouraging diversity in the workplace. . . . According to *Workforce 2000*, only 15 percent of those entering the workforce by the year 2000 will be white men. Employers . . . who choose to limit their labor market to white males will find themselves competing for a decreasing number of workers.

Workforce 2000 also predicts a shortage of people with skills necessary in a high-tech work environment. Thus, employers will also be competing for skilled employees. Historically, when supply is low and demand is high, prices increase. Therefore, it is costly for employers to fail to value and encourage diversity. Employers who expand their recruitment and selection nets to include men and women from all ages and ethnic groups will be at a competitive advantage.

Employers increasingly recognize that in the global marketplace, a diverse workforce can provide a competitive edge. The U.S. workforce, will all its heterogeneity, provides many potential employees who know the language, culture and values of a country in which an employer might want to do business. Furthermore, diversity provides a richness of ideas and variety of views—a fertile growing medium for creativity.

Theodore H. Curry II, *Corrections Today*, August 1993.

In addition to missing out on changes in existing markets, companies that are not aware of market diversity risk losing out on new business. One black manager in charge of production of a widely distributed directory told us how her company lost an important piece of new business. Even though the desired new market was in a southwestern city, the project team failed to tap into the city's predominant Hispanic community. The company lost its bid to a competitor that had an Hispanic manager in charge of the project and had given members of the Hispanic community input into the process.

Managers are increasingly coming to recognize that their ability to represent their organizations' customers and clients is a major issue in marketplace competitiveness. The perception of this ability, by potential customers in particular, can also be a factor in an organization's competitiveness. A manager who is of the same sex or ethnic background as a customer may have greater credibility because that similarity implies shared experiences and, consequently, greater understanding and integrity. Shared experiences such as speaking another person's native language, rearing children, or coping with day-to-day discrimination are sometimes recognized and appreciated by an increasingly diverse customer base in much the same way that membership in certain fraternities or military units has been recognized over the years. These nontraditional kinds of experiences may actually be as valuable in terms of preparing people for senior management roles as any traditionally recognized experiences. In any case, customers may perceive that someone of their own sex or ethnicity is better able to serve their needs, and this can influence them to switch to or stay with one organization rather than another.

Finally, with respect to potential marketing advantages, some executives in our study believe that using diversity to improve their marketing capability within ethnically diverse domestic markets will help them market more effectively internationally. They are looking for ways to apply their experience in the United States to help them enter and build a share in foreign markets. If they can develop responsiveness and an image to improve marketing in our own culturally rich country, then it should be easier for them to gain new markets in foreign cultures. This advantage in a growing global marketplace is yet another important reason for advocating diversity.

Cost Savings

Many executives believe that an effective approach to fostering diversity will save money over the long term and often even in the short run. While the costs associated with specific aspects of doing business are difficult to pinpoint, estimates of cost savings in areas such as personnel are increasingly used to justify investment in diversity. The cost involved in recruiting, training, relocating, and replacing employees, along with providing a competitive compensation package, is a major expense for most organizations. In many cases personnel costs consume at least one-half to two-thirds of an organization's budget; this is especially true for service organizations. Reducing these costs can make a big difference in profitability.

How can fostering diversity contribute to cost cutting? Many managers we interviewed expect diversity efforts to reduce the high turnover rate of nontraditional employees and the costs that go with it. One manufacturing manager in our study was concerned that his company seemed to be training engineers for competing companies, which were luring away some of the most talented employees. He believes that more attention to young engineers, especially women and people of color, will keep this from happening as often. According to P. Schmidt, women and people of color were resigning from Corning Incorporated at twice the rate of white men, prompting that company to institute some key diversity practices in 1987. The cost of Corning's exodus was estimated at $2 to $4 million a year to recruit, train, and relocate replacements. Other sources estimate the cost of turnover per person to be $5,000 to $10,000 for an hourly worker and anywhere from $75,000 to $211,000 for an executive at around the $100,000 salary level. The cost to replace more senior executives is probably much higher. . . .

Avoiding Legal Fees

Personnel costs are also more painful to executives when the money spent is being wasted. Big settlements to discrimination claimants, for example, frequently represent costs that would not have been necessary had the organization taken action to promote diversity. In 1991, a jury awarded the record sum of $17.65 million in damages to a woman employed by Texaco who claimed she was passed over for management promotions. In a 1988 case, State Farm Insurance was expected to pay $100 to $300 million to women who were allegedly denied hiring or advancement. The allegation that female employees were denied benefits when they were pregnant will cost AT&T an estimated $66 million, according to an article in the *Wall Street Journal*. The staggering sums paid in damages and awards are accompanied by costs simply to open a legal case (approximately $25,000) or fees to settle ($50,000) or to take a case through trial ($100,000).

High legal fees and settlements emphasize that failing to address diversity can be an expensive proposition. According to Ronni Sandroff, nearly 90 percent of all Fortune 500 companies have received complaints of sexual harassment, and more than a third have been sued. The cost per company per year in absenteeism, low morale, and low productivity is estimated at $6.7 million. Job-related stress, which contributes to increased turnover and absenteeism as well as a host of other negative effects, is another expensive problem that diversity efforts can help alleviate, particularly for nontraditional employees.

Although a diversity effort is expensive, it can result in significant savings that will offset the expenses. Short- and longer-term savings in personnel and legal costs can make diversity an attractive business strategy from a fiscal point of view.

Increased Productivity

Although it is difficult to assess the impact of diversity on productivity, many executives in the organizations we studied expect greater productivity from employees who enjoy coming to work, who are relaxed instead of defensive or stressed in their work setting, and who are happy to be working where they feel valued and competent. The cost of changing an organization's climate for nontraditional employees may be high, but the promise of a significant payoff in increased productivity is what keeps the effort alive. For example, according to L.H. Chusmir and D.E. Durand, if a 12 percent productivity gain could be achieved among female employees by reducing barriers for women, who comprise 44 percent of the workforce, the result would be a 5 percent productivity gain overall.

Despite the complexities of human motivation and ability to perform and the difficulty of measuring human productivity, a compelling case can be made that diversity efforts do have a positive impact. There is strong reason to think, for example, that people are motivated to work harder and more productively when they believe they can be successful. In *Ensuring Minority Success in Corporate Management*, Donna Thompson and Nancy DiTomaso argue that a multicultural approach has a positive effect on employees' perception of equity, which in turn affects their morale, goal setting, effort, and performance. Organizational productivity is consequently improved. Other research also ties employees' perceptions to elements of productivity. Robert Eisenberger and his colleagues, for example, found a positive relationship between employees' perception of being valued and cared about by their organization and their attendance, dedication, and job performance.

Innovation, one aspect of productivity that concerns many managers, is apparently affected by diversity. Cox and Blake present evidence linking diversity to enhanced creativity and innovation. Moreover, in the study led by Robert Eisenberger, employees who felt valued and supported by their organization were more innovative without any direct reward or personal recognition. Other research on innovation by Philip Birnbaum and Robert Ziller showed that heterogeneous groups (in terms of race, age, values, background, training, and so on) are more productive than homogeneous groups. A number of executives we interviewed were convinced that diversity would enhance their organization's ability to find innovative solutions to business problems and to create a wide range of goods and services. A

208

construction manager said, "Any time you broaden the organization with people with different backgrounds, you strengthen the organization.". . .

To the extent that diversity efforts can alleviate the problems and improve the perceptions of employees—both the nontraditional employees who have borne the brunt of discriminatory treatment in many organizations and their white male counterparts, who must also be prepared and motivated to perform—productivity will be improved.

Better Quality of Management

Simply including nontraditional employees in fair competition for advancement can improve the quality of management by enlarging the pool of talent from which to choose. In our study, one Native American woman, who is in charge of a technical area, noted that in her company, "There is a tremendous pool of people we haven't utilized. We have clerical people with Ph.D.'s and M.B.A.'s. We can start tapping those people."

Diversity activities may unblock some highly qualified and able nontraditional employees who are stuck in clerical and other low-level jobs. For example, in one company we studied, a diversity program was designed to help identify and advance high-potential employees. The program identified a woman who had been a clerk in the company for the preceding twelve years and had never been considered for a management position. The director of an engineering unit in the company estimated that now that the woman was unblocked, she would reach at least the fifth level of management within five years.

A number of managers we interviewed maintain that including nontraditional managers in fair competition will strengthen the cadre of all managers, including those who are white men. A diversity program, with its enhanced competition for jobs, can encourage the more competent white men to perform even better, while the less competent ones are weeded out. The senior vice president of a health care organization, a white man, pointed out that a diversity program stands to benefit all strong-performing individuals, including white men. . . .

New personnel practices, especially those tied to a diversity effort, are likely to be closely scrutinized by cost-conscious managers who need to be convinced that they are warranted. Some diversity-related practices, therefore, are more carefully thought out than the practices already in place. This often comes about through the use of task forces and employee groups that are part of a diversity effort. Such groups help design, review, or endorse personnel practices to ensure that they are thorough and fair. One manager praised the role of an employee group in assuring that new practices are as good as they can be: "You try stuff out on this group regarding decisions you're considering, and they speak for employees. Better decisions are made sometimes because of their input. For example, there was a new compensation plan in the works. The compensation people were going to make a change, and I brought them into this group. The group worked through not only the impact on women and minorities but also the general administrative details for all managers that made it a better plan." Often, simply asking, "Is this fair and appropriate for women and for people of color?" can help an organization strengthen its human resources in general, its human resource practices, and its broader business practices.

Increased Fairness

A significant benefit of diversity, simply put, is increased fairness. This is both a business and an ethical issue. On the one hand, as the connections between fairness and better business performance become clearer, it is easier to invoke fairness as a goal of diversity. On the other hand, many managers we interviewed expressed a strong belief that their organizations should act with fairness for its own sake regardless of whether it made better business sense. One chief executive of a high-technology company put it this way: "There is a philosophical difference now, which comes from the heart. It is a sense of fairness in methods and practices. We care about what people think and feel. That is progress."

Other managers we interviewed described their pride in creating a more open, flexible, responsive, and responsible work environment where people can be happier, not just more efficient or productive. Such an organizational climate is one of the less publicized benefits of successful diversity efforts.

Finally, the managers we interviewed pointed to the benefits of diversity beyond their organizations. Some managers want their organizations to be agents for change, to make the world a better place. One black administrator, for example, told us that more black men in her state go to prison than to college because, she said, the school system is failing that group. The diversity effort in her institution is aimed at getting more blacks and other underrepresented groups into educational leadership positions. The effect of this on children, she feels, will be to help them overcome their feelings of inferiority created by stereotyping and get greater benefit from the educational system.

Although some managers may argue that business has few if any obligations to the larger community, other managers insist that being a good community citizen eventually benefits their business. One white male business executive in our study expressed a very strong view about the role of business in the community and how diversity efforts can benefit both. He said, "The bigger picture we have to deal with is the minority situation in this country. [In this area] the situation is so desperate and so in need of role models, that if we in corporations can't advance minorities so they can turn around and do what needs to be done in their communities, I don't see any of us surviving."

Diversity efforts have the potential to play a significant role in solving the problems that plague organizations and society at large. Although support for diversity is increasingly tied to business issues, social responsibility is still an incentive for many executives. However, much remains to be done before diversity is fully realized and the benefits noted here can be reaped.

"There is little systematic evidence that [diversity management] policies produce long-term benefits."

Diversity Management Is Counterproductive

Frederick R. Lynch

"Diversity management" refers to corporate policies designed to increase the inclusion and tolerance of growing numbers of minorities and women in the workplace. In the following viewpoint, Frederick R. Lynch describes diversity management as one manifestation of the political correctness that he says is sweeping the country. Lynch contends that diversity management programs increase tensions between employees and produce resentment in many white men who correctly perceive that the policies discriminate against them. Lynch is a visiting associate professor of government at Claremont McKenna College in California and author of *Invisible Victims: White Males and the Crisis of Affirmative Action* and *The Workforce Diversity Crusades: The Second Coming of Affirmative Action*.

As you read, consider the following questions:

1. According to Lynch, what percentage of major corporations and government agencies have diversity management programs?
2. What is "managerial accountability," as defined by the author?
3. How does diversity management function as a "protection racket," in the author's view?

Frederick R. Lynch, "Workforce Diversity: PC's Final Frontier?" *National Review*, February 21, 1994. Copyright ©1994 by National Review, Inc., 150 E. 35th St., New York, NY 10016. Reprinted by permission.

In researching his novel on sexual harassment [*Disclosure*], Michael Crichton was stunned to discover that none of the corporate executives he talked to was aware of the rising influence of feminism. When Crichton mentioned legal scholar Catharine MacKinnon, they scoffed that she was simply a "professor."

Ignoring ivory-tower ideological trends has cost business billions of dollars. Twenty years ago, the radical egalitarians of Political Correctness began the long march from the universities to the think tanks and the media, and on into social policy via the courts and government agencies. And now PC is in the White House.

PC long escaped serious criticism by manipulating white guilt and threatening [to label] potential critics as "racist." This ideology is built upon a colorized class struggle in which white males (formerly the "bourgeoisie") oppress women and minorities (formerly the "proletariat"), and lack of equal results in terms of either ethnicity or gender is primarily the result of deeply embedded racism and sexism. This world view, in turn, has produced a host of expensive policies to achieve proportional results, in everything from hiring to mortgage lending.

But things can always get worse. President Clinton's rhetoric about "workplace fairness" and his publicized efforts to build a government that "looks like America" signal the arrival of a new future-oriented proportionalism, known as "managing diversity." Diversity management leaves behind the bad press of a backward-looking, shrill affirmative action, and looks forward to an impending majority–minority America. It helps business harness this demographic destiny by exorcising the invisible demons of institutional racism/sexism and by cleansing white-male culture. Thus restructured, multicultural employers will retain and promote more minorities and women, gaining "the diversity advantage" in matching workforce ethnicity with an increasingly diverse customer base. "We've got to get right with the future!" commands *Miami Herald* publisher David Lawrence.

A Partly Organized Policy Crusade

Diversity management is more than a fad, yet less than an established field. It's a partly organized policy crusade with a mix of highly credentialed professionals, committed ideologues, curious CEOs and consultants, and employed and unemployed affirmative-action officers. Diversity consultants (most of whom are minority and/or female) offer a range of specialties from keynote speeches (stars fetch up to $10,000), to one-day mini-anthropology courses (for about $1,500 to $3,000), to long-term organizational makeovers (average: about $225,000).

Estimates vary widely, but about 30 to 50 per cent of major corporations and government agencies have some such programs on the books. Apple, Avon, Digital, DuPont, Hughes, and others have made workforce diversity an explicit corporate goal. Hughes has a Director of Diversity and U.S. West has a Director of Pluralism. Prudential Insurance is one of several corporations that link executives' performance evaluations (and/or bonuses) to their records on promoting female and minority employees. Some consultants urge corporations to follow the lead of major universities, such as Michigan and California, and use set-aside "targets of diversity" positions to increase workforce diversity.

Some of the issues that diversity management arose to address are real. There *is* heavy immigration into the United States. There *are* ethnic and gender tensions in the workplace. Employers in areas like Los Angeles and New York *do* face bewildering cultural variations among employees and customers. Cultures *do* contain taken-for-granted rules that can cause substantial frictions.

Little Help

Despite the grand rhetoric of its advocates, there is little evidence that diversity management can solve the problems it purports to address. In fact, it may make them worse. As diversity programs proliferate across corporate America, group infighting has become a problem second only to "backlash" by white men. . . .

Nor will converting the workplace into an arena for the practice of identity politics do much to improve competitiveness or help minorities advance in the business world, where a deficit of business skills, not a proliferation of racism, is the overwhelming reason many minorities fail to advance. Diversity managers address this gap by making race and ethnicity qualifications in their own right. But the resources spent maintaining the fiction of equal preparedness would be better used to assist minorities lacking the business skills to compete on merit alone.

Heather MacDonald, *The New Republic*, July 5, 1993.

How do we deal with these changes? Who accommodates whom? Should employees continue to assimilate into organizational cultures premised on Western values? Or should we "celebrate differences" and critique organizational cultures allegedly created by and for white males in order to make other people more comfortable?

Sondra Thiederman and Tom Kochman are fairly non-ideological PhD pros who offer sensible cross-cultural instruction about the thoughtways and habits of black, minority-immigrant, and female employees and customers. (They're careful to talk about diversity *within* cultural groups and not to create new stereotypes—an admitted problem in the diversity biz.)

But the more ambitious gurus of diversity management—such as Elsie Cross, R. Roosevelt Thomas (*Beyond Race and Gender*), and Ann Morrison (*The Glass Ceiling, The New Leaders*)—see assimilation as a cover for white male domination. Consultants' proposals for expensive "cultural audits" and subsequent changes in formal and informal rules and procedures are rooted in multiculturalism's axiom that there are no universal or objective standards. Therefore, all "qualifications" such as grades, test scores, and diplomas are suspect.

So distorted are the laws—not to mention the ideals—concerning nondiscriminatory equal treatment that cynical CEOs do not blink when diversity consultants prescribe culturally adjusted "fair treatment" of employees rather than Eurocentric "equal treatment." For example, it might be unfair to evaluate equally white males and Asians on such criteria as "taking initiative" or "showing originality"; many Asians, it is held, are reluctant to challenge authority. (CEOs do wince, however, at diversity consultants' fondest dream: "managerial accountability"—tying performance evaluations and pay to achieving diversity goals.)

Are these programs effective? Testimonials abound, but there is little systematic evidence that the policies produce long-term benefits. On the contrary, a recent UC Irvine survey of Orange County firms that tried diversity training found that it *increased* conflicts among employees. The field is rife with stories of "blow-ups"—as occurred when several senior executives at a California utility stormed out of a simulation exercise after being told to sit on the floor as members of an "oppressed group." There can also be incredible abuses. *Campus* magazine recently reported that a University of Cincinnati trainer persistently badgered a white male graduate student, impugning the student's family and stating that the recent death of his father "removed one more racist influence" from his life.

Why Is Diversity Management Spreading?

In the absence of compelling evidence that the policies are effective, why are they spreading?

First, diversity management has thrived in a political vacuum. The Reagan and Bush Administrations were unable or unwilling to challenge proportioned arguments. Former civil-rights commissioner John Bunzel recalls being told by a Reagan Administration official that "no one here knows how to talk about this stuff." Reverse-discrimination complaints from rank-and-file whites beyond the Beltway were ignored or stigmatized. There was no substantial respectable resistance to the pressure for diversity. So it spread.

Second, diversity management was given a powerful economic

rationale by, ironically, the neoconservative Hudson Institute in its *Workforce 2000*. Shortly after this impressive report was issued, in 1987, R. Roosevelt Thomas Jr., then at the Harvard Business School, named and formally launched the new field with his seminal 1989 *Harvard Business Review* article, "From Affirmative Action to Affirming Diversity." Thomas likened the changing American workforce to a new fuel mixture flowing into an engine; the engine, he argued, would have to be rebuilt to utilize diverse talents more efficiently.

Third, CEO skepticism about *Workforce 2000* projections could be squelched by pointing to the rapid transformation of sections of southern California and Florida into Third World enclaves. "The future is now in L.A.!" diversity consultants fondly chirped, until the 1992 riots shattered the multicultural mecca. (Honolulu is being considered as a replacement.)

Fourth, as with affirmative action, court decisions and government action loom increasingly large. The 1991 Civil Rights Act and recent court cases have increased the risk of employers' losing discrimination lawsuits on the grounds of lack of workforce proportionality. Even before Clinton's election, government regulators were sending signals that it was not enough to hire women and minorities; they must be retained and promoted as well. This was the obvious implication of the Department of Labor's 1991 "Glass Ceiling Report.". . .

A Protection Racket

In part, then, diversity management has become a kind of protection racket. Consultants claim that diversity training can prevent or reduce costly court settlements and ease government compliance problems. Again, there's no proof of this; but it seems reasonable that judges and federal regulators would smile on diversity training as demonstrating "good faith efforts" toward diversity.

No one knows for sure, but perhaps half or more of all diversity training is directly the result of past, present, or feared future legal problems. This may be a source of the widespread grumbling among consultants about diversity management being "stuck in the one-day training mode" rather than moving on to more sweeping organizational reform. Employers may be buying only as much protection as they think they need.

As a result, while some consultants get rich, most don't. Even well-known authors such as Anita Rowe and Lee Gardenswartz admit, "You can't make a living off this alone." And the field is flooded with newcomers. A poll of consultants by the newsletter *Cultural Diversity at Work* found 50 per cent registering "some complaint of trainer incompetence." Indeed, the stars worry about hordes of neophytes getting into trouble and giving the entire field a bad name. "If you're going to open a can of worms," warns Anita Rowe, "you'd better know how to make worm soufflé."

Diversity and Affirmative Action

Diversity management's major problems, however, stem from its deep ambivalence toward its disreputable twin, affirmative action. Tensions related to this issue run like a fault line beneath the diversity movement.

Even the definition of "diversity" sets off tremors. As suggested in the title of his book *Beyond Race and Gender*, R. Roosevelt Thomas wants to expand diversity efforts to include age and generational differences, family problems, and education. But veteran affirmative-action officers with civil-rights backgrounds bristle at all this, fearing that an expanded focus will dilute, even endanger, gains made for minorities and women.

In any case, diversity management has acquired the affirmative-action stigma. Consultants fret about being seen as professional minorities rather than minority professionals. The usually savvy Lewis Griggs, a suave, white male Stanford MBA, stumbled on this landmine and precipitated a partial walkout from his 1991 workshop on "gaining access to the white male power structure." Pressed to reveal the secret of his own access, Griggs innocently admitted that he was a white male selling to other white males. "I know their language, their culture." This was formally consistent with the multicultural theories underlying the "diversity" movement, but it was not appreciated.

The success of white males like Griggs is received with mixed emotions. PC's race and gender determinism dictates that only women and minorities can do diversity work because only they have experienced true oppression. But consultants are desperate to counter the number-one rated problem: "backlash" or "resistance" by white male workers.

White males nearly picked apart a one-day workshop for middle-management municipal workers I observed in suburban L.A. Through a combination of silence and increasing sniping about reverse discrimination they rattled the two trainers. "Don't scapegoat!" one trainer finally fired back.

The personnel manager intervened at one point. "We don't have quotas," she snapped, "we have goals." Several people laughed.

"White male inclusion" is much discussed in print and at conferences. But diversity management is so pickled in PC that most trainers can't comprehend, much less admit, that for two decades millions of white males have been excluded from jobs or promotions by tactics such as race-norming of test scores, set-aside positions, etc. "We know it doesn't happen," argues California consultant Frances Kendall. "It's all in their heads."

Many diversity advocates have wearied of arguing and now quietly rationalize white-male resistance to PC approaches as "anxiety" over "loss of privilege." Says Anita Rowe: "Being a white male is like being born on third base and imagining you've hit a triple." Such threadbare rationalizations of real social conflicts suggest major trouble for clients down the line.

The more radical forms of diversity management are tied to the fortunes of multiculturalism and PC. Like the original Stalinist version, American PC arose in the 1970s to shield egalitarian ideals and reforms by denying or suppressing contradictory facts. But the explosion of crime among urban youth, out-of-control immigration, the difficulties of single-parent families, and the inefficiencies and resentments bred by quotas now defy denial or rationalization. To borrow Roosevelt Thomas's metaphor, the engine of business will not run on a mix of real and politically colored data.

One timebomb is the fact that affirmative-action formulae designed to help blacks now hurt them in cities where their numbers are declining relative to immigrant minorities. Thus, Latinos in L.A. are demanding their "fair share" of government jobs—from blacks.

Indeed, diversity management may be haunted by its slogan: "The future is now in L.A." Right now, L.A.'s multicultural future looks grim. Even before the 1992 "rainbow riots," immigration was fueling a growing disparity between taxpayers (aging whites) and tax receivers (mostly immigrants). Gated communities, random violence, and overcrowded immigrant apartments suggest Brazilification.

So obvious is massive white flight out of southern California that Jay Leno recently quipped: "People in Los Angeles share a dream: moving to Seattle." If rising laughter and ridicule signal a breakdown in ruling ideas, PC is in trouble.

"Youth apprenticeships will help their participants . . . build more satisfying lives for themselves."

Apprenticeships Would Increase Opportunities for Youths

Edward E. Barr

In the following viewpoint, Edward E. Barr argues that American education fails to prepare students for the nation's increasingly specialized, dynamic, and technological job market. Moreover, by emphasizing college preparation, Barr contends, the current education system evinces "class and racial overtones" because it neglects non–college bound students, who are disproportionately low-income and minority youths. To assist these underserved students, Barr advocates a youth apprenticeship program, based on the German system, that would identify non–college bound students in early high school and supplement their academic studies with on-the-job training. Barr is president and CEO of Sun Chemical Corporation.

As you read, consider the following questions:

1. According to the author, what two constraints threaten the idea of youth apprenticeship?
2. What are the virtues of work, according to Stephen Hamilton, as quoted by Barr?
3. According to sociologist James Coleman, cited by the author, are differences in expenditures between schools closely related to differences in academic performance?

From "Ramping Up the American Economy," Edward E. Barr's speech to the New York University School of Business, February 9, 1993. Reprinted with the author's permission.

Economist Lester Thurow, in his book *Head to Head* declared that in the 21st century "the education and skills of the work force will end up being the dominant competitive weapon." I agree, which is one reason for focusing my concerns on an educational concept which has long been discussed; one which has been extremely successful in certain other societies; and one which is not unknown—albeit little used here in the United States.

The most meritorious characteristic of this concept is its proven ability to help youth who do not go on to college to make a safe passage from adolescence to adulthood. . . .

The concept I am endorsing is *youth apprenticeships*—especially:

- Why they can better exploit our actual work places as learning environments.
- How they can provide mentor relationships and adult role models for our often unoriented youth.
- And, speaking as a CEO of a company that has experienced the difficulties in hiring the routinely ill-prepared products of our secondary schools, how they can instill in the nation's future employees the flexible vocational skills, and dependable attitudes, essential in today's world.

Some of the concepts, even the phraseology I will employ, are drawn from the various writings of Stephen Hamilton, professor of Human Development at Cornell University. Hamilton has become the nation's outstanding advocate of the "necessity of helping young people make the crucial connection between school learning, community participation, and a satisfying, constructive life's work."

In fact, while still Governor of Arkansas, Bill Clinton gave this tribute to Hamilton's landmark 1990 book, *Apprenticeship for Adulthood:* "Too many of our young people aren't moving from school to good jobs with a good future today. Apprenticeship is an idea which has worked in other countries. We ought to try it here.". . .

Not Conventional Programs

Since there are few people who haven't encountered the word "apprenticeship," and since everyone has his or her own image of what it entails, *let me list the programs to which I am not referring*.

1. Cooperative education at the *collegiate* level, made notable at institutions like Cincinnati and Northeastern Universities, and a score of community colleges. These commence *after* high school, or, at best, in *late* adolescence.

2. Vocational education and work-study programs in our high school systems. Let it suffice to say that these tired and conventional programs, too often captive of old-line bureaucracies, and which train for narrow occupational fields and *specific* jobs, do

little more than give the concept of apprenticing a bad odor.

3. Traditional apprenticeship programs, which currently prepare some 300,000 young people *already out of high school*, to be licensed carpenters, electricians, bricklayers and similar craftsmen. The International Brotherhood of Electrical Workers, for example, began developing a full apprenticeship program in 1957, and has a commendable record for turning out highly skilled, well-paid journeymen. One critical characteristic of all these programs, however, is that the average enrollee enters in his late 20's, sometimes pushing 30.

The *youth apprenticeship* concept, in contrast to the existent programs, is designed to steer non–college bound students, *as early as their second year in high school*, into skilled jobs. This sharply diminishes the risk that non–college bound students will drift, having received no occupational skills or work place socialization before or after high school graduation.

American Education: The Worst of Both Worlds

[Critics] argue that apprenticeship modeled on the German dual system shortchanges 16-year-olds by pushing them into lifetime career decisions they are ill-prepared to make. They stoutly maintain that a solid academic education—something rarely given today by U.S. high schools—is the best ticket to success, whether the student chooses college or moves directly into the workplace. . . .

The counterargument is that schools already "track" students by assigning them to "slow learner" classes as early as third grade. . . .

As for the argument about academic education, half of America's high school students graduate with a general education diploma—the worst of both worlds.

Edwin Kiester Jr., *Smithsonian*, March 1993.

The idea seems, to me at least, so attractive that one wonders why it hasn't caught on long ago. Aside from the resistance of interests adverse to change, or the diminution of their empires, there appear to be two formidable constraints:

- It seemingly goes against the grain of the American belief in universal upward mobility;
- U.S. companies, which would assume substantial financial as well as oversight responsibilities under the program, historically have competed by simplifying work procedures and lowering costs.

Hamilton notes that "youth apprenticeship runs against the U.S. industrial mindset of viewing labor as a cost to be minimized." On the contrary, he says, "you have to view workers as an investment, and when you do, you try to get as much output from them as possible, and you train them accordingly."

I firmly believe a refocus is long overdue in U.S. secondary education to engage the interests and involve our less academic youth. "The most glaring structural problem with American education," *The Economist* declared in November 1992 in a special survey of the issues,

> is that it does not know what to do with pupils who are not bound for college. . . . In importing the German university system, in the late 19th and early 20th centuries, America made the disastrous mistake of forgetting to import the apprenticeship system as well. For apprenticeships smacked of class-stratification, and America was hypnotized by upward mobility.

The consequence for our country is that about half of our 18-year-olds are stuck with the stark choice of either going to college, or with poor preparation going directly into the job market. This wasn't so formidable for the latter group while low skill, but still relatively high paying assembly line type jobs were reasonably plentiful. What has broken down in the scheme of things is that higher basic qualifications, more precise skills, and the maturation that comes with familiarity with work-place practices are now required in our increasingly sophisticated, information technology–dominated industrial culture.

Looking Abroad

In fixing our deficiency, we are well-advised to look abroad. Most of us are aware—at least vaguely—that the world's most successful and extensive apprenticeship system is found in Germany. A quick summary of that system is in order.

Youth in Germany can choose to enter a vocational school track and begin their three-year, sometimes longer, apprenticeships as early as the age of 15. This decision is preceded by extensive counseling and evaluation of alternative apprenticeship career tracks. It is not inflexible and it permits a change to another career track by the 70 percent of German students in the program.

While clearly not a universal option chosen by all German youth, 85 percent of those who do not enter the academic collegiate preparatory track go into apprenticeships. Interestingly, some 20 percent of Germans graduate from college, very close to the 24 percent that actually completes Baccalaureate education in our country, where approximately 50 percent begin to pursue some form of college education.

The standards are set mainly by industry and are uniform throughout the country. The student enters into a contract with a firm that provides a highly structured program of on-the-job training, generally for three days a week, and state-provided theoretical training for two days a week.

Real Time

The apprentices work in real time, with real responsibilities, alongside adult colleagues, and acquire from these mentors their work habits and attitudes. Adolescent boredom fades during the program, in large part because the students are given adult-type assignments, and see the linkage between learning theory and facts, and earning a living. The traumatic schoolwork transition is neutralized, and a culture is fostered in which training is respected and skilled work revered.

The costs of the German programs are divided between the local government groups which provide the theoretical schooling, the employers who are assessed a percentage of their payroll expenses, and the apprentices themselves who work for only a nominal salary.

Successful graduates receive a journeyman's certificate—the ticket to adult employment—only when they pass a demanding written and practical exam at the end. By 18 or 19, when they assume adult jobs, they possess very high levels of academic and vocational skills, and as anyone who has visited German companies is aware, they know what it means to work. . . .

I don't want to leave the impression that the German system of apprenticeship is without faults. Many observers recoil because of what they perceive as caste-influenced characteristics. A specific concern also resides in the fact that many small firms cannot afford the price tag to train a recruit.

Therefore, some fine tuning appears to be in order. In Denmark, for instance, they give greater emphasis to theoretical training (because it lasts a lifetime) than to practical skills (which are soon outdated). They have constructively cut the number of apprenticeship categories from 300 to 80, while there still are 375 officially defined occupations in Germany. The Danes also have engineered the financing procedures such that the participating educational institutions are forced to compete for students. We have this program in our Danish Chemical Company, and I know it works!

I will not recount the many reasons, or cite the dreary examples, of the difficulty of importing foreign models to a distinct culture like our own. Nonetheless, we would be wise to take some leaves from the book of German experience. . . .

An especially remarkable fact about the German experience was reported recently by [an] enthusiastic supporter, Ray Marshall, who served as Labor Secretary under President Carter. "Fully one-third of German university-trained engineers came up first through their apprenticeship system and then attended

223

university, a path that would be unthinkable for most U.S. engineers."

Marshall's point is doubly significant because it disabuses those who decry the German approach by claiming it tracks students into irrevocable life decisions.

Students Are Not Uniform

There is still another hand-up in American educational philosophy and preoccupation which inhibits the adoption of youth apprenticeships. This is the egalitarian assumption that all youth are capable of learning at levels that most other societies reserve for the school system's most achieving students. This was a fundamental premise of the monumental, influential, and otherwise excellent 1983 study, "A Nation at Risk," which galvanized much-needed attention on the educational crisis in the United States.

One of its praiseworthy recommendations was to toughen up the standards of our schools, increase the rigor and number of required courses, and promote a greater student mastery of basic academic knowledge and skills. I am absolutely in accord with these objectives, but unfortunately the "Risk" study mistakenly overlooked, and its prescriptions for action did not provide for, the fact that *all* students do *not* respond uniformly to tough academic curricula, programs and schools.

Not all youth can learn the same material in the same way. In addition, as important as the academic curriculum is for collegiate preparation, the school environment only very tangentially addresses the need to instill what Hamilton refers to as "worker virtues." Moreover, particularly in our inner cities but by no means confined to those settings, there are multiple non-school influences on youth which wash over and many times overwhelm our schools.

Youth apprenticeships incorporate the premise that the effects of our schools must be buttressed by what happens in other spheres of life as well. Two of these, the family and community at large, are receiving much attention of late and also should be necessary components of a total strategy. What youth apprenticeships bring into play is that additional societal sphere— known as the work place.

"Virtues of Work"

Without jettisoning concern or attention to student mastery of necessary knowledge and skills, Hamilton points out, a major function of youth apprenticeships is captured in the German word *Arbeitstugende*, meaning the "virtues of work." The apprenticeships help youth internalize "the need to be punctual, diligent, responsible, and receptive to supervision." Hamilton

224

concurs that if such virtues "are yoked to passivity and subordination, they deserve to be stigmatized," but he rejects any facile dismissal of them. The "virtues of work" are as important, he insists, to middle class youth who have been known to coast through school, watch TV excessively, and spend much of their time "having fun," as they are to those raised in socially and economically disadvantaged families.

No one can guarantee that participants in such youth apprenticeships will refrain from drug and alcohol use, premature motherhood, delinquency, or the criminal and other negative behavior that is increasingly so disruptive among our high school youth. Nor will these programs absolutely eradicate the situation where many high school students drop out formally, or mentally, even when they succeed in graduating officially. But my response to this disheartening situation, which has not only eluded solution but gotten much worse, is a bit of wisdom from the Torah which is loosely translated as "what is the alternative?"

Our high schools for non-college bound youth essentially serve as warehouses, or like holding patterns over an overcrowded airport. They keep them for some additional years out of the adult job market, until they are dispirited enough to be eased into whatever employment is available.

This is all a waste! Under the prevailing regimen, too many non-college bound youth are prepared with nothing that comports with the requirements of a dynamic, fast-changing, increasingly technological society. Restless and dispirited, is it any wonder that their behavior and work attitudes are unattractive to prospective employers?

Skilled and Flexible

My final argument for youth apprenticeships derives from the changing nature of manufacturing today. In the past, manufacturing flourished by separating complex tasks into their simplest components, with omnipotent managers making the strategic decisions and telling the workers what to do. The workers became semi-skilled cogs operating single-purpose equipment in the industrial machine, and their educational preparation was not of great moment.

This has all changed. The key to competitive success for advanced societies like ours is "flexible specialization," not mass production. The developing countries now can, and do, run mass production machinery at much lower cost. As a consequence they are weaning away more and more of our so-called smokestack industries. The alternative long-term markets for the production of countries like the United States are up-scale. Our work force, using multi-purpose equipment, must become proficient at supplying in timely fashion, on short production runs, a variety of high quality goods to essentially affluent customers. The work force must have highly developed, craft-like skills, and the judgment to participate in decision-making and quality control.

This means that for the U.S. to be competitive, we must not only reorganize production, but begin to generate large cadres of highly motivated, skilled and flexible workers. Amidst all the calls for educational reform going back to the decade of the 1950s, and despite all the increased investments in education made by the nation, we seem to have missed that target.

Non-College Youth Are Neglected

A better prepared, more sophisticated work force does not mean more academic preparation for college, or college attendance itself, as important as these objectives are for other youth. Indeed, it would be "criminal" to steer a still higher proportion of the educational dollar to higher education. Given the cost to society of U.S. collegiate education—tuition, endowment contributions, rich subsidies from federal, state and local government—non-college youth are already relatively neglected. They "have been consistently overlooked and undertrained." According to Hamilton, a large number receive "no public support during their transition to adulthood."

There are clear class and racial overtones to this discrepancy, moreover, when we consider the disparate income and racial composition of the college as opposed to the non-college-going populations. It is not unfair to conclude, therefore, that the national overwhelming emphasis on college education has undercut a necessary attention to work force preparation. Richard Hyse, a former economics professor at SUNY [State University of New York] Oswego, has written:

> First, it degrades any type of blue-collar work to a nonhonorific status, making any apprenticeship system by definition fit only for the intellectually less endowed, the dropouts, the inner-city unreachables. With this de-emphasis also comes an abandonment of craft codes, which acted as quality controls and a source of personal pride.

More money in itself is not the answer, especially if these investments aren't in the right place. Sociologist James Coleman has conclusively shown that the differences in expenditures between schools are almost wholly unrelated to differences in academic performance. The relationship between money and results is further made equivocal by the fact that the German government spends a lower proportion of its budget on education (9.1 percent) than any other European community government, but can still point to an educational system envied by most of the world.

226

I think the Germans must be doing something right in this sphere, and will therefore sum up why I think we should emulate them:

First—we would be steering a precious and fragile portion of our youth on the path towards [meaningful work]. It has been estimated that if Americans were involved in youth apprenticeships to the same relative extent as their German counterparts, not 300,000 but 6,000,000 would be enrolled.

Second—institution of a significant youth apprenticeship movement would set in motion an overdue shakeup, not only of the secondary school system and its vocational education component, but would inevitably result in a long-needed, many-fold increase of corporate investment in human resources.

Third—in addition to financial participation, these apprenticeships will draw industry into playing a more crucial role in providing focus, content and a supportive setting for the upbringing of our youth.

Fourth—because they commence early in adolescence, before hormonal changes run the full course, before they get discouraged over future prospects, or get caught up in some of the more pernicious distractions of contemporary life, these apprenticeships can have significant beneficial effect on the behavior of problem youth.

And, finally—by explicitly dealing with their socialization and internalization of "worker virtues," youth apprenticeships will help their participants both build more satisfying lives for themselves, and contribute a vital, better prepared resource to society.

The great challenge facing the nation is to prepare a changing population of young people to do a new kind of work. Failure will imperil our economic health, social progress and democracy itself. It is not a college education which can prepare such workers. Sadly, for the non-college bound American youth, neither is it the traditional high school diploma. Moreover, the forms of education that are reasonably effective with advantaged youth, are seldom able to assist large numbers of disadvantaged youth achieve similar goals. Poor and minority youth need more support and encouragement.

The situation clearly calls for a dramatic change. That's why I believe the youth apprenticeship approach is required "to connect schools to work places and to provide young people with clearer paths from school to work." My purpose has not been to provide a precise, technical prescription for the organization of an apprenticeship system, but rather to make a case for its serious adoption as a fundamental and major aspect of U.S. secondary education.

*"Apprenticeship will narrow [students']
opportunities to acquire the kinds of general
intellectual skills they need most."*

Apprenticeships Would Reduce Opportunities for Youths

Harvey Kantor

In the following viewpoint, Harvey Kantor disputes the popular argument that a national apprenticeship system would increase opportunities for non-college bound youths—especially inner-city blacks—by providing them with marketable skills. Kantor maintains that such a system would reduce the opportunities of its participants because it would provide them with a limited set of skills rather than a comprehensive academic education. It would also perpetuate inequality, according to Kantor, by formalizing the current belief among many that working-class and minority students are not likely to attend college. Kantor is an associate professor at the University of Utah in Salt Lake who specializes in educational history and policy.

As you read, consider the following questions:

1. What two assumptions are the arguments for apprenticeship premised on, according to Kantor?
2. The author notes that most jobs are found through personal contacts. For what two reasons does this hurt young African Americans seeking work, according to Kantor?

Excerpted from Harvey Kantor, "The Hollow Promise of Youth Apprenticeship," the complete version of which appeared in *Rethinking Schools*, vol. 8, no. 1, Autumn 1993. For more information, contact *Rethinking Schools*, 1001 E. Keefe Ave., Milwaukee, WI 53212. (414) 964-9646. Reprinted with permission.

President Bill Clinton's School-to-Work Opportunities Act proposes to create over a five-year period as many as 300,000 youth apprenticeships for those who have been called the "forgotten half" of American youth—the more than 50% of high school students who do not go on to college and whose life chances have been diminished by changes in the American economy. Patterned after similar programs in Europe, especially the system in Germany where upwards of one-half of all high school students are apprentices, Clinton's proposal would combine paid work and on-the-job training with related classroom instruction in the last two years of high school and a third year of "professional-technical" education. At the end of that time, according to the Clinton plan, students would receive a certificate of occupational competence in addition to a high school diploma and would have the option of going on to college or entering the workforce in their chosen field. . . .

But, despite its apparent potential, there are good reasons to question whether apprenticeship can do much more than previous vocational programs to get young people to study more, to improve their job prospects, or to make the economy more productive. In fact, by focusing attention so exclusively on education at the expense of other public policies designed to end racial discrimination, encourage high wages and full employment, and foster the reorganization of work, it may actually do more to dim than to brighten the prospects for genuine economic reform. . . .

Apprenticeship and the Youth Labor Market

The arguments for apprenticeship are premised on two assumptions about the problems non–college bound high school graduates face when they enter the labor market. One is that the difficulties young people experience early in their work careers are damaging to their long-term economic prospects and contribute to a good deal of their anti-social behavior. The other is that many of these problems can be ameliorated by new institutional arrangements that help young people make a smoother transition from school to work. Both of these assumptions are highly problematic, though neither of them is entirely unfounded.

To begin with, although many young people spend their initial few years after high school in unskilled, poorly paid jobs in what economists call the secondary labor market, there is little evidence that these early experiences necessarily lead to serious economic difficulties later on. Rather, as young people get older, many move out of these secondary labor market jobs into better-paying, more stable employment in the preferred, or what is often referred to as the primary, sector of the economy. In fact, while those concerned over the transition from school to work have tended to view youth unemployment and job hopping as "pathological," since the 1930s most studies of the youth labor market have concluded that for the majority of young people this period in their work career is a temporary one and that many eventually "settle down into permanent employment" [according to W. Norton Grubb].

This pattern of employment is partly a reflection of the maturation process. Many of the young men interviewed by the economist Paul Osterman in his study of the youth labor market, for example, were initially more interested in short-term jobs to get money for recreation or buying a car than in stable employment. Only as they matured and began to think more about assuming adult responsibilities did they develop an understanding that a steady job was desirable and become more attached to the labor force and committed to looking for better-paying, more stable employment.

It would be wrong to attribute the characteristics of the youth labor market chiefly to youthful instability, however. As Osterman and several others have pointed out, more important is the structure of the labor market and the nature of the demand for labor. Put simply, many young people work in secondary labor market jobs after high school not because they are uninterested in more stable, better paying work but because most employers are not interested in hiring young workers for jobs with better compensation and opportunities for advancement. For these jobs, employers generally prefer to hire slightly older workers who they believe are more reliable and responsible and thus a better risk for investment in training and promotion. This benefits workers in their mid-twenties by enhancing their opportunities for more financially remunerative and secure employment, but it also means that most students just out of high school are confined to less desirable jobs in the secondary labor market (jobs that pay low wages and offer little security and that provide few rewards for stable work behavior), at least until they grow older. . . .

A Misplaced Focus

Given the evidence that employers do not readily offer adult jobs to teenagers and that dead-end youth work does not inevitably portend future economic problems for many youth, much of the policy focus on smoothing the transition from school to work for high school graduates not only seems "doomed to remain . . . at the mercy of individual enthusiasts" [in the words of Thomas Bailey] but also seems somewhat misplaced. The chief focus of public policy should be on generating enough employment for those youth who are having unusual difficulty making the transition to adult employment in the preferred sectors of the labor market—especially the disproportionate numbers of minority youth, particularly young African Americans, who are experiencing greater and greater difficulty both finding work and holding any stable, better-paying jobs at all.

Indeed, whatever significance is accorded to the problems white youth face in the secondary labor market, there is no disputing the obstacles young African Americans encounter in finding and holding work even as they get older. Not only are Black unemployment rates more than double the rates for similarly educated white youth, but over the last two decades the labor force participation rate for young African Americans—especially for young African-American males—has worsened considerably, both absolutely and relative to their white peers. Whereas in the 1950s Black and white men ages 18 to 24 not in school participated in the labor market at roughly the same rate (about 90%), in 1983, only 72% of 18- to 24-year-old African-American males not in school were in the labor force, compared to 89% for whites. In short, although many African-American youth also develop greater attachment to the labor force as they get older, today they are much more likely than in the past or in comparison to whites to have stopped looking for work and dropped out of the labor market altogether. But whether the barriers young African Americans face in the labor market can be overcome mainly by improving the institutional linkages between school and work is questionable.

What Choice?

Most of the high schools that will participate in apprenticeship programs will be public, and public high school students are more likely to come from low-income and minority backgrounds. The rate of college enrollment by minority public high school students is already low, but the presence of youth apprenticeship programs may further discourage minority youth from entering college and pursuing the high-tech or professional skills that the programs are unlikely to provide. As a Portland attorney arguing for the elimination of tracking put it, "If you were told all your life you're not college material, then when you are given a choice, what choice would you make?"

Michael A. Stoll, *Dollars & Sense*, November/December 1993.

Although advocates of apprenticeship believe that linking education more closely to the workplace will benefit a variety of students, one of their chief selling points is that it will be especially beneficial for low-income, minority youth, particularly

Black youth living in inner cities. This is partly because they believe that apprenticeship will link effort in the classroom with rewards in the workplace and thereby give minority students greater incentive to study and achieve in school. In addition, they argue that job-based education programs like apprenticeship will help minority youth improve their prospects in the labor market not only by equipping them with vocational skills but even more important by providing them with access to the kinds of employment opportunities they now lack because they are excluded from the informal networks necessary to obtain jobs and move into meaningful careers.

Although these arguments have merit, the employment difficulties facing young minority workers are more deeply rooted than any of them assume. First, a large body of popular and scholarly literature supports the notion that lack of skills is a major problem for many minority youth. But skills or the lack of them do not seem to be the primary consideration for many employers when they hire young workers, even for jobs in the primary labor market. In Osterman's study, for example, the majority of young workers in primary jobs did not know how to do their job when they were first hired, but were trained by their employer. This suggests that while apprenticeship might help young minority workers build skills, it is unlikely that raising their levels of "human capital" will dramatically improve their job prospects. What apprenticeship might do is teach attention to detail, work-discipline, and other work-readiness behaviors that employers believe minority youth lack. This implies, however, that the chief value of the system is [as Osterman says] "socialization, not skill building."

Personal Contacts

Much recent research also supports the argument that most jobs—both in the primary and secondary labor market—are found through personal contacts. Osterman's study of the youth labor market points out, for instance, that youth do not search for work in an "impersonal labor market" but "move through channels already traveled by people they know." In secondary jobs, friends are the most frequent source of referral, while parents and relatives are more helpful in finding jobs in the primary market. This makes sense since secondary jobs are more likely to be in small retail stores which employ youth from the local neighborhood or in bigger firms which have large numbers of minimum-wage jobs and are known to hire young workers for unskilled work. By contrast, primary firms are more interested in stability, and employers believe that parents are more likely than friends to be a reliable means of control.

For two reasons, this structure of employment undoubtedly

hurts young African Americans seeking work. One is that they are more likely than whites to live in inner-city neighborhoods where there has been a substantial loss of the kinds of small businesses and industries that typically provide employment opportunities for young workers. The other is that even though the occupational distribution of African Americans has improved considerably since World War II and become more similar to that of whites, African Americans continue to be underrepresented in the most desirably sectors of the labor market. As a result, young Blacks have less access to the informal job networks that help white youth find jobs and that are necessary for securing employment not only in the secondary market but in the primary labor market as well. . . .

Discrimination and Employment Policies

But the absence of job networks and inadequate socialization are not the only reasons many African-American youth have such a hard time entering the labor market and finding better-paying, higher status jobs. At least two others are equally, if not more, important, though there does not seem to be much apprenticeship can do about them. One is the persistence of racial discrimination. Sometimes this is explicit. Many white employers and workers, for example, resist hiring people of color—especially Black men—to supervise whites. In other cases, employers equate race with characteristics that disqualify minority workers for employment, particularly in higher level positions. As the sociologists Joleen Kirschenmann and Kathryn Neckerman discovered in their interviews with employers in Chicago, many employers associate race with inner-city schools, which in turn signifies poor education, inadequate work skills, and insufficient commitment to the work ethic. Either way, however, race compounds the employment problems facing minority youth, since it militates against hiring African Americans and other minority workers for entry level jobs or promoting them to more financially rewarding, higher status positions.

Youth apprenticeship advocates contend that the relationship between skilled mentors and apprentices will help combat these discriminatory practices. Because apprenticeship is not a strictly private relationship, argues Stephen Hamilton, one of the foremost supporters of youth apprenticeship in the United States, the employer must assure that the apprentice has every opportunity to learn what is needed for certification as a skilled worker. But this hardly guarantees equal treatment on the job, as Hamilton himself acknowledges. Nor does it guarantee equal access to the most desirable apprenticeships. On the contrary, Thomas Bailey reports that, in Germany, Turks and other recent immigrants, who occupy a similar position in the German labor market as African Americans and other minorities do in the United States, are not only underrepresented in the apprenticeship system; among those who do participate they are also concentrated in apprenticeships in those occupations that offer the least chance for promotion and that consistently have the highest unemployment rate among students who successfully complete their apprenticeships.

A Full Employment Policy Is Needed

The other problem is the absence of a full employment policy. Because young African Americans and other minority youth are generally at the bottom of the hiring queue, tight labor markets substantially improve their employment prospects, both absolutely and relative to whites. Yet once inflation began to accelerate in the late 1960s and early 1970s, successive administrations have tried to control it chiefly by letting unemployment rise. The result has been devastating for young Blacks and other low-income minority youth, since they are the first fired and last hired when labor markets turn slack. Today unemployment has dropped to about 7% nationwide compared to 11% in the early 1980s, but policymakers remain convinced that lower unemployment rates would mean higher inflation, so they have avoided stimulating the economy to reduce unemployment any further even though this harms young Blacks looking for work.

Full employment is, of course, hardly a panacea for racial inequality in the labor market. Expanding aggregate demand will not by itself increase the availability of "good" jobs. Nor will it necessarily prevent whites from trying to monopolize them by restricting African Americans and other people of color to the lower levels of the job hierarchy. This requires more affirmative policies that change the position of people of color in the labor queue and that intervene more directly in decisions about how to allocate workers to different jobs. But it is hard to see how policies such as apprenticeship can improve the employment prospects of those minority youth just entering the labor market without a commitment to continuous full employment as well. . . .

Narrowing Opportunities

It is difficult to dispute much of what the advocates of apprenticeship have to say about the shortcomings of American schools and their failure to prepare high school graduates for work. High schools today do not do a very good job engaging the majority of students in academic learning. Nor, except for those headed for liberal arts colleges, is there much relationship between what happens in the classroom and the jobs students get when they enter the labor market. One result is that many students have little incentive to study hard or achieve in school.

Instead, they drop out or else simply put in seat time until they graduate.

For these students, a job-based education program like apprenticeship does indeed seem to offer a much-needed alternative to the academic orientation of the high school curriculum. There is some evidence, for example, that those students bored with academic work find vocational classes more appealing. But despite its promise to make education more relevant and useful to non–college bound students, in practice it is not likely that apprenticeship will invigorate the traditional high school curriculum to accommodate either their economic needs or their diverse interests and learning styles. Rather, by channeling them into job-specific training, it seems more likely that apprenticeship will narrow their opportunities to acquire the kinds of general intellectual skills they need most both at work and in social life.

Advocates argue that apprenticeship will create a learning environment that provides for the development of both specific and general skills. But rather than broaden the character of the curriculum to meet the needs of a diverse population, the introduction of work-oriented programs has functioned over the years to fragment the curriculum and deepen the division between college and non–college bound students. In fact, many of those who have studied the history of vocational education contend that it has done little to unify practical and academic education or eliminate the gap between those headed for work and those headed for college. Much more often, they say, vocational education has fostered a differentiated system of schooling, with low-income and minority boys channeled into industrial education programs, low-income and minority girls channeled into traditional female courses and occupations, and white middle and upper-class students placed in college-oriented academic programs.

Adding to Inequality

Despite the pleas of apprenticeship advocates, there is little reason to think that youth apprenticeship will be much different. Although advocates stress that even the most academically capable students can benefit from practical job-based education and that apprenticeship graduates will be able to go on to college, most proposals for apprenticeship make it plain that the chief raison d'etre of the program is to serve working-class and minority students who they believe are not likely to pursue a baccalaureate degree. In their view, these students are not academically capable and have been poorly served by the current educational system but will benefit from a less academic, more vocationally oriented education.

Indeed, some contend that this will actually make American

education more democratic. They argue that making explicit provision for the non–college bound will promote more opportunity than the existing system, which pretends to give access to the same education to every student but in reality provides many students with little useful training at all. If there is a case to be made for apprenticeship, however, it is not that it will equalize opportunities for the least advantaged. Although it comes cloaked in the rhetoric of concern for the "neglected majority" and the "forgotten half," this approach to education and work will only add "another dimension of inequality" to an already unequal system.

In the end, if there is a democratic approach to changing the relationship between education and work, it is not to subordinate education even further to vocational concerns, as apprenticeship ultimately proposes to do. Despite the claims of its advocates, this will not equalize educational opportunities or improve the economic prospects of poor and minority youth; it will only reproduce the inequities that apprenticeship claims to address. A more democratic alternative for a changing economy is to provide all students with the kinds of skills they need to develop fully and manage technological change. This means offering them an education that will equip them not only with specific vocational skills but, in John Dewey's words, with the "initiative, ingenuity, and executive capacity" they need to be "masters of their own industrial fate."

Such an education by itself is not sufficient, however. It is also necessary to develop policies around schooling and the economy that intervene more directly in labor markets rather than focus on schooling and training alone. Among other things, this requires policies to combat racial discrimination at work, a commitment to full employment and to macroeconomic and other pro-employment policies such as reducing the work week and changing the pattern of government expenditures that will help sustain it, and support for unionization as well as for experiments to improve the quality of work life such as works councils and worker participation in management. This is the only way for policy to respond actively rather than reactively to the social and economic problems that apprenticeship hopes to solve and that have generated interest in job-based plans for education in the first place.

Periodical Bibliography

The following articles have been selected to supplement the diverse views presented in this chapter.

Derrick Bell	"The Freedom of Employment Act," *The Nation*, May 23, 1994.
Bonita L. Betters-Reed and Lynda L. Moore	"The Technicolor Workplace," *Ms.*, November/December 1992.
Peter Brimelow and Leslie Spencer	"When Quotas Replace Merit, Everybody Suffers," *Forbes*, February 15, 1993.
Jeffrey S. Byrne	"Affirmative Action for Lesbians and Gay Men: A Proposal for True Equity of Opportunity and Workforce Diversity," *Yale Law & Policy Review*, vol. 11, 1993. Available from 127 Wall St., New Haven, CT 06520.
Ellis Cose	"A Hostile and Welcoming Workplace," *Business and Society Review*, Winter 1994. Available from Management Reports, Inc., 25-13 Old Kings Hwy. N., Suite 107, Darien, CT 06820.
The CQ Researcher	"The Glass Ceiling," October 29, 1993. Available from 1414 22nd St. NW, Washington, DC 20037.
Jerry Dennehy	"Between Youth and Experience," *Newsweek*, November 15, 1993.
Esther B. Fein	"Older People Laboring for Acceptance in Jobs," *The New York Times*, January 4, 1994.
John Frantz	"Davis-Bacon: Jim Crow's Last Stand," *The Freeman*, February 1994. Available from the Foundation for Economic Education, Irvington-on-Hudson, NY 10533.
Beatrice Johnston-Hernandez	"Women Fight Free Trade," *Third Force*, May/June 1994.
Karen Judd and Sandy Morales Pope	"The New Job Squeeze: Women Pushed into Part-Time Work," *Ms.*, May/June 1994.
George R. LaNoue	"Social Science and Minority 'Set-Asides,'" *The Public Interest*, Winter 1993.
Los Angeles Times	"Work Force Diversity: Getting Along and Getting Ahead," May 16, 1994.
Heather MacDonald	"The Diversity Industry," *The New Republic*, July 5, 1993.

Elaine McCrate | "Closing the Pay Gap," *Dollars & Sense*, January/February 1993.

Sharon Nelton | "Winning with Diversity," *Nation's Business*, September 1992.

Karen Nussbaum | "Removing Barriers for Working Women," *The Christian Science Monitor*, March 24, 1994.

Vic Perlo | "Racism and Unemployment," *Political Affairs*, July 1994.

Steven E. Rhoads | "Would Decentralized Comparable Worth Work?" *Regulation*, no. 3, 1993. Available from the Cato Institute, 1000 Massachusetts Ave. NW, Washington, DC 20001.

Rochelle Sharpe | "The Waiting Game: Women Make Strides, but Men Stay Firmly in Top Company Jobs," *The Wall Street Journal*, March 29, 1994.

Shawn Steel | "Jim Crow in Los Angeles," *National Review*, June 27, 1994.

R. Roosevelt Thomas Jr. | "From Affirmative Action to Affirming Diversity," *Harvard Business Review*, March/April 1990.

Laurie Udesky | "Sweatshops Behind the Labels," *The Nation*, May 16, 1994.

Richard Vedder and Lowell Gallaway | "Declining Black Employment," *Society*, July/August 1993.

Steven Yates | "The Ethics of Affirmative Action," *The Freeman*, July 1994.

How Should Work and Society Be Reconciled?

Work

Chapter Preface

In a matter of decades, society has undergone profound transformation, particularly so in the American family and workplace. For example, from roughly 1960 to the late 1980s, the percentage of all married mothers in the workforce rose from 28 percent to 65 percent, and the number of minor children living with one parent rose from 9 percent to nearly 25 percent.

Such change has made the task of raising children—considered by many a full-time job in itself—even more difficult. In response, working parents increasingly seek relief from employers in the form of "work-family" programs, such as flexible work schedules and child-care resources, to help them meet the demands of both their jobs and their children. In the words of work-family program consultant Fran Sussner Rodgers, "The challenge is to do whatever it takes to make it possible for people to contribute the most at work and care for their families."

However, businesses have exhibited mixed attitudes toward "family-friendly" programs, ranging from enthusiastic support to open contempt. According to *Wall Street Journal* writer Sue Shellenbarger, most companies resist such programs, and even so-called support often amounts to mere lip service. Writes Shellenbarger, "The prevailing corporate culture in most businesses . . . reflects the traditional family structures of the 1950s: a wife who cares for the children at home while the husband goes off to work."

Whether employers resist or embrace work-family programs, the demands of job and home will likely continue to compete for the attention of many Americans. Solutions to these conflicting interests are among the issues discussed in the following chapter on how work and society should be reconciled.

240

> *"We must* expect *people to work. We must tell healthy people . . . that cash assistance can't go on forever."*

Welfare Reform Should Require Recipients to Work

Donna E. Shalala

Donna E. Shalala has served as secretary of the Department of Health and Human Services since 1993. In the following viewpoint, a speech to the National Job Opportunity and Basic Skills Training (JOBS) Directors Conference on July 19, 1993, Shalala argues that the goal of the federal government's welfare reform strategy is to reduce the welfare rolls and provide recipients with jobs. Shalala contends that welfare must be a temporary, transitional program that reinforces the ideas of work, family, and responsibility—values that should be passed to future generations. She states that after some time period (the Clinton administration proposed an initial two-year limit for young parents in June 1994), welfare recipients should be obligated to find private sector or community service jobs.

As you read, consider the following questions:

1. How will an increased Earned Income Tax Credit provide work incentives, according to Shalala?
2. According to Shalala, how could the child support system be improved?

Donna E. Shalala, "Welfare Reform: A Priority for the Clinton Administration," *Children Today*, vol. 22, no. 2, 1993. Courtesy of Office of Human Development Services, U.S. Department of Health and Human Services.

I'm pleased to have the opportunity to talk about welfare reform—one of the Clinton Administration's top priorities. One of *my* top priorities.

First, I'd like to tell you about a woman from Virginia who wrote a very thoughtful letter to President Clinton right after the election.

She told the President that she has relied on AFDC [Aid to Families with Dependent Children] for nine years while caring for her severely disabled, fourteen-year-old son, Jarrod. This woman has received only four child support payments from her ex-husband in all those years. The grand total of the last one was *four dollars and sixty-one cents.*

She wants to work, but, realistically, she can't afford to lose her son's health benefits. She wrote to the President: "The only hope I have to gain employment is to wait until Jarrod's 18th birthday in 1996, when his qualification for SSI [Supplemental Security Income] and Medicaid is no longer dependent on total family income."

This story demonstrates how far welfare has wandered from the transitional program it was intended to be—and how little hope it inspires. There are millions of other stories like it. Stories about people who struggle to leave welfare—only to be pushed back by a barrage of work-related expenses. Like child care, transportation to work, and rent increases for those who live in subsidized housing.

Welfare Reform and Values

Our welfare reform strategy is based on a simple notion: *welfare must be a temporary, transitional program that builds on core American values—work, family, opportunity, and responsibility.* Values we want to preserve and pass down to generation after generation, so that we always remain strong and united as a people.

Our current system doesn't reinforce these values, and no one knows it better than you [directors]—who are working on the front lines implementing JOBS [Job Opportunities and Basic Skills] programs in all 50 states and territories.

You know that some welfare recipients face huge *barriers* in trying to join the workforce. And that others were the children of welfare recipients and barely know there is another way.

Since the late 1980s, the number of families on welfare has grown steadily. So has the number of families in poverty and the amount of money federal and state governments spend supporting the poor. And so has the paperwork, the complexity, and the perverse incentives that make the welfare system such a nightmare for administrators and recipients.

Aid to Families with Dependent Children is a 22-billion-dollar-

242

per-year system that too often penalizes work, stigmatizes recipients, and many times locks families into a cycle of dependency.

It's time to find a better way.

After years of attacking the problem in only a piecemeal way, it's time to find fundamental solutions. Comprehensive solutions. Solutions that build on the best and most effective work that *you* are doing with your customers.

President Clinton has a deeply felt commitment to welfare reform. As Governor of Arkansas, his innovative ideas enabled thousands of people to move into jobs—and were influential in the development of the Family Support Act of 1988.

Everyone Wants Change

We owe both the President and New York Senator Daniel Patrick Moynihan a debt of gratitude for their vision and tenacious work on a program that pointed us in the direction of continuous change. Many of your own governors have laid out similar visions.

My personal commitment is just as passionate. In the 1980s, when I was president of Hunter College in New York, we developed a program to provide single parents with an undergraduate education—and social service support. The program created futures, and moved bright young people from the welfare rolls to the tax rolls.

Everybody wants change—recipients, legislators, tax payers, and all of you who provide social services. Later in your careers, I hope you will look back on this as a watershed moment in the history of our welfare system. A moment that you helped shape with your work and your voices and your minds.

In June 1993, the President appointed a Working Group to develop a comprehensive welfare reform plan. The group is led by David Ellwood, the Assistant Secretary for Planning and Evaluation at HHS [Health and Human Services]; Bruce Reed, White House Deputy Policy Advisor; and Mary Jo Bane, Assistant Secretary for Children and Families.

These are major policy thinkers who know the human face of welfare, and I firmly support the work they are doing. They will help us develop a plan that is bold and that is fair.

It will be a plan that addresses the diverse *causes* of welfare, and not just the *consequences*. A plan that keeps people from having to enter the welfare system in the first place, while enabling others to get the short-term help they need.

Making Work Pay

Our work is guided by four basic principles:

First, *work must pay*. The way things are right now, having a full-time job does not guarantee that you will live above the poverty line. As a result, people lose their incentive to work.

That's not right. And it doesn't reflect those very values I was talking about. Everyone has something to contribute. And in our great country, no one who works hard and plays by the rules should have to raise children in poverty.

Our proposal to dramatically increase the Earned Income Tax Credit, or EITC, will give people an economic incentive to choose work instead of welfare. The EITC is a work-based, refundable tax credit designed to make sure that work pays for low-income families. The President's economic plan makes a strong investment in this bipartisan program.

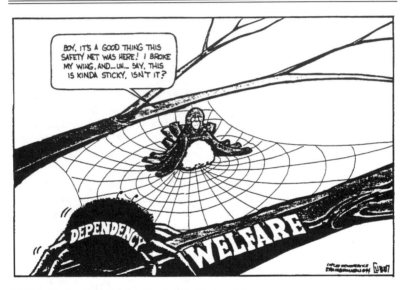

©Cullum/Copley News Service. Reprinted with permission.

Our EITC expansion will essentially lift above the poverty line all families with four persons or fewer in which the head of the household is working full-time, year-round. It will be a building block of comprehensive welfare reform—a powerful first step at encouraging people to join and stay in the labor market.

Health care reform will also enable people to move from welfare to work. For years, we've ignored the link between the health care crisis and welfare dependency. High health care costs—and lack of insurance for low-wage workers—drag down many Americans as they struggle for self-sufficiency. As a result, people who *want* to work must stay on welfare for years, simply because Medicaid is their only source of health security.

The President's health care plan will remedy this injustice. We will ensure that all Americans receive comprehensive health care at a reasonable cost. Under our system, work will pay— and it will provide health coverage.

Better Child Support Enforcement

Our second welfare reform principle is that we must build a far better system of child support enforcement. Right now, twelve million children have parents who could pay child support but do not. This is a national disgrace.

Both parents have a responsibility to provide for their children. As President Clinton has said, governments don't raise children; people do.

When one parent abandons that responsibility, we all pay the price—but the person who suffers most is the child. We must tighten up on enforcement while making awards more equitable.

Too many children do not have a legal father—over 500,000 children born *each year.* As a result, these children are often deprived of financial support, not to mention love, encouragement, and guidance.

We must improve our capacity to establish paternity at the hospital, right after childbirth. This is critical. There is no better place to get fathers—especially very young men—to accept legal responsibility right away for their children.

Strengthen Education and Training

Our third principle is one that hits home to you. We must strengthen education and training—and provide other support necessary for recipients to move into the workforce.

In this area, your work is critical. Today, 520,000 Americans are enrolled in JOBS programs to help them reenter the workforce and regain independence and dignity. I admire the work you do—offering families a passageway into the mainstream.

But to make the welfare rolls shrink, we need to increase the number of AFDC recipients active in programs to help them get jobs—and hold them. Although the requirements of current law are being met, less than sixteen percent of all non-exempt AFDC mothers are actually enrolled in JOBS programs. That is not nearly enough.

We need more of the great JOBS success stories that come from your programs. Stories like that of Joyce McLaughlin, a Louisiana mother of three who found herself homeless after separating from her husband. Desperate to support her children, Ms. McLaughlin moved into a shelter in her home town and applied for AFDC. It was a bitter pill to swallow, since she had worked for much of her adult life.

Then she learned about a local JOBS program called Project

Independence. The program provided some transitional support—child care assistance and bus passes—which allowed her to hunt for work. Now she works full-time and has moved her family into an apartment.

Then there's Beverly Curtis, a 19-year-old mother from Oklahoma. Ms. Curtis moved rapidly off welfare with the help of a JOBS program that combines training and work experience. She quickly landed a clerical job at a law firm. After a month, she got an even better job as a computer operator.

Beverly Curtis and Joyce McLaughlin are only two of the millions of Americans who just need a little help to get back on the road to independence.

That's how the system is supposed to function—providing transitional support to families in trouble, heading off further pain and hardship. And then, parents' or guardians' getting *opportunities* to find *work*—and piecing their lives back together again.

The *families* stay together, and the children learn lessons about courage and *responsibility* that they will pass on to their children.

Work. Family. Opportunity. Responsibility. That's what I call success stories. We can make these stories the rule, and not the exception, for millions of Americans.

Expect People to Work

But that won't happen without the fourth principle, which may be the most important of all. We must *expect* people to work. We must tell healthy people—in no uncertain terms—that cash assistance can't go on forever.

Once the major elements of welfare reform are in place, it is critical to set time limits, after which we should require able-bodied recipients to find jobs in the private sector or, if necessary, in community service.

I want to emphasize this point in a loud, strong voice. I've heard people question whether the Clinton Administration has the "stomach" to impose time requirements. You bet we do.

There has to be a time-certain period, beyond which people don't draw a check for doing nothing when they can do something.

A New Sense of Responsibility

We need to create a new sense of responsibility among *all* Americans—including those receiving public assistance. And there's no more compelling reason to do this than our children.

We have to remember the children of Joyce McLaughlin, and of Beverly Curtis. We must offer these children a vision of hope and responsibility. Welfare reform will help renew these values for our children—who will make up the society of tomorrow.

Reforming welfare won't be easy, and it won't happen overnight. It will take time and courage and leadership. There will be disagreements. There will be unexpected challenges. And we will need your support and your ideas along the way.

We will accomplish this landmark social achievement—and it will be worth it. As the President has said: We must reform welfare "not by punishing the poor or preaching to them, but by empowering the poor to take care of their children and improve their lives."

"Welfare reform . . . deals too generously with those recipients who are most competent and motivated, and too harshly with those who are least competent and motivated."

Welfare Reform Should Not Stress Work

Neil Gilbert

Many Americans agree that welfare reform is needed but are divided on how to pursue it. In the following viewpoint, Neil Gilbert argues that reform strategies that set time limits on welfare and provide incentives to work are no more likely to succeed than previous reform programs. Gilbert argues that instead of instituting costly incentives and punitive time limits designed to persuade all welfare work, reformers should instead distinguish between different types of welfare recipients and devise a specialized plan that ensures the well-being of children. Gilbert is Chernin Professor of Social Welfare at the University of California at Berkeley and is a contributor to *Commentary* magazine.

As you read, consider the following questions:

1. In Gilbert's opinion, how could welfare reform programs result in increased costs and dependence on welfare?
2. How should welfare cases be treated differently, according to the author?
3. What concerns does Gilbert express about children in welfare families?

Neil Gilbert, "Why the New Workfare Won't Work." Reprinted from *Commentary* (May 1994), by permission; all rights reserved.

Almost everyone agrees that work must replace welfare. Following President Clinton's lead, both Democrats and Republicans have embraced the idea of a two-year limit on welfare, during which recipients of Aid to Families with Dependent Children (AFDC) would be given education, training, child care, and job-placement services. Afterward, when entering the labor force, they would continue to qualify for transitional services like Medicaid and child care during the first year of employment, as is currently the case under the Family Support Act.

This approach is a variation on workfare experiments that have disappointed policy-makers since the 1967 work-incentive program. Although the reforms now in fashion are more stringent in their demands, and more generous in their incentives, they are no more likely to succeed than earlier schemes.

A Quick Fix

The ultimate question is: what happens to welfare recipients who follow the program, but are unable to secure employment after the two years? According to current thinking, they should be required to participate in some form of public-works program established by the state. This is a tough-sounding quick fix that will surely create more problems than it solves. For those who have not found a job after two years are likely to include many AFDC mothers who are among the least skilled and least motivated in the welfare population. The social and economic costs of employing them in public works will be staggering.

Thus, estimates by the Congressional Budget Office indicate that expenditures for on-the-job supervision of these workers and day care for their children would amount to $6,300 per participant. With the average AFDC grant already about $5,000, participation in mandatory work programs would hence more than double the costs for each welfare recipient. Smoke-and-mirrors proposals to finance this plan through taxing food stamps and cutting other welfare benefits suggest just how desperate the administration is becoming as it starts to calculate the costs of public works. And beyond fiscal concerns, the cynicism and demoralization bred by make-work would surely undermine the already shaky standards of public bureaucracies.

Other aspects of the current thinking on welfare reform are also hardly likely to go according to plan. In particular, proposals for reform organized around incentives to work and a two-year limit on public support are plagued by three problems: they ignore success; they create perverse effects; and they require a level of callousness that social-agency personnel are unlikely to countenance.

For many families, AFDC serves not as a poverty trap, but as a temporary support in hard times; in fact, about 48 percent of all

AFDC spells last less than two years. True, this success rate can be somewhat misleading, since one-third of short-term cases will enroll in AFDC again some time in the future and, in any event, most AFDC costs are attributable to long-term recipients. Nevertheless, reform measures that ignore the substantial number of successful cases are only likely to increase program expenses still further. By providing various transitional services and other incentives to work, they will raise the costs of public support for families who previously, in the absence of these benefits, would have left the rolls.

©1994, Kirk Anderson. Reprinted with permission.

At the same time, if incentives are high enough, they may perversely encourage those who are already in low-paying occupations to leave work for AFDC, and then recycle back into the labor force in order to qualify for the transitional benefits.

Finally, for those welfare recipients who refuse to participate in either training or public works, how are public agencies to enforce mandatory work requirements? Answers to this question are harsh and unsatisfactory. The Republican Task Force on Welfare Reform, for example, would impose sanctions on those who fail to participate by initially reducing the family's AFDC grant and food-stamp benefits by 25 percent, and after six months dropping them from AFDC altogether. But proposals of this sort disregard the question of what will happen to the children on welfare, for whom the AFDC program was originally devised.

Whatever hard lines policy-makers may draw, moreover, workers in welfare agencies are unlikely to impose sanctions that would virtually drive families with children onto the street. And if these sanctions *were* enacted, one may confidently predict that the two-year limit would become to welfare in the 1990's what deinstitutionalization was to mental illness in the 1960's, the deferred costs of which now plague our cities.

The essential problem with the transitional-incentives and time-limits approach to welfare reform is that it deals too generously with those recipients who are most competent and motivated, and too harshly with those who are least competent and motivated. I would suggest an alternative—one that begins with the need to distinguish among AFDC families, and seeks to ensure the well-being of children.

Two Classifications

Families enter the AFDC program for different reasons and remain on the rolls for varying periods of time. About 60 percent of AFDC spells begin because of either a decline in family earnings or a divorce (or separation) of married couples with children. I would argue that these cases should be treated differently from the 30 percent of AFDC spells that begin when an unmarried woman has a child.

The reason is simple. Welfare applicants who were married or employed for some period of time prior to enrollment in AFDC are generally independent citizens who had been abiding by social conventions and trying to follow the rules. It is reasonable to presume that they are competent and motivated to become self-sufficient. Thus, they should be considered a separate group, awarded AFDC benefits, and left alone for two years to reorganize their lives. A high proportion of them will be among the 48 percent of recipients who leave the welfare rolls of their own volition in less than two years. Those remaining on AFDC after two years could then be enrolled in the first phase of intervention, leading to what might be termed "managed dependency."

Out-of-Wedlock Births

As for women who enter the AFDC program because of out-of-wedlock births, they are another matter. For one thing, they are younger and more likely to become long-term recipients than those in the other group. For another thing, their children are at great risk of harm. Children in single-parent families are twice as likely to be abused as those in households where both parents are present; when the single parent is a teenager, the risk is even higher. This group should be targeted for special intervention, if for no other reason than to protect the children.

Instead of forced labor and make-work schemes, however, the intervention would be divided into two phases. In the first, practical assistance would be offered to mothers and protection would be provided for their children by means of regular home-health visits, assistance in home management, encouragement of school drop-outs to complete their high-school requirements, and development of systematic plans for reintegration into the labor force.

After three years, those still on AFDC would enter the second phase. Here, greater social controls would be employed, reflecting the recipients' emerging status as "wards of the state." Home visiting to supervise child-care practices would continue, and the level of public-assistance grants would remain the same. But during this phase, a case manager would be assigned to exercise increased regulation over each family's financial affairs, which would entail payment of rent and utilities and weekly allocations of food stamps. There would also be increased monitoring of outside resources available to recipients, which would reduce their AFDC grants.

Tightening social control through case managers and home-health visitors would certainly raise the costs of AFDC. But this would still be a relatively inexpensive way for society to protect vulnerable children, while giving notice that long-term public dependence would be accompanied by greater public surveillance. Increasing the role of public authority in recipients' lives would make welfare less attractive to some who might otherwise be employed.

Beyond AFDC Adjustments

This is a modest goal, but those who demand more would do well to recognize that tinkering with AFDC is not the answer. Although AFDC may help to sustain the never-married, single-parent culture of poverty, it did not create this unhealthy pattern of behavior, and forces larger than those generated by welfare reform will be required to eliminate it.

Indeed, a serious effort to reduce welfare must go well beyond adjustments in the AFDC program. The best and fairest incentive would be to increase the work-related benefits of low-paying jobs of the kind that many welfare recipients might perform. Progress along these lines is already under way with the expansion of tax-based social transfers, such as the earned income tax credit. Working families also need the security of medical protection, which those on welfare receive through Medicaid. Finally, there is widespread agreement that absent fathers should be held responsible for the financial support of their children (though resources for such support are often quite limited among fathers of children in the AFDC population).

Even with all this, dependency will not disappear. Whether due to personal deficiencies or forces beyond their control, people in need of care will always be with us. At the very least, however, social policies aimed at alleviating dependency should not condemn children for the hard luck or personal frailties of their parents.

"Corporate attention to work-family issues is greater than ever before."

Business Supports Work-Family Programs

John L. Adams

John L. Adams is the chairman and chief executive officer of Texas Commerce Bank, a commercial bank chain. In the following viewpoint, Adams maintains that work-family issues—and their impact on economic well-being—are a higher priority for business than ever before. He states that corporate leaders are increasingly addressing work-family issues and successfully implementing family leave, flexible scheduling, on-site child care, and similar work-family programs. Adams insists that responsiveness to work-family needs is essential to recruiting and retaining quality workers.

As you read, consider the following questions:

1. How can work-family issues vary among different families, according to Adams?
2. In the author's opinion, why are some businesses wary of work-family programs?
3. Why does Adams believe business should aim to create a sense of community?

Excerpted, with permission, from "Juggling Job and Family," John L. Adams's speech to the National Council of Jewish Women, September 1993. The complete text appears in the December 1, 1993, *Vital Speeches of the Day*.

Balancing work and family is a greater challenge today than ever before. Some people find themselves at wits' end juggling jobs and tending to the needs of their children and parents. . . .

It's been said that total commitment to family and total commitment to career is possible, but fatiguing. That observation is more true today than ever. And it offers a challenge to corporate leaders—how can we help make the commitments more possible, and less fatiguing, for our employees, while achieving profitability?

The term "work-family" is a relatively new addition to the business lexicon. It defines a realm of issues that, for many companies, didn't exist in the past. Of course, some companies have recognized and addressed the family needs of workers for many years. But for others, work-family is shorthand for a new array of corporate initiatives, and it's a term that is destined to be with us well into the future.

Three Families

I'd like to offer a context for our exploration of work-family, what new realities it presents, and what it means to the new bottom line. The context is three families. The financial writer Sylvia Porter has said the average family exists only on paper, invented by statisticians for the convenience of statisticians. Our families confirm her point:

One is a two-career couple with a small child. He's a marketing manager, she's a finance specialist. Their job sites are fifteen miles apart, each about the same distance from home.

Family number two is a middle-aged couple. He's a manufacturing production worker, she's a secretary. Their children are grown. Her mother has been diagnosed with Alzheimer's disease.

The third family is made up of a single woman and her two children. The mother was trained as a computer operator through a program at a nearby community college.

What does "work-family" mean to these families? For the two-career professionals, it means figuring out how their child is cared for when one or both of them must work late, which is a common occurrence, or how they can make it to her soccer game.

For the folks with the sick parent, it means finding help in caring for her. Without it, one of them may have to quit work.

For the single mother, balancing work and family means finding reliable, affordable child care so she can take the bus ride to her job and be able to focus on her work once she's there. What does she do when the day care center calls and says one of the kids is sick?

Three families, three different sets of needs. All three face the frustrations of juggling work and family responsibilities. And all three are typical in our companies today. Let's keep them all in mind as we discuss work and family. Because the challenges in their lives are today's new realities. And how well they meet those challenges will have a dramatic effect on how well they contribute to the new bottom line.

Greater Attention

Without a doubt, the issues of work-family balance and the extent of corporate responsibility to workers are higher on our agendas than ever before. One need only look at recent news coverage to confirm this:

- A recent issue of *Business Week* had a cover story on work and family;
- In June 1993, the *Wall Street Journal* presented a 14-page special report on work and family;
- Articles in *Inc.* magazine, the *Dallas Morning News* and *Spirit* magazine have addressed work-family programs, workplace discrimination against mothers, and the effects of the Family and Medical Leave Act;
- And on September 3, 1993, the *Wall Street Journal* reported on the National Study of the Changing Workforce by the Families and Work Institute. The study reveals broader-than-expected conflict between work and family life, and suggests that workers place high value on flexible scheduling and attention to personal needs.

The enactment of the Family & Medical Leave Act brings added excitement. While it's too early to fully assess its impact, the mere existence of the law heightens the importance of work-family issues.

I think most of us believe that corporate attention to work-family issues is greater than ever before. There is mounting, encouraging evidence that companies both large and small are implementing, and benefiting from, work-family programs. Despite the advances, though, there still is far to go in convincing companies of the value of such programs and motivating them to take action. According to the *Wall Street Journal*, a nationwide survey in 1992 of firms with more than 50 employees showed that only 7.2 percent of the companies surveyed had on-site or near-site child-care programs. And two-thirds of the businesses said "no" when asked if they might ever offer employees even such minimal child- or elder-care help as referrals and workshops.

It's reasonable to believe that these numbers have improved since the survey. But while more companies may have seen the light, many still resist taking action on child-care, elder-care, and other work-family issues.

Opponents of work and family programs say that employers should not involve themselves more deeply in workers' lives, that to do so opens a Pandora's box of raised expectations, employer liability, invasion of privacy, and even accusations of unfairness in providing work-family programs.

Some corporate leaders see themselves caught in a dilemma of achieving the "lean and mean" organization desired by shareholders and the financial markets, while simultaneously putting scarce resources to meeting employee support needs. To this argument, let me suggest that while they try to get leaner and meaner, companies should pay even more attention to work-family issues, rather than avoid them. I'll elaborate on this idea in a bit.

Another common concern about work-family programs deals with small companies. Because their resources can be more limited than those of large corporations, they often cannot afford to extend greater benefits and flexibility to workers. But there are many small company successes, and we'll touch on a couple in a moment.

Corporate Cops

Faith Wohl epitomizes a new kind of crusader: She is a corporate cop, upholding work-family policies for 90,000 DuPont workers nationwide.

It's a job that's relatively new in companies—and one that's growing quickly. There are probably about 200 corporate cops walking the work-family beat these days, just about all of them created in the past four years, estimates the Families and Work Institute in New York. And the number is expected to expand further as more companies set up work-family programs.

Major companies initially hired such managers to simply *address* work-family conflicts, to raise people's awareness of the issues and to devise programs that could help employees. But companies have found that wasn't enough. So these executives have become *enforcers*, with a mission to eradicate management's entrenched resistance to flexible schedules, work-at-home arrangements, job sharing and parental leaves.

Julie Amparano Lopez, *The Wall Street Journal*, June 21, 1993.

There are still other challenges to work-family. One is applying programs fairly across an organization. How do you offer the same opportunities to shift workers that you do to nine-to-fivers? And what benefits do you make available to childless workers?

Finally, businesses today employ a huge "shadow workforce"

of temporary and contract workers, most with no benefits beyond a paycheck. One-third of families are in this category. How do we meet their needs?

While all of these arguments and issues must be considered, corporate response to work-family issues is building momentum. And regardless of how much or how little change has occurred in any individual company, ultimately all business will have to address work-family issues as part of the new bottom line.

The Changing Family

Why are corporate leaders more and more addressing work-family issues in their business planning and management? One obvious reason is the changing family. When the drive to American industrial dominance began to build steam in the 1950s, the country was comfortable with the notion of a working husband and a wife at home with kids. It made sense in the wake of World War II. The men had come home. Rosie the Riveter could leave the factory. They both wanted children, and American prosperity enabled single-earner families to lead comfortable lives.

Today, we must deal with new realities. Remember the guy who wouldn't dream of his wife's working? He's the same guy who now wakes her up in the middle of the night to suggest that she ask her boss for a raise.

Fewer than 22 percent of married-couple households consist of a male breadwinner and female homemaker. In the 1950s, the figure was 80 percent. Fifty-eight percent of mothers with children under six now hold paying jobs. The figure was 20 percent in 1960. And 68 percent of mothers with children under 18 work outside the home.

Today, the majority of families rely on two incomes to maintain a middle-class standard of living, and a significant number of families need two incomes just to pull themselves above the poverty line. Two working parents, and single parents, bring an array of needs with them into the workforce that didn't exist before.

Corporations can choose to ignore work-family issues or strive to hire workers who don't need or demand assistance. Indeed, good companies with good jobs can often get employees who will routinely work late, virtually giving their lives over to the company.

But relying on a strategy of only hiring such hard-chargers is not practical. The evidence is mounting that responsiveness to work-family needs is essential to recruiting and retaining good workers—at all levels. Let me elaborate on this. Business success certainly depends on the highly motivated professionals who manage work groups, develop business plans and aspire to the pinnacle of the organization. But remember the three families I described earlier. A successful business also needs productive line workers and efficient secretaries and clerks. Work-family programs help attract and retain professionals, production workers, clerks, and secretaries alike.

At a more philosophical level, work-family programs may be crucial to sustaining our basic business and societal structures. If we, as corporations, and as a society, want a productive economy, we must support people's efforts to work, to rise above welfare and poverty. We must help reduce their frustrations and worry, and actively create an environment that lets them enjoy their work. Today, that means being sensitive to, and assisting with, workers' family needs.

For Good Business

Responding to work-family issues is not just compassionate. It's good business. Recent studies of such companies as Johnson & Johnson and AT&T show that helping employees resolve work and family conflicts boosts morale and increases productivity. The J&J study found that absenteeism among employees who used flexible time and family-leave policies was, on average, 50 percent less than for the workforce as a whole. It also found that 58 percent of the employees surveyed said such policies were "very important" in their decision to stay at the company. The number jumped to 71 percent among employees using the benefits.

AT&T found that the average cost of giving new parents leave of up to one year was 32 percent of an employee's annual salary, compared with 150 percent to replace the leave-taker altogether. The Johnson & Johnson research highlights one of the consistently reported benefits of work-family programs—employee recruitment and retention. Other important benefits also emerged, including helping women advance and promoting teamwork.

While the array of work-family programs can be bewildering for employers, and the effectiveness of various programs may require further research, two things are clear:

Whatever the work-family program—flexible scheduling, on-site day care, child- and elder-care referral, family leave—you can find companies that are successfully implementing it.

Second, whether employers are today committed to work-family or not, they will have to address employees' increasing insistence on, and need for, such programs.

In my career at Texas Commerce Bank, I have seen and been involved in the evolution of our response to work-family needs.

One exciting effort that we're a part of is the local initiative of the American Business Collaborative for Quality Dependent

Care. The collaborative has brought 12 Dallas/Fort Worth–area companies together in a two-year, 1.2-million-dollar effort to improve the quality and availability of dependent care programs such as child care and elder care. Nineteen different projects are targeted for collaborative support.

For those companies participating, the initiative is a way to help attract and retain a productive, motivated workforce that will ensure their competitiveness now and in the future.

At Texas Commerce Bank, I believe we are making a sincere, sensible effort to enact work-family programs. With a new, comprehensive program initiated in January 1993, we're providing employees with family leaves of absence, flexible work scheduling, dependent care, and employee assistance. Like many companies, we're still learning what programs are most beneficial to employees, which ones are most efficiently implemented, and how far we can stretch our resources. . . .

Small Companies

Earlier I mentioned that small companies may fear they do not have the resources to implement work-family programs. But small companies, blessed with energy and creativity, should not sell themselves short. [U.S. Supreme Court Justice] Oliver Wendell Holmes was a rather small man, but there was nothing diminutive about his spirit. Once when he was present at a gathering of unusually tall men he was asked, as a joke, if he did not feel somewhat small and insignificant in the company of such big guys. "Indeed I do," replied Dr. Holmes tartly. "I feel like a dime among a collection of pennies."

Well, some small companies are proving they can compete with the big guys when it comes to innovative work-family programs. Take G.T. Water Products of Moorpark, California. The 28-employee plumbing products manufacturer provides an on-site school with extended care, adoption assistance, flexible scheduling, and benefits for part-timers. Four hundred seventy-five–employee Lancaster Laboratories in Pennsylvania offers on-site adult day care and child care, emergency counseling, and a dependent-care assistance plan. Such examples suggest that companies of all sizes can implement work-family programs that make sense for them. . . .

I think there is another new reality that demands consideration. I suggested that going "lean and mean" should lead companies to pay even more attention to work-family issues, rather than avoid them. The reason is simple. Having fewer workers means every worker is more important than ever.

We have to care about our people; they're our most important asset. We have to rely on a diverse workforce with new needs. And in all of our organizations, especially the lean and mean ones, we have to ensure the productivity of the people we have. Everyone counts today, and we have to get the best from them.

A Sense of Community

In closing, I'd like to refer to a book published a couple of years ago—*Love and Profit* by James Autrey. Autrey's work seeks to help managers make the workplace more creative, more caring and, as a result, more productive.

One chapter of *Love and Profit* begins by suggesting that "the Job is the New Neighborhood, and friends and coworkers are the new extended family."

Autrey goes on to say that today people are in a sudden, compulsive search for connection and a sense of community. He argues that business has an unprecedented opportunity to create a special place, which in the old days we thought of as just a place to work.

"Despite rising costs," Autrey writes, "we must come to grips with issues of child care, parental leave, employment of the disabled, education and training of workers for fast-changing jobs, and accommodation of aging workers who do not want to retire."

"We managers," he concludes, "have the opportunity to lead and direct people in that ever more powerful bond of common enterprise, and at the same time to create a place of friendship, deep personal connections, and neighborhood."

And he offers, of all things, a new management bumper sticker. It would read: "If you're not creating community, you're not managing." Work-family is about creating community.

"While waving the family-friendly banner with one hand, [companies] are tossing out the chicken soup with the other."

Business Does Not Adequately Support Work-Family Programs

Jaclyn Fierman

Despite an increased need for work-family programs such as child care, telecommuting, and flexible work time, few businesses are providing such benefits, Jaclyn Fierman argues in the following viewpoint. Fierman contends that businesses, faced with the need to remain competitive, are disinclined to invest in work-family programs; and that when such programs are made available, employees are often reluctant to take advantage of them due to pressure from coworkers and supervisors. Fierman is an associate editor for *Fortune*, a biweekly business magazine.

As you read, consider the following questions:

1. According to Fierman, how have families changed in the past two decades?
2. What job is flextime impractical for, according to Anne Kinney, cited by the author?
3. What is the biggest advantage for companies claiming to support work-family programs, in Fierman's opinion?

If only good-guy companies finished first. Work at Tandem Computers probably surpassed most people's idea of a dream job. At its printed circuit-board assembly plant in Watsonville, California, there were free-flowing beer parties on Fridays, a swimming pool, and ergonomically designed chairs for every weary back. Best of all was the benevolent CEO, James "Just call me Jimmy" Treybig. When employees complained that working long hours over the Christmas holidays to meet year-end deadlines cut into their family time, the big-hearted Texan responded, "I'll see what I can do."

What Treybig should have done for these folks, he now realizes, was insist they radically improve productivity. Instead, he sent them home to their eggnog and outsourced the work. To his surprise, he saved a considerable amount of money. Two years ago Treybig sold the Watsonville plant to SCI Systems, which kept on—at lower pay—just two-thirds of the 270 people Tandem once employed. Says Treybig: "You can't bend so far to protect people's lifestyle that you cost them their jobs."

The man who once described Tandem as a "socialist" company has straightened up. Reminded of *Fortune*'s 1987 story, *How Jimmy Treybig Turned Tough*, his response was, "Yes, but not tough enough." In 1993, when Tandem's losses hit $500 million, he began the truly tough process of trimming salaries by 5% and eliminating 1,800 out of nearly 11,000 jobs. He also cut back on his famed Friday beer busts. Quarterly get-togethers welcome family but emphasize business. . . .

Any boss worth his options knows that productivity depends as much on satisfied workers as smart processes. So out of enlightened self-interest, most companies have devised policies that give people some slack in juggling work and family commitments. But as Treybig discovered, paternalism can fail employers. It can also fall short for employees. At many companies, people worry they will jeopardize their careers if they take advantage of perks like job sharing and lengthy maternity leaves. Says Sheila Madden, Tandem's manager of corporate staffing: "There is a natural tension between family goals and corporate goals."

Mixed Messages

Is the tension resolvable? Can a company be both competitive and caring? As employers bolt from lifetime commitments to employees and seek to renegotiate that contract, they're sending mixed messages. While waving the family-friendly banner with one hand, they are tossing out the chicken soup with the other.

And the soup is disappearing just when the labor force could use more of it. Six million single mothers leave their youngsters and go to work today, double the figure of 20 years ago. Over roughly the same period, the number of working couples with children under 18 has risen nearly 60%, to more than 14 million families; as an added stress, some of these families also care for elderly parents. Work/Family Directions in Boston, which sets up child and elder care support systems for companies, found that about 15% of employees in large companies have an aging or infirm dependent.

Business as Usual

With an onslaught of women, single parents and two-paycheck couples in the work force, corporate support for families, it seems, is exploding. There's just one problem: For most workers, life hasn't changed much at all. All this hoopla—and it's business as usual? What's going on here? Put part of the blame on corporate hype. At some companies, family-friendly programs have never been much more than public-relations gimmicks, corporate paint jobs aimed at giving the firms a '90s look. More often, though, the reasons are more subtle—if no less powerful. Many companies don't even *pretend* to be changing, often because they are philosophically opposed to getting involved in their workers' personal lives. Others balk at the perceived cost; more than 70% of the companies surveyed in 1992 by the Society for Human Resource Management of Alexandria, Virginia, believed that most work-family programs were too costly to implement.

But the most important reason for the lack of progress is more fundamental: The way most companies do business is antithetical to a family-friendly workplace, and few companies have had the will—or perhaps the knowledge—to make the necessary changes. As a result, chief executives make pronouncements, companies issue new rules—and the managers on the front line ignore them.

Sue Shellenbarger, *The Wall Street Journal*, June 21, 1993.

If these overextended workers feel abandoned, their employers could justifiably say the same. A Roper poll of 1,027 women and men for *Working Woman* magazine in November 1993 found that ambition isn't what it used to be. Nearly 80% defined success as having a happy family life or relationship. Dead last among seven choices, says Roper's Nick Tortorello, "were the very things people prized in the Eighties: money, career, and power." Says Jeffrey Sonnenfeld, director of the Center for Leadership and Career Studies at Emory University in Atlanta: "The edge has come off baby-boomers. They're trying to recapture lost areas of their life."

Bosses can't necessarily extract the extra mile, but they can—

and do—demand extra time. Harvard economics lecturer Juliet Schor, author of *The Overworked American*, says that people today work more than they did 25 years ago—the equivalent, in fact, of a 13th month each year. In a survey of 10,000 managers and professionals at major corporations, Work/Family Directions found that working mothers averaged 44 hours a week on the job and 31 on family responsibilities; fathers put in 3 more hours at the office but logged just half as much time as their wives on child care and household chores.

When *Fortune* polled over 200 CEOs, close to 80% said they will have to push their people harder than ever before to compete in the Nineties. That's particularly true at downsized companies, where fewer people do just as much work. After announcing layoffs at Sprint's benefit-laden long-distance division in 1993, President Ronald LeMay exhorted employees "to be introspective about the adequacy of your commitment . . . 40-hour workweeks are a relic of the past."

Even as they squeeze, employers remain well intentioned. Rare is the midsize to large company that doesn't offer—at least on glossy paper—some sort of child care assistance and flexible scheduling like part-time, telecommuting (working off-site or from home), compressed workweeks (40 hours in four days), or flextime (the freedom to start an eight-hour day slightly early or late). A survey of 1,034 U.S. businesses by the employee benefits consulting firm Hewitt Associates found that 78% offer child care support and referral programs; 60%, some kind of flexible scheduling; 20%, elder care programs; and 9%, on-site child care.

Halfhearted Endorsement

But good luck finding companies where use of these programs is either widespread or wholeheartedly embraced by management. A survey of employees at 80 major companies by Work/Family Directions showed that fewer than 2% of eligible employees take advantage of job sharing, telecommuting, and part-time work options. Though virtually all the companies say they allow part-time work, only 51% have formal policies, and just 1.7% of employees at those companies take advantage of the option. Flextime is the most popular benefit: About a quarter of the companies offer it, and 24% of those eligible seize the opportunity. "There are penalties for using these policies," says Dana Friedman, co-president of Families & Work Institute in New York City, another group lobbying for a workplace with as much give as get. "You lose your seniority, and co-workers resent the hell out of you."

A senior tax accountant at Ernst & Young says she felt a chill from some colleagues when she went part-time after her son was born. "People resented me for going home after work instead of heading out for a few drinks the way I used to," she says. And a former vice president at Bankers Trust, now a full-time mother, admits she used to have misgivings about working mothers. "I feel guilty saying this," she says, "but before I had children I resented women who were on the phone with their babysitters, husbands, and pediatricians."

Employees often pay a price for taking what's offered them even though the companies, paradoxically, appear to reap some benefits. WMX Technologies in Oak Brook, Illinois, sponsors support groups for parents that address everything from discipline to schoolwork. The company estimates the counseling saves it $1,600 a year per participant by lowering absentee and turnover rates and the use of medical benefits. Corning [Inc.] says its full plate of family-friendly programs has cut turnover in half since 1986. And Aetna [Life & Casualty Co.] estimates its family-leave policy saves it roughly $2 million a year in replacement costs.

Public Relations

Perhaps the biggest payoff for companies that purport to make life easier for their employees is the public relations bonus. Witness the clamor to make *Working Mother*'s annual list of what it says are the 100 best companies to work for in the U.S. In 1993 more than 1,000 companies submitted their family-friendly credentials for consideration, twice the number that applied in 1992. Having a nice-guy reputation helps with recruiting, and surveys show that people will even sacrifice higher pay for more flexibility in their lives.

But not everyone believes the companies on *Working Mother*'s list deserve their gold stars. Just ask the long-distance operators and customer service representatives at Sprint, which appeared on the 1992 roster. Although people at headquarters can use all sorts of flexible policies, long-distance operators say they are put on warning if they arrive even 15 minutes late to work. Says Ronnie Brown, 28, a single mother who works in Sprint's customer service office in Dallas: "When we saw that Sprint made the list, we said, 'Do we work for a different company, or what?' There's a double standard here."

Sprint doesn't debate that charge. Certain work, it says, simply doesn't lend itself to flexible hours. "We offer very generous family benefits at Sprint," says corporate employee relations manager Anne Kinney. "But flextime for operators isn't an option. We have to run a business." *Working Mother* dropped Sprint from its 1993 list. Says deputy editor Betty Holcomb: "It became clear to us that Sprint wasn't following through the way it should have."

Even when top management broadly defines its benefits and

makes them available across the board, lieutenants down the line may not feel obliged to dispense the largess. "I call it supervisor sabotage," says Berkeley sociologist Arlie Hochschild. "Senior managers say 'If I worked long hours with children, so can you.'"

Corning, purported to be a saint among sensitive employers, has found practicing its policies considerably harder than printing them up. Says Wendy Luce, who used to manage one of the company's ceramics plants: "Management tends to be very traditional. They still want line managers in the plant from 7 A.M. to 10 P.M." Supervisors, in turn, expect the same from their troops. "Just because we have the policies doesn't mean everyone has bought into them," says Sherry Mosley, manager of Corning's work/life balance department.

Long Hours Count

Diehard supporters of family-friendly policies can unwittingly sabotage the works. What's an ambitious employee to think if the boss regularly works through the dinner hour? Catalyst, which tries to further women's progress in the workplace, honored the Bank of Montreal for its commitment to flexible policies and the advancement of women. Yet bank president Tony Comper regularly works 65 to 70 hours a week. Go figure how employees—who feel subtle pressure to work equally hard—find time to tuck in their kids, much less rear them.

Truth be told: Face time counts. Putting in long hours, even if you're twiddling your thumbs, is still viewed by many bosses as a sign of loyalty. Marcia Kropf, a vice president of Catalyst, conducted focus groups with up to 200 people at a dozen major companies. "We'd hear over and over," she says, "that men who take off in the afternoon from three to four-thirty to play squash but stay at their desks until seven are seen as more committed than women who work nonstop but leave at five."

Does anyone out there walk the talk? Morrison & Foerster, the second-largest law firm in San Francisco, with some 550 attorneys, comes close. Other companies might well benefit from studying the firm, a model of partnership, not paternalism. MoFo, as employees call it, embraces more than women and children in its family-friendliness. When partner Arturo Gonzalez, 33, son of a railroad laborer, was a summer associate at the firm after his second year at Harvard law school, his older brother was arrested and convicted after four trials of murdering his ex-wife's lover. "A partner here helped me work on the case," says Gonzalez. After joining the firm, he defended his brother pro bono on company time. The brother, who spent 7½ years in jail, is now a free man.

Mothers also get a break at MoFo. Women can remain on the

partnership track even if they work part time. The hitch is this, says MoFo partner and former part-timer Rochelle Alpert: "Litigation is not a Monday, Wednesday, Friday business. When the matter required it, I put in grueling hours."

Such give and take pervades the partnership. "We grew up together in this firm, and we're willing to cover for each other when it's necessary," says MoFo Chairman Peter Pfister. "That's far more important than any policies on paper." While the atmosphere is nurturing, the firm's success depends on each attorney's willingness to pull his or her weight. In other words, a company can support its employees' needs. But only if the work gets done. And only if most people, most of the time, don't ask for chicken soup.

"I feel [two careers] is worth it from a personal standpoint and from what I observe of the family's standpoint."

Working Mothers Benefit Families

The Myers family, interviewed by Judith Valente

In the following viewpoint, the Myers family of Winnetka, Illinois, describes the advantages and disadvantages of having two parents who are working professionals. The Myerses find it difficult to balance the demands of two careers and the needs of three children. They contend that a primary hardship is finding the time for various needs such as child care, household duties, and family and personal time. However, the family believes that two incomes satisfy the needs of all family members and that having both parents working is the most suitable option for them. Judith Valente is a staff reporter for the *Wall Street Journal* daily newspaper.

As you read, consider the following questions:

1. How have Phyllis and Scott resolved the conflict of pursuing separate careers?
2. Why do Elizabeth and Katherine believe that women's careers are important?
3. According to the Myerses, what are the financial benefits of having two incomes?

Imagine a successful dual-career couple, and people like Phyllis and Scott Myers come to mind.

Dr. Myers, 44 years old, and Mr. Myers, 47, live in Winnetka, Illinois, with their three children—twins Katherine and Elizabeth, 14, and 5-year-old Jonathan. Their combined six-figure income has allowed them to buy a huge house in one of Chicago's loveliest suburbs. They have the means to hire housekeepers, take skiing vacations and provide Elizabeth the chance to study in France.

But the Myerses have also paid a price for their comforts and success. Dr. Myers, who holds a Ph.D. in education, laments the fact that she has surrendered many of her career goals for her family, yet feels she still doesn't have enough time for her home life. Mr. Myers wishes he had more time to nurture his marriage. Katherine and Elizabeth complain that their parents sometimes miss their basketball games and that their mother brings work home from the office.

Dr. Myers is executive director of the One-to-One Learning Center for children and adults with learning problems, two miles from her home. She has worked outside the home all of her married life, except for 2½ years after her twins were born, during which time she attended classes at the University of Chicago and wrote her doctoral dissertation. Her current workday runs from 8:15 A.M., when she puts Jonathan on the bus for his half-day school program, to 6:30 P.M. She comes home for about an hour during the day to feed Jonathan, do laundry and prepare that evening's dinner.

Mr. Myers is a principal partner in a 30-member law firm in downtown Chicago, a 50-minute train commute from his home. When trying a difficult case, he says, he has worked as many as 26 days in a row without weekends off. His workday normally runs from 7:30 A.M. to 6:30 P.M.

Though housekeepers have at times helped with the cooking and laundry, Dr. Myers says help is difficult to find and keep. The family is currently without a housekeeper.

Here, before the fireplace in their living room, the Myerses (except for Jonathan, who is watching a video upstairs) discuss with *Wall Street Journal* staff reporter Judith Valente the difficulty of balancing careers and family life.

More Pluses than Minuses

Valente: Has it been worth it to you to pursue two demanding careers? Or, knowing what you know now, would have you done things differently?

Dr. Myers: It's a trade-off. But all together, yes, I feel it is worth it from a personal standpoint and from what I observe of the family's standpoint.

What has made it worth it?

Dr. Myers: It's what I want to do with my life. I want a more varied life than the life of staying home. I also feel there is more of a peer relationship with your spouse when you are both [working]. With regard to the children, I think there are more pluses than minuses. One of the big pluses is that the kids are fairly independent and can solve problems on their own to a greater extent, I think, than if I was around all the time. Obviously, there is also a monetary benefit and a lifestyle benefit.

Scott, how has it been for you?

Mr. Myers: From a financial standpoint, the fact that we haven't had a lot of pressing financial concerns has certainly made life easier. I confess, I wonder how people do it. When I see families of four, five, six children, making $20,000 a year—I think, "My God." What's stressful is when you're trying to be somewhere, and she's trying to be somewhere. Inevitably, there are conflicts.

Girls, what do you think about the long hours your parents work?

Katherine: Well, we have to figure out rides and how to get places by ourselves.

Is that hard?

Katherine: Not really.

Do your friends have the same problem?

Elizabeth: We have to do more of it. With our friends, a lot of times, their parents can drive them home. They don't really have to figure out, when they're going somewhere, how they can get home.

Dr. Myers: Yes, but you get places too.

Elizabeth: Yeah, right, on a bike.

Do most of your friends have mothers who work?

Katherine: In the town we live in, more mothers are at home because they can do it on their budget.

What would you like: Mom at home, Mom at home part time, Mom working full time?

Katherine: We might get on each other's nerves if she was home all the time. I don't think she'd be happy home all the time because it would be just kind of boring. I don't want to sit home when I get older.

Why is that?

Katherine: Because I think a woman is entitled to a professional side of her life. I don't want to sit around the house. I mean, [homemakers do] work and everything, but to me it wouldn't be very fulfilling.

Conflict with Children

When you look at your Mom, do you ever think she has too much to do, that it's extremely hard juggling work and a family?

Elizabeth: Sometimes we want to talk to her when we come

271

home from school and we get kind of annoyed that she's on the phone. Also, even though she works pretty close, it's kind of hard for her to come home. If we were sick or something, she could come pick us up, but it would be hard.

Dr. Myers: Remember when you got mad at me that one time because you were sick and I said, "I'll pick you up in an hour at the end of my meeting"? You weren't real happy about that.

Elizabeth: Yes.

Dr. Myers [to Elizabeth]: There was an interesting thing that you said when we first talked about this interview; do you mind if I say what it was? Why don't you repeat it?

Elizabeth: When I was little, in first grade, I used to be jealous that everyone else's mom was home and I was mad because Mom had to work and wasn't home all the time. But then when I got older, I liked it better that she worked because she had other functions besides her family.

Working Mothers Are a Positive Influence

Both the daughters and the sons of wage-working mothers have been found to have a more positive view of women and less rigid views of sex roles; the daughters (like their mothers) tend to have greater self-esteem and a more positive view of themselves as workers, and the sons, to expect equality and shared roles in their own future marriages. We might well expect that with mothers in the labor force *and* with fathers as equal parents, children's attitudes and psychologies will become even less correlated with their sex. In a very crucial sense, their opportunities to become the persons they want to be will be enlarged.

Susan Moller Okin, *Justice, Gender, and the Family*, 1989.

What age where you when you changed your mind?

Elizabeth: Probably third grade, around nine years old.

Katherine: She was usually there when we'd come home for lunch in grade school.

Dr. Myers: There wasn't a lunch program in the school, so I had to get home [on their lunch hour]. For a while, we had students live in, but they were gone during the day. It's always a juggling act. The child care, the house care is always on your mind. We've used just about every model that there is for child care. But a lot of the time, I was having to come home for lunch every day to be here to get them on and off buses.

Was that hard on you?

Dr. Myers: You're never in the place you're supposed to be, and you are always feeling guilty about where you are. You're always rushing around. You're always late. At those times, I get quick to snap [at the children], when it's just one more detail to handle and you've already handled the 19th and 20th one. So, one rule that we finally came up with is that I wasn't going to solve any problems or help you with school work after 9 P.M. Remember?

Katherine: Yeah.

Why did you make that a rule?

Dr. Myers: I don't have any pleasantness left in me after 9. I found myself in a pattern of—I don't want to say exploding but—

Being short?

Dr. Myers: Yes.

Elizabeth: You'd come home from work and you'd say you're not going to talk for 20 minutes.

Dr. Myers: One of the things about living close to where you work, and not having much of a commute, is that you just have no time by yourself.

Katherine: I thought you liked the close commute.

Dr. Myers: I do. I'd like to have a close commute *and* come home to an empty house for 20 minutes. You guys used to always greet me at the door with a problem. Remember, Katherine? You'd say, "Mom, I have to do this," or, "I need this for tomorrow." I'd say, "Give me a break."

A Typical Day

What is a typical day for you, Phyllis, now that you no longer have a housekeeper?

Dr. Myers: Today, I put Jonathan on the school bus at 8:15. I went to work. When I came home at noon to take him off the bus, I put in a load of laundry. Jonathan and I had a quick lunch. I fixed dinner. Then, I took Jonathan to his baby sitter. Then I went back to work.

He comes home for lunch?

Dr. Myers: He comes home and stays home. He just turned five and only has school half a day. He's in junior kindergarten.

You come home on your lunch hour and prepare dinner?

Dr. Myers: It's not very relaxing. But I do feel fortunate that I get to talk with Jonathan and play with him a little bit. Then I go back to work.

What time do you get home?

Dr. Myers: Most days it's 6:00 or 6:15.

Did the housekeeper cook?

Dr. Myers: She would throw a chicken in the oven.

Mr. Myers: Make salads.

Elizabeth: I remember when you came home for lunch with us, you'd be home for 10 minutes and then go back to work.

273

Dr. Myers: Yes. I just wanted to check in. I used to work an hour away. I kept the same job, but we moved closer [to the office] so I could be nearer to the family.

Did you give up a nicer house or—?

Dr. Myers: No, it didn't have that trade-off. It strapped us financially [because the new neighborhood was more expensive]. Scott and I have made a big point of putting the kids first in terms of seeing that they're not being sacrificed because of our careers. But that puts the two of you next and puts yourself last. You don't have the mental health of having time to just sit down and read a book or relax. That takes its toll.

Scott, was there ever a point at which you discussed whether or not you should be a dual-career family, or was it just understood?

Mr. Myers: We never really had any discussion. It wasn't really a choice that anybody made, other than that was the way it was going to be. I don't remember ever really consciously talking about it.

Dr. Myers: The discussions have really been about whose is the primary career and whose is the secondary career. It's an issue I'm still not totally comfortable with.

Whose career is more important?

Dr. Myers: Scott's. And we discussed that early on, even before we got married. He said his career would be more important and that's it.

Mr. Myers: I don't remember that fiat.

Dr. Myers: I do. I've chosen to develop my career as one that has flexibility. Far more than his does. I can get to their [school events] during the day, which I think is real important for kids.

Mother's Career

What about you girls? What do you think of the trade-offs your mother has made?

Elizabeth: She always worked. I can't really say what it would be like not to have her work.

Katherine: It doesn't seem like we had a significant loss. I've never felt any kind of hole out there that needs to be filled emotionally.

Elizabeth: We had housekeepers, baby sitters.

Dr. Myers: I think kids need some distance from their parents to grow. It's really important for kids to make mistakes, accept their mistakes and learn from them. I think that a real plus of my working is that you children are learning to be self-sufficient and feel good about decisions you make.

Katherine: It's true women can offer things professionally, for the advancement of society.

Elizabeth: It was also good that we had a role model. Mom always says when she was growing up, there were no sports or anything for girls. Your choices were to be a teacher, a nurse or a model.

Phyllis and Scott, Have there been any strains on your marriage?

Dr. Myers: We've discussed that really at length. What has been difficult on our relationship is the lack of nurturing. You have to be so focused on getting things done. At the dinner table, I'm talking about the schedule for tonight and tomorrow. There's not much humor in that. There's not much play or nurturing.

There is not a lot of time for just pure fun?

Dr. Myers: And spontaneity.

Mr. Myers: I think that's true. When two people are in careers where they have significant time demands on them—which both of ours clearly do—it limits the amount of time available for other purposes. A housekeeper can help with household chores, but there are certain logistics that only the parents can figure out. By the time you are finished, it's 10 o'clock at night.

How would you like things to be?

Dr. Myers: In the best of all worlds, it would be a 28-hour day. One more hour for sleeping, an hour more for the children, an hour more for my spouse, and an hour just to myself. You are so wasted by the end of the day, you really don't have time for each other. It becomes very much of a business relationship with what has to get done and what the next day will bring. The disposal needs fixing or whatever.

Mr. Myers: It's always something.

What would help?

Dr. Myers: One thing that I've noticed is that businesses are having small-group discussions or noon-time workshops where employees talk about these issues. I often give parenting workshops. Just being able to hear other people with the same concerns, and listen to how they cope, helps a lot. You don't feel so alone.

Is there anything you yourselves can do differently?

Dr. Myers: I can make fewer demands on what the house needs to look like. I'm afraid we may make excessive demands on [our daughters] to help out at home. I also need to back off on demands for the job. When you're at the top and you delegate authority, you expect everything to be handled the way you would have done it. At some point you have to back off. It may or may not be the way I would have done it, but I've got to accept it. It's also part of turning 40—learning to accept less as being more. . . .

Financial Freedom

We've talked a lot about the trade-offs. What do you see as the benefits of being a two-earner household?

Elizabeth: Vacations. I'm going to France this summer on the exchange program for school and I'm sure that is a benefit from having both parents work. Because no doubt it is very expensive.

What else?

Katherine: Maybe we couldn't afford this house if we didn't have two incomes. We go skiing. That was fun.

Where?

Mr. Myers: Colorado, Utah.

Dr. Myers: With dual careers, you have more mobility to make changes. It gives you the freedom to say, "Is this really what I want to do?" You aren't operating with the pressure of being the only breadwinner.

Elizabeth: That's one of the reasons I want to work when I grow up. If I get divorced or something, then I won't be depending on someone else. I'll have my own income and I can feel self-sufficient. I'd rather feel self-sufficient than let child support pay for my kids. I'll already have a job.

Katherine: I enjoy working. I'm goal-oriented. I know I want to do something professionally. I don't think I'd get the same satisfaction out of staying at home.

An Economic and Cultural Necessity

The rise in working mothers is a change that leaves the nuclear family intact—an internal, rather than an external, alteration. And it is a change that brings economic benefits, not disadvantages. In fact, the two-paycheck family, as even its detractors increasingly admit, is largely the product of economic necessity—as men's wages stagnate, divorce rates remain high, house prices rise and the costs of college soar.

The two-working-parent family is beginning to be considered a cultural necessity as well, rather than an ideologically charged choice. One needn't be a strident feminist to conclude, as Richard T. Gill and T. Grandon Gill do in *The Public Interest*, of all places, that "in a long life expectancy, low birth rate society, there really is no serious alternative to major lifelong working careers for most women. The career of full-time wife, mother and homemaker has simply ceased to be an adequate life project."

Ann Hulbert, *The New Republic*, August 16, 1993.

Would you like to have families as well as careers?

Katherine: I haven't decided.

Elizabeth: I'm going to have one. But I'm going to get my career started before I get married. I'd like to go into the medical-science field. I thought about becoming an obstetrician, but they can get sued a lot. I would really like to research cures and make some breakthroughs and find ways to help people that are sick.

Katherine: I think I'd like to go into law or politics. I think the country needs some leadership.

Would you two have done anything differently than your parents did?

Elizabeth: I think I will probably work full time. Mom only works part time.

Dr. Myers: I work *flexible* hours.

Elizabeth: But Dad works more hours than you do. You work more at home.

Dr. Myers: I feel a little piqued when I hear that. You say that because Dad works 50 to 60 hours a week. But if he worked a more-typical workweek of 40 hours, as I do, you wouldn't think that. The girls see me on the phone at home, and I'm working, but they don't necessarily consider that work.

How about you Scott? Any regrets?

Mr. Myers: No. Other than that I would have probably practiced in a place with better weather.

Dr. Myers: I don't know that I've fully come to terms with [putting many career goals aside]. I do regret it sometimes. If I'd write the book I know is in me, it [might] satisfy that part of my career energies.

"Women simply are no longer willing to sacrifice their roles as mothers to their careers."

Stay-at-Home Mothers Benefit Families

Elena Neuman

Increasingly, women are reconsidering career choices and leaving the workforce to care for their children at home, Elena Neuman argues in the following viewpoint. Neuman interviews several working mothers and experts who contend that a primary reason more mothers are staying home is to ensure the healthy development and well-being of their children. Many such mothers believe that working outside the home could cause their children to experience emotional and behavioral problems later in life. Neuman maintains that the failure of feminism to achieve such goals as quality day care and the sharing of child care responsibilities by fathers has also spurred women to become full-time mothers. Neuman is a freelance writer in Washington, D.C.

As you read, consider the following questions:

1. Who are the "new breed of full-time mothers," according to Neuman?
2. According to Arlene Rossen Cardozo, cited by Neuman, how did feminism fail to accommodate families?
3. According to the author, how has the status of housewives changed?

When Carlie Sorensen Dixon, a young partner in a Washington law firm, took a three-month maternity leave in 1987 for the birth of her first son, she fully intended to return to her clients and a flourishing tax law practice. Years later, she's still at home.

In 1993, three months after returning from her maternity leave, Jacquie Singleton, a nightclub manager in Tampa, Florida, decided to trade her sequin gowns and tuxedo suits for "baggy, stay-at-home mom clothes."

In Downers Grove, Illinois, Linda Rush is taking time off from her job as a manager for a direct-marketing company to raise her two children. She plans to resume her career when her youngest enters school.

As Americans debated the pros and cons of the 1993 Family and Medical Leave Act, the nanny problems of failed attorney general nominee Zoe Baird and former Vice President Dan Quayle's thoughts on family values, thousands of working women chose a traditional solution to their child care problems: They stayed home.

They are a new breed of full-time mothers. Far from the June Cleaver image of happy homemakers who give Tupperware parties and attend PTA meetings, these women are professionals who have decided, often at great financial sacrifice, to take a break from their careers to embark on what they consider a much more challenging and rewarding endeavor—raising their children. They are predominantly middle-class and married, with bachelor's or graduate degrees, and most came of age at the height of the feminist movement and have every intention of reentering the work force when their children start school.

Mothers Groups Abound

According to the network of mothers groups that formed over the past decade to represent them, the number of professional moms is skyrocketing. The membership of Illinois-based FE-MALE—Formerly Employed Mothers at the Leading Edge—grew 54 percent in 1993 and 60 percent in 1992. The 6-year-old organization, which has 2,000 members and 102 chapters nationally, recently changed its name from Formerly Employed Mothers at Loose Ends. "The old name no longer fits the mind-set of our members or women in general," says Rush, who is FEMALE's national publicity director.

In the past 3 years, the 20-year-old mothers organization MOPS International, or the Mothers of Preschoolers, has nearly doubled in size, with 28,000 members nationwide. Both Mothers First, a Washington-area support group for full-time mothers, and Mothers at Home, a 10-year-old group that publishes a 15,000-circulation newsletter called *Welcome Home*, claim unprecedented growth in membership since 1990. "The phone's been ringing off the hook," says Beth Osborne, communications chairwoman of Mothers First.

Other groups abound, such as Home by Choice, Moms Club, the National Association of Mothers' Centers and the Lawyers at Home Forum. And in early 1994, another mothers-at-home group was launched: The National MothersCare Network, the first national federation of full-time moms groups, will act as a watchdog against what members feel are inaccurate and derogatory portrayals of stay-at-homers and will attempt to publicize their image of modern motherhood. "We're not wealthy women who like to sit in front of soap operas all day and eat bonbons," says Dixon, who is helping to launch the group. "Most of us have given up substantial incomes in order to take on long days at home—without lunch or coffee breaks—with our kids."

P.C. VEY

" DON'T WORRY, YOU'RE MOTHER'S JUST ON THAT NEW WORK TWELVE HOURS A DAY, COME HOME AND COLLAPSE INTO YOUR FOOD' DIET. "

"There's definitely something new and subtle going on," says Barbara Dafoe Whitehead, vice president of the Institute for American Values, who specializes in family issues. "Confident women are now challenging some of the rigid tenets of what women should or shouldn't do with their work lives and family lives. I sense among younger women a much more critical attitude about all of the things that older feminists accepted as truth. There is a growing familism; we're beginning to rethink where our main values lie. And it's very recent—in the last two or three years."

Women Workers Decline

In 1991, for the first time this century, the percentage of women in the work force dropped, according to the Bureau of Labor Statistics. During the last half of 1990 and into the first quarter of 1991, 74 percent of women aged 20 to 44 participated in the labor force, down 0.5 percent from the year before. While women's work force participation jumped back in 1992, data show that the rate of increase in the 20 to 39 age group is slowing, according to bureau economist Howard Hayghe. "Mothers are finding alternative methods of employment that are allowing them to stay home more with their children," says Hayghe. "They're finding part-time work, home-based businesses and freelance work."

Many family researchers say the trend is much more pronounced than the bureau's data indicate, primarily because the agency counts individuals who work as little as one hour per week for profit or 15 hours or more without pay in a family business or on a farm. Mothers on extended maternity leave or those who baby-sit one night a week, do two hours of temp work, or tutor a friend's child for a nominal fee would all be considered part of the work force.

"One almost has to make a conscious effort to not be counted in order to escape inclusion in the BLS figures," says William Mattox, vice president for policy at the Family Research Council. "But if you look at recent polls, it becomes evident that at an attitudinal level, a change has definitely taken place."

A 1991 *Washington Post* poll found that 55 percent of Americans believed a child is likely to suffer if his mother works outside the home, up from 48 percent in 1989. A 1990 Gallup Poll for the *Los Angeles Times* showed that 73 percent of the public believed children fare best when they have a mother at home. And a 1990 Times-Mirror poll found that 73 percent of respondents believed too many children are being raised in day care, up from 68 percent in 1987.

In particular, women's attitudes toward their work and family have changed. In the past 3 years, Yankelovich Partners, a Connecticut consulting firm that studies societal changes and publishes an annual survey of working women, found striking changes in the attitudes of mothers toward their work. For 20 years, about 30 percent of women surveyed said they would quit their jobs to care for their children if they didn't need the money. In 1989, the number grew to 38 percent. By 1991, it had jumped to 56 percent.

The Failure of Feminism

"There has been a value shift lately," says Martha Bullen, coauthor of *Staying Home: From Full-Time Professional to Full-Time Parent*, which surveyed 600 stay-at-home mothers across the country. "In the eighties many women felt they ought to be out there competing with men and showing they could climb as high and fast as they could, perhaps to prove their feminist principles to themselves. But today, in the nineties, the emphasis is changing to the family. Women simply are no longer willing to sacrifice their roles as mothers to their careers."

But why now? As far back as 1981, feminist founding mother Betty Friedan said in *The Second Stage* that feminist theory must make room for the importance of families. And throughout the eighties, child care gurus from Dr. Benjamin Spock to T. Berry Brazelton have been warning about the ill effects of surrogate child care on children's psychological development.

Some attribute the new familism to the failure of feminist theory to adequately address the procreative side of women's lives. "Feminism has not accommodated the new thinking about family in its theory or rhetoric," says Arlene Rossen Cardozo, author of *Sequencing: A New Solution for Women Who Want Marriage, Career, and Family*, which advocates that women have a career and a family—just not at the same time. The term "sequencing" has now been adopted by theorists as a description for professional and other working women who take time off to raise children and then return to careers. "The feminist movement was never meant to embrace all women," says Cardozo. "Children were never factored into the original equation. Sure women can be like men if there aren't any children involved."

At its height in the seventies and early eighties, feminist careerism was based on three factors: changing society's attitudes about maternal care-giving; fathers sharing equally in child care responsibilities; and the availability of widespread, quality day care. None of these goals has been fulfilled.

According to national surveys, working women still bear the burden of child rearing and home maintenance. The amount of time fathers devote to primary child care has remained unchanged since 1965. In fact, a 1988 study by University of Virginia sociologists Steven Nock and Paul Kingston found that contrary to feminist hopes, fathers in one-income households spend more time with their children than do fathers in two-career homes. As a result, the eighties saw the rise of the so-called superwoman—the 10-hour-a-day working woman who would come home to a "second shift" involving child care, cooking and cleaning.

"We hear a lot of lip service to fathers' sharing equally in the tasks associated with parenting and house chores, and that's just not happening on a large scale," says Ellen Bravo, national executive director of 9to5 National Association of Working Women. "What society has really said to women is that having both a family and a job is something they're going to have to do alone. And that's a lot."

Many stay-at-home moms have decided to leave the work force after a series of child care difficulties ranging from undependable nannies to slipshod day care. In addition, the lack of flexible work arrangements such as job-sharing, flextime and tele-commuting jobs has left mothers without many options.

Ironclad Discipline

A family needs more than an impressive job title and a diploma in Latin: it demands commitment, real, dogged self-denial that brooks no competition. Women my age, who used to talk gravely of juggling family and career, have begun to realize that juggling gets tiring after a while, and if you catch the career and drop the family, it will break. . . .

Housewives, for all the love they bring to their work, are trained in the stern school of necessity. Children must be fed, must have clean clothes, must be washed and dressed and nursed when they're sick, every day, on time, whatever else has to give way; there is no argument and no reprieve. This ironclad discipline, which nothing but love can teach, turns the wheels of a million households, and is almost entirely lacking in the feckless and untrained graduates who seek jobs each year.

Kathleen Wagner, *Fidelity*, April 1992.

"At the moment, the progress of integrating family needs into the workplace is proceeding at a snail's pace," says Deborah Swiss, a consultant on work-family issues and coauthor of *Women and the Work/Family Dilemma*, which surveyed more than 900 female graduates of Harvard's law, business and medical schools. "That's why many women are leaving the workplace."

Swiss found that even among the nation's most elite professional women, there is frustration and confusion over how to bridge work and family. While 85 percent of the Harvard professionals said they believed reducing the hours of work would be detrimental to a woman's career, no less than 70 percent of them decreased their hours after their first child was born. A surprising 25 percent of MBA respondents left the workplace entirely. Swiss also found that the women who left the work force had made a more comfortable peace with their decision than had the part-timers.

Baby Busters

The coming of age of Generation X, successors to the baby boomers, has also contributed to the stay-at-home trend, according to William Dunn, author of *The Baby Bust: A Generation Comes of Age*. People in their 20s are the latchkey kids, children of divorce and children of full-time career mothers who yearn for the family lives they feel they missed. "They did not grow up in the Ozzie and Harriet family, and they're well aware of what they missed," says Dunn.

Moreover, because they are entering the work force during a period of slow economic growth and job insecurity, these baby busters are less wedded to jobs and careers than were the baby boomers. "All this makes them more introspective, more independent and, in terms of the women, less inhibited about making the choice to drop out of the economy for several years to raise a family," says Dunn. In fact, a 1990 *Time* magazine poll on the twentysomething generation found that 63 percent of 18- to 29-year-olds hope to spend more time with their children than their parents spent with them.

"Thinking people are looking around at all of the problems children and youngsters are facing in American society and realizing that children aren't faring well in our country," says Brenda Hunter, a psychologist specializing in parent-infant attachment and the author of *Home By Choice*. "The fastest-growing segment of the criminal population consists of children. The SAT scores have dropped 80 points in the last 20 years and the suicide rate has tripled for 15- to 24-year-olds. People aren't stupid, they're concerned."

According to Hunter, research since 1980 on infants in day care shows that babies placed even in good-quality nonparental care for more than 20 hours a week are at risk for emotional and behavioral problems later in life. A Texas study of 236 third-graders who had spent more than 30 hours a week in day care during infancy found that the children were harder to discipline and had poorer work habits and peer relationships than did children who stayed at home. And Jay Belsky, a human development professor at Pennsylvania State University who once maintained that day care was harmless, now believes that early and extensive day care poses a serious risk to healthy psychological development.

Says Osborne of Mothers First, "A lot of people I know are

seeing the problems that we're having in society and saying, 'Maybe parents being at home could have a beneficial impact.'"

Happy at Home

But above and beyond concerns that their children won't develop well psychologically, most mothers who choose to stay home say they do so primarily because they feel they would be missing their kids' wonder years if they worked. "I'm not home just because I think my children need me," says Julie Heflin, a Washington lawyer who is caring full-time for her two preschool sons. "I feel there's a big part of me that would miss out if I were at work, even if somebody could do exactly the same job with my kids as I could."

These women talk about personal fulfillment, contentment and quality time. They talk about meeting diverse women through mothers organizations and learning new skills. "My world has completely changed," says Dixon. "It's gone from a world where I was governed by external demands and ideas of success, identity and power to a very comfortable, happy, low-key life where my world is governed by being a good parent to my kids and leading a balanced, interesting life.

"Our society has given us the message that a career is the road to happiness," she continues. "And I wasn't unhappy practicing law. But it didn't hold a candle to this. These three kids are five times more interesting than a legal problem or extra money in the bank. Everything's different than I thought."

Former professionals such as Dixon, as well as sociologists, are finding that the stigma associated with staying home—what they call the "I'm just a housewife" syndrome—seems to be fading. "There's no question," says Bullen, "that making this choice is easier today than it was five years ago."

Hunter agrees: "I don't think that women at home feel as downtrodden or as beaten down by cultural attitudes as they did in the last two decades. There's been a real shift away from feminist dogma toward individual preferences."

If the [recent] past is any indication, women in increasing numbers will leave the work force—temporarily—to devote themselves to their children. At least that's what the mothers groups would like. "Hopefully, the exodus will continue and we'll be large enough in number to one day be a force to be reckoned with," says Heflin, cochairwoman of the Washington-based Lawyers at Home Forum. "Right now people look at us cockeyed and say, 'You did what?' But I think it's going to be more common, and society will support it."

Periodical Bibliography

The following articles have been selected to supplement the diverse views presented in this chapter.

Joshua Abramowitz "The Democrats' Welfare Trap," *National Review*, April 4, 1994.

Teresa Amott "The War on Welfare: Clinton's Carrots and Sticks," *Dollars & Sense*, November/December 1993.

Christopher J. Check "Rediscovering Family in the Information Age," *The Family in America*, July 1994. Available from the Rockford Institute, 934 N. Main St., Rockford, IL 61103-7061.

Ann Hulbert "Home Repairs: Parents, Work, and the Durability of the Family," *The New Republic*, August 16, 1993.

Mickey Kaus "Tough Enough: A Promising Start on Welfare Reform," *The New Republic*, April 25, 1994.

Peter T. Kilborn "More Women Take Low-Wage Jobs Just So Their Families Can Get By," *The New York Times*, March 13, 1994.

Karen Levine "Is Today's Workplace Really Family-Friendly?" *Parents*, August 1993.

Beth Lovern "Confessions of a Welfare Mom," *Utne Reader*, July/August 1994.

William R. Mattox Jr. "The Family-Friendly Corporation: Strengthening the Ties That Bind," *Family Policy*, November 1992. Available from the Family Research Council, 700 13th St. NW, Suite 500, Washington, DC 20005.

Karen Moderow "Moms at Home," *Moody*, February 1994. Available from the Moody Bible Institute, 820 N. LaSalle Blvd., Chicago, IL 60610.

Theresa Monsour "Friendly Persuasion," *Working Mother*, February 1994.

Revolutionary Worker "Clinton's Welfare Warfare on the Poor," June 26, 1994. Available from PO Box 3486, Merchandise Mart, Chicago IL 60654.

Sue Shellenbarger "Family Feud," *The Wall Street Journal*, June 21, 1993.

Jill Zook-Jones "The Maternal Imperative," an interview with psychologist/infant specialist Brenda Hunter, *Christianity Today*, March 7, 1994.

For Further Discussion

Chapter 1

1. Ray Marshall and Marc Tucker argue that the U.S. education system should provide students with work skills. Peter Shaw contends that the purpose of education is to produce, not skilled workers, but "citizens capable of thinking on their own." Do you consider education a high priority? Why or why not? What role do you think education will play in your future?

2. Wilfried Prewo uses unemployment statistics to bolster his argument for youth apprenticeship programs. Kenneth A. Couch cites employment statistics to back up his opposition to such programs. Whose use of statistics is more convincing? Why?

3. Robert B. Reich uses anecdotal examples to illustrate his belief that technological advances have raised the demand for workers with greater skills. John B. Judis quotes statistics purporting a surplus of college-educated workers to counter Reich's argument that workers with more skills are needed. Which type of argument do you find more compelling? Why?

Chapter 2

1. Chuck Williams is identified as a member of the National Committee of the Communist Party, USA. Does this information influence your assessment of Williams's argument that the contingent workforce is a function of corporate exploitation of workers? Explain.

2. Many commentators advocate government intervention to create jobs and reduce unemployment. Others believe that free-market mechanisms, not government intervention, are the most effective means of achieving high employment and low unemployment. Based on the viewpoints in this chapter, do you believe that the effects of government intervention on employment are positive, negative, mixed, or negligible? Give two examples to support your conclusion.

Chapter 3

1. Richard Edwards concludes that labor unions are declining both in membership and in influence. John B. Judis concludes that unions may be on the upswing. They each use a different type of evidence to reach their conclusions. Whose evidence do you find more compelling? Explain why.

2. On what basis does Kevin Clarke conclude that unions are still necessary? What kind of evidence does he use to support his conclusion? What regions of the country and what industries does Clarke argue need unions the most? Why?

3. In his viewpoint, economics professor Leo Troy predicts a gloomy future for unions. He says they "will be limited to a few industries" and their "impact on the economy and society in general will be substantially reduced." On what kind of evidence does Troy base his argument? How and why are his beliefs different from those of Kevin Clarke?

4. Irving Bluestone is the retired vice president of the United Auto Workers. He is also a professor of labor studies. Barry Bluestone is a professor of political economy. How are their backgrounds reflected in their viewpoint? Compare their point of view with that of Mike Parker and Jane Slaughter. Both sets of authors support unions. What might account for the differences in their conclusions about labor-management partnerships?

5. Labor secretary Robert B. Reich argues that the Wagner Act has become a tool for corporations to undermine unions. *Nation's Business* writer David Warner asserts that without the Wagner Act, businesses would fail because of lost productivity or skyrocketing labor costs. Whose argument do you find more compelling? Why?

Chapter 4

1. Gertrude Ezorsky asserts that affirmative action is an appropriate means of compensating blacks for the past injustice of slavery. Herman Belz contends that affirmative action is not an appropriate compensation for past injury because it compensates people who were not directly harmed by the injustice. Do you believe affirmative action is an appropriate compensation for slavery? Why or why not?

2. Elaine Sorensen argues that the comparable worth policy implemented in Minnesota achieved its goal of increasing the pay of women relative to that of men. Steven E. Rhoads maintains that the policy in Minnesota harmed employee relations and disrupted the free-market mechanism by which rising and falling wages rectify shortages and surpluses of labor. Assuming that both of these assessments are true, do you think comparable worth policies should be more widely adopted? Explain.

3. Edward E. Barr contends that apprenticeships would foster economic and racial equality by providing poor and minority

youths with useful skills and job opportunities. Harvey Kantor argues that apprenticeships would promote inequality by channeling poor and minority youths into vocationally oriented programs instead of providing them with the academic education offered to other students. Which argument do you find more convincing? Why?

4. Barr is president and CEO of a large corporation. Kantor is an associate university professor who specializes in educational history and policy. Cite one passage from each of their viewpoints in which you believe these professional affiliations are reflected.

Chapter 5

1. On what aspects of welfare reform do Donna Shalala and Neil Gilbert agree? How do they disagree? How is welfare failing or succeeding, according to the authors? Which makes the more persuasive case, and why?

2. John J. Adams writes that commitment to both family and career is possible but more fatiguing than ever before. What do you think are the hardships confronting workers who try to balance family and job needs? What are some of the difficult choices these workers often face?

3. Phyllis and Scott Myers express how difficult it is to meet family and career responsibilities. Despite their high income, the Myerses face many of the same dilemmas as other full-time working couples. Are there any similarities between the Myers family and your family or those of your peers? Explain.

Organizations to Contact

The editors have compiled the following list of organizations concerned with the issues debated in this book. The descriptions are derived from materials provided by the organizations. All have publications or information available for interested readers. The list was compiled on the date of publication of the present volume; names, addresses, and phone numbers may change. Be aware that many organizations take several weeks or longer to respond to inquiries, so allow as much time as possible.

American Association for Affirmative Action (AAAA)
11 E. Hubbard St., Suite 200
Chicago, IL 60611
(312) 329-2512

The AAAA is a group of equal opportunity/affirmative action officers concerned with the implementation of affirmative action in employment and in education nationwide. Its publications include the quarterly *Newsletter*.

American Economic Foundation (AEF)
50 Public Square, Suite 1300
Cleveland, OH 44113
(216) 321-6547

The foundation is a nonprofit research and educational organization that advocates free-market economic priciples. It encourages comprehension and appreciation of the private enterprise system through individual economic self-education. It publishes the economic primer *How We Live*, the leaflet "Ten Pillars of Economic Wisdom," and various booklets and pamphlets.

American Federation of Labor–Congress of Industrial Organizations (AFL-CIO)
815 16th St. NW
Washington, DC 20006
(202) 637-5000

The AFL-CIO is a federation of national and local labor unions. It organizes labor unions, and its various committees and departments conduct research and education services for unions. Its publications include a biweekly newsletter, *News*.

Association for Union Democracy
500 State St.
Brooklyn, NY 11217
(718) 855-6650

This group works to ensure the legal rights of union and other labor organization members and advocates greater democracy within unions. It publishes and disseminates literature on the legal rights of workers and union members, and it consults with and educates union members to help them reform their organizations. Its other publications include the bimonthly journal *Union Democracy Review* and many books.

Brookings Institution
1775 Massachusetts Ave. NW
Washington, DC 20036-2188
(202) 797-6000

The institution is a private, nonprofit organization devoted to nonpartisan research, education, and publication in economics, government, foreign policy, and the social sciences. Its principal purpose is to contribute informed perspectives on the current and emerging public policy issues facing the American people. Its publications include the *Brookings Review*.

Center on National Labor Policy
5211 Port Royal Rd., Suite 103
North Springfield, VA 22151
(703) 321-9180

This public policy group promotes principles of free enterprise in labor policy making. It opposes what it views as the excessive power of unions, seeks to stop government grants to unions and government interference in and regulation of labor policy, and strives to prevent public employee strikes. It publishes the quarterly *Insider's Report*.

The Conference Board
845 Third Ave.
New York, NY 10022
(212) 759-0900

This fact-finding institution conducts research and publishes studies on business economics and management. Its Work and Family Information Center researches changes in work and family relationships. Its publications include the monthly *Across the Board*, the monthly *Conference Board Briefing*, and other specialized journals.

Economic Affairs Bureau
One Summer St.
Somerville, MA 02143
(617) 628-8411

The bureau publishes and distributes educational materials that interpret current economic information from a progressive, socialist perspective. It publishes the monthly *Dollars & Sense*.

Economic Policy Institute (EPI)
1730 Rhode Island Ave. NW, Suite 200
Washington, DC 20036
(202) 775-8810

EPI conducts research and promotes education programs on economic policy issues, particularly the economics of poverty, unemployment, and American industry. It supports organized labor and believes that government should invest in infrastructure and education to improve

America's economy. It publishes periodic *Briefing Papers*, *Studies*, and the triannual Economic Policy Institute *Journal*.

Employment Policies Institute (EPI)
607 14th St. NW, Suite 1110
Washington, DC 20005
(202) 347-5178

EPI is a nonprofit research organization that believes entry-level employment opportunities often provide the best job-training and education programs for young Americans and those seeking to move from welfare to work. It also believes that a government-set minimum wage destroys these opportunities. EPI publishes *Employment Effects of Minimum and Subminimum Wages*.

Employment Policy Foundation
1015 15th St. NW, Suite 1200
Washington, DC 20005
(202) 789-8685

This educational arm of the Labor Policy Association and the Equal Employment Advisory Council researches employment policies, produces studies on employment, and conducts seminars on equal opportunity employment issues. It promotes the interests of employers regarding federal equal opportunity/affirmative action practices. It publishes numerous books and studies, including *Managing Diversity in an Equal Opportunity Workplace*.

Families and Work Institute
330 Seventh Ave., 14th Fl.
New York, NY 10001
(212) 465-2044

The institute is a nonprofit research and planning organization dedicated to developing new approaches to balancing the continuing need for workplace productivity with the changing needs of American families. More than forty research reports are available for sale, including *The Changing Workforce: Highlights of the National Study, Work and Family Trends*, and *An Examination of the Impact of Family-Friendly Policies on the Glass Ceiling*. For a list of publications please write or call.

Family Research Council
700 13th St. NW, Suite 500
Washington, DC 20005
(202) 393-2100
fax (202) 393-2134

The council provides information to the public on issues such as parental responsibility, the impact of working parents on children, the effects on families of the tax system, and community support for single parents. Its publications include the monthly *Washington Watch*, the bimonthly *Family Policy*, and reports and policy analyses.

Human Resources Development Institute
815 16th St. NW
Washington, DC 20006
(202) 638-3912

This training institute of the AFL-CIO works to ensure that labor unions fully participate in employment and training programs funded under the Job Training Partnership Act (JTPA). Its publications include the quarterly *Accountability* and the bimonthly newsletter *HRDI Advisory*.

Industrial Relations Research Association (IRRA)
7226 Social Science Bldg.
University of Wisconsin
Madison, WI 53706-1393
(608) 262-2762

The IRRA is a nonpartisan membership organization that brings together those involved in academics, labor law, public policy, union administration, and economics to share ideas, issues, research, and practices in labor relations. It publishes an annual *IRRA Research Volume* as well as a quarterly newsletter.

Institute of Labor and Industrial Relations (ILIR)
University of Michigan
1111 E. Catherine St.
Ann Arbor, MI 48109-2054
(313) 763-1187

The ILIR conducts research in the informal economy of workers who make their living outside of normal work patterns, forecasts employment and unemployment trends, and conducts education and training services for the professional and personal development of workers. It publishes numerous books and policy papers that focus on low-wage work in the inner cities.

International Center for Research on Women (ICRW)
1717 Massachusetts Ave. NW, Suite 302
Washington, DC 20036
(202) 797-0007
fax (202) 797-0020

ICRW is a nonprofit organization dedicated to promoting women's full participation in social and economic development. It conducts research and analysis aimed at improving the situation of poor women in developing countries. Its numerous publications cover the topics of woman-headed households, economics, and women in economic development.

International Labor Rights Education and Research Fund
100 Maryland Ave. NE
Washington, DC 20002
(202) 544-7198

The fund's research and education programs work to promote U.S. trade policies that ensure economic justice for workers in developing countries. It publishes the quarterly *Worker Rights News* as well as books, resource material, and articles in other periodicals.

Labor Policy Association
1015 15th St. NW
Washington, DC 20005
(202) 789-8670

This association of human resource officers conducts research on matters relating to federal employment policy and maintains a task force to study current employment issues. It publishes the quarterly *Status of Issues*.

Labor Research Association
145 W. 28th St.
New York, NY 10001-6191
(212) 714-1677

This association supports labor unions by conducting research and compiling statistics on economic and political issues. It publishes periodic studies and reports and the bimonthly *Economic Notes*.

National Alliance of Business
1201 New York Ave. NW
Washington, DC 20005-3917
(202) 289-2888
fax (202) 289-1303

The alliance works to shape social policies that will improve education, strengthen job training, and instill in workers the values essential to success in the modern workplace. It publishes the monthly *WorkAmerica* newsletter, the biweekly *Business Currents* report, and numerous books on education reform, workforce quality, and job training.

National Association of Private Industry Councils
1201 New York Ave. NW, Suite 800
Washington, DC 20005
(202) 289-2950

This association of private industry councils seeks to develop job-training opportunities in the private sector for the unemployed and economically disadvantaged. Its publications include the monthly newsletter *NAPIC Reports On*.

National Center for Employee Ownership
1201 Martin Luther King Blvd.
Oakland, CA 94612
(510) 272-9461

This nonprofit information and education organization, whose membership includes companies, unions, and academics, promotes an increased awareness and understanding of employee-owned companies. It publishes the bimonthly *Employee Ownership Report* newsletter, the quarterly *Journal of Employee Ownership Law and Finance*, and the books *Employee Ownership Reader* and *Creating an Ownership Style of Management*.

National Committee on Pay Equity (NCPE)
1126 16th St. NW, Suite 411
Washington, DC 20036
(202) 331-7406

NCPE is a national coalition of labor, women's, and civil rights organizations and individuals working to eliminate sex- and race-based wage discrimination and to achieve pay equity. Its publications include a quarterly newsletter, *Newsnotes*, and numerous books and briefing papers on the issue of pay equity.

National Employment Law Project
475 Riverside Dr., Suite 240
New York, NY 10115
(212) 870-2121

The project implements litigation and advocates policies to promote the employment rights of the poor and disabled and to fight employment discrimination and abusive discharge. It publishes the quarterly *Employment Law News* as well as books and monographs on employment law.

National Institute for Work and Learning
1255 23rd St. NW, Suite 400
Washington, DC 20037
(202) 862-8845

The institute believes that the full development of human resources demands that education and work be treated as lifelong pursuits. It seeks to promote active collaboration between institutions of learning and work. Its projects include Partnerships for Youth Transitions and Worklife Education and Training, and its publications include numerous books and studies.

National Right to Work Committee
8001 Braddock Rd., Suite 500
Springfield, VA 22160
(703) 321-9820

This labor reform group conducts research and education programs to promote the belief that people should not be compelled to join labor unions in order to obtain jobs. It publishes the monthly *National Right to Work Newsletter* and the quarterly *Insiders Report*.

New Ways to Work
149 Ninth St.
San Francisco, CA 94103
(415) 552-1000

Seeking to create a work world that better responds to the needs of workers, this group promotes the concepts of flextime, job sharing, work sharing, and compressed workweeks. Its publications include the quarterly *Work Times* and many reports, studies, and brochures.

9to5 National Association of Working Women
614 Superior Ave. NW
Cleveland, OH 44113-1387
(216) 566-9308
fax (216) 566-0192

The association is the leading membership organization for working women. It utilizes class-action lawsuits and public information campaigns to achieve change on issues such as discrimination against pregnant women and sexual harassment in the workplace, computer safety, and pay equity. It publishes books and reports on issues such as contingent work and sexual harassment.

Public Service Research Council
1761 Business Center Dr., Suite 230
Reston, VA 22090
(703) 438-3966

This lobbying organization conducts research and public affairs programs on public sector (government) employment, specifically on such issues as strikes, unions, and political spending. It opposes unionism in the public sector. The council publishes the monthly newsletter *Forewarned*.

Rockford Institute
934 Main St.
Rockford, IL 61103-7061
(815) 964-5811

The institute advocates traditional roles for men and women and maintains that mothers who work or place their children in day care harm their children. It publishes the monthlies *Family in America* and *Religion and Society Report*.

U. S. Department of Health and Human Services
200 Independence Ave. SW
Washington, DC 20201
(202) 619-0257

The secretary of health and human services advises the president on health, welfare, and income security plans, policies, and programs of the federal government. The department's many administrations and agencies can provide information and statistics on children and families, health care, or social security and welfare/workfare.

U. S. Department of Labor
200 Constitution Ave. NW
Washington, DC 20210
(202) 219-6411

The Department of Labor administers a variety of federal labor laws guaranteeing workers' rights, a minimum wage, freedom from discrimination, and unemployment and workers' compensation insurance. Its public affairs office provides information on the department's policies and actions.

W.E. Upjohn Institute for Employment Research
300 S. Westnedge Ave.
Kalamazoo, MI 49007-4686
(616) 343-5541

Funded by the nonprofit W.E. Upjohn Unemployment Trustee Corporation, this institute studies the causes and effects of unemployment, ways of insuring against unemployment, family employment issues, labor relations, and workforce equality. It publishes numerous books, monographs, and national and local studies, and it compiles statistics on unemployment.

Wider Opportunities for Women (WOW)
1325 G St. NW
Washington, DC 20005
(202) 638-3143

WOW works to expand employment opportunities for women by overcoming sex-stereotypic education and training, work segregation, and discrimination in employment practices and wages. It publishes *Women at Work* periodically as well as books and fact sheets.

Workers' Defense League (WDL)
218 W. 40th St., Rms. 203-204
New York, NY 10018
(212) 730-7412

This labor-oriented civil rights organization conducts educational campaigns to defend workers' rights and provides legal counseling to workers on employment-related problems. It publishes the quarterly *WDL News* as well as reports and pamphlets on workers' legal rights.

Work in America Institute, Inc.
700 White Plains Rd.
Scarsdale, NY 10583-5058
(914) 472-9600
fax (914) 472-9606

The institute strives to improve U.S. productivity and the quality of working life through national research and a membership that brings together leaders from labor, management, government, and academia. Its publications include numerous books and policy studies and the monthly *Work in America* newsletter. It also provides an information research service.

Bibliography of Books

Katharine G. Abraham and Susan N. Houseman — *Job Security in America: Lessons from Germany.* Washington, DC: Brookings Institution, 1993.

Teresa L. Amott — *Caught in the Crisis: Women and the U.S. Economy Today.* New York: Monthly Review Press, 1993.

Eileen Appelbaum and Rosemary Batt — *The New American Workplace: Transforming Work Systems in the United States.* Ithaca, NY: ILR Press, 1994.

Lotte Bailyn — *Breaking the Mold: Women, Men, and Time in the New Corporate World.* New York: Free Press, 1993.

S. Anthony Baron — *Violence in the Workplace: A Prevention and Management Guide for Business.* Ventura, CA: Pathfinder Publishing, 1993.

Herman Belz — *Equality Transformed: A Quarter Century of Affirmative Action.* New Brunswick, NJ: Transaction Publishers, 1991.

Francine Blau and Marianne Ferber — *The Economics of Women, Men and Work.* Englewood Cliffs, NJ: Prentice-Hall, 1986.

Barry Bluestone and Irving Bluestone — *Negotiating the Future: A Labor Perspective on American Business.* New York: Basic Books, 1992.

Rae Lesser Blumberg, ed. — *Gender, Family, and Economy: The Triple Overlap.* Newbury Park, CA: Sage, 1991.

Harry Browne and Beth Sims — *Runaway America: U.S. Jobs and Factories on the Move.* Albuquerque, NM: Resource Center Press, 1993.

Allan C. Carlson — *From Cottage to Work Station: The Family's Search for Social Harmony in the Industrial Age.* San Francisco: Ignatius Press, 1993.

Susan D. Clayton and Faye J. Crosby — *Justice, Gender, and Affirmative Action.* Ann Arbor: University of Michigan Press, 1992.

Joseph F. Coates, Jennifer Jarratt, and John B. Mahsiffe — *Future Work: Seven Critical Forces Reshaping Work and the Work Force in North America.* San Francisco: Jossey-Bass, 1990.

Dorothy Sue Cobble — *Women and Unions: Forging a Partnership.* Ithaca, NY: ILR Press, 1993.

Ellis Cose	*The Rage of a Privileged Class: Why Are Middle-Class Blacks Angry? Why Should America Care?* New York: HarperCollins, 1993.
Robert W. Crandall	*Manufacturing on the Move.* Washington, DC: Brookings Institution, 1993.
Kenneth C. Crowe	*Collision: How the Rank and File Took Back the Teamsters.* New York: Scribner, 1993.
Peter F. Drucker	*Post-Capitalist Society.* New York: HarperCollins, 1993.
Richard Edwards	*Rights at Work: Employment Relations in the Post-Union Era.* Washington, DC: Brookings Institution, 1993.
Paula England	*Comparable Worth: Theories and Evidence.* New York: Aldine de Gruyter, 1992.
Richard Allen Epstein	*Forbidden Grounds: The Case Against Employment Discrimination Laws.* Cambridge, MA: Harvard University Press, 1992.
Gertrude Ezorsky	*Racism and Justice: The Case for Affirmative Action.* Ithaca, NY: Cornell University Press, 1991.
Ben Fine	*Women's Employment and the Capitalist Family.* New York: Routledge, 1992.
Thomas Geoghegan	*Which Side Are You On? Trying to Be for Labor When It's Flat on Its Back.* New York: Farrar, Straus & Giroux, 1991.
Claudia Goldin	*Understanding the Gender Gap: An Economic History of American Women.* New York: Oxford University Press, 1990.
Philip Harvey	*Securing the Right to Employment.* Princeton, NJ: Princeton University Press, 1989.
Barry T. Hirsch	*Labor Unions and the Economic Performance of Firms.* Kalamazoo, MI: W.E. Upjohn, 1991.
Jane C. Hood, ed.	*Men, Work, and Family.* Newbury Park, CA: Sage, 1993.
Gerald Horne	*Reversing Discrimination: The Case for Affirmative Action.* New York: International Publishers, 1992.
Mickey Kaus	*The End of Equality.* New York: Basic Books, 1992.
Len Krimerman and Frank Lindenfield, eds.	*When Workers Decide: Workplace Democracy Takes Root in North America.* Philadelphia: New Society Publishers, 1992.

Paul Krugman

The Age of Diminished Expectations: U.S. Economic Policy in the 1990s. Revised and updated edition. Cambridge, MA: MIT Press, 1994.

Louise Lamphere, Alex Stepick, and Guillermo Grenier, eds.

Newcomers in the Workplace: Immigrants and the Restructuring of the U.S. Economy. Philadelphia: Temple University Press, 1994.

Martin J. Levitt with Terry Conrow

Confessions of a Union Buster. New York: Crown, 1993.

Frederick R. Lynch

Invisible Victims: White Males and the Crisis of Affirmative Action. Westport, CT: Greenwood Press, 1989.

Ray Marshall and Marc Tucker

Thinking for a Living: Education and the Wealth of Nations. New York: Basic Books, 1992.

Lawrence Mishel and Jaqueline Simon

The State of Working America, 1992-93. Armonk, NY: M.E. Sharpe, 1993.

Lawrence Mishel and Ruy A. Teixeira

The Myth of the Coming Labor Shortage: Jobs, Skills, and Incomes of America's Workforce 2000. Washington, DC: Economic Policy Institute, 1991.

Lawrence Mishel and Paula B. Voos, eds.

Unions and Economic Competitiveness. Armonk, NY: M.E. Sharpe, 1992.

Phyllis Moen

Women's Two Roles: A Contemporary Dilemma. New York: Auburn House, 1992.

Ann M. Morrison

The New Leaders: Guidelines on Leadership Diversity in America. San Francisco: Jossey-Bass, 1992.

Ann M. Morrison et al.

Breaking the Glass Ceiling: Can Women Reach the Top of America's Largest Corporations? Updated edition. Reading, MA: Addison-Wesley, 1992.

Cynthia Negry

Gender, Time, and Reduced Work. Albany: State University of New York Press, 1993.

Russell Nieli, ed.

Racial Preference and Racial Justice: The New Affirmative Action Controversy. Washington, DC: Ethics and Public Policy Center, 1991.

William E. Nothdurft

School Works: Reinventing Public Schools to Create the Workforce of the Future. Washington, DC: Brookings Institution, 1990.

Robert B. Reich

The Work of Nations: Preparing Ourselves for 21st-Century Capitalism. New York: Knopf, 1991.

Steven E. Rhoads

Incomparable Worth: Pay Equity Meets the Market. New York: Cambridge University Press, 1993.

James C. Robinson

Toil and Toxics: Workplace Struggles and Political Strategies for Occupational Health. Berkeley: University of California Press, 1991.

Juliet B. Schor

The Overworked American: The Unexpected Decline of Leisure. New York: HarperCollins, 1991.

Isaac Shapiro and Robert Greenstein

Making Work Pay: The Unfinished Agenda. Washington, DC: Center on Budget and Policy Priorities, 1993.

Helen E. Sheehan and Richard P. Wedeen, eds.

Toxic Circles: Environmental Hazards from the Workplace to the Community. New Brunswick, NJ: Rutgers University Press, 1993.

Arthur B. Shostak

Robust Unionism: Innovations in the Labor Movement. Ithaca, NY: ILR Press, 1991.

Richard Lewis Siegel

Employment and Human Rights: The International Dimension. Philadelphia: University of Pennsylvania Press, 1994.

Elaine Sorensen

Comparable Worth: Is It a Worthy Policy? Princeton, NJ: Princeton University Press, 1994.

Elaine Sorensen

Exploring the Reasons Behind the Narrowing Gender Gap in Earnings. Washington, DC: Urban Institute Press, 1991.

Christopher L. Tomlins and Andrew J. King, eds.

Labor Law in America: Historical and Critical Essays. Baltimore: Johns Hopkins University Press, 1992.

Melvin I. Urofsky

A Conflict of Rights: The Supreme Court and Affirmative Action. New York: Scribner, 1991.

Margaret Weir

Politics and Jobs: The Boundaries of Employment in the United States. Princeton, NJ: Princeton University Press, 1992.

301

Index

Abrams, Charles, 170
Adams, John L., 254
Aetna Life & Casualty Company
  work-family policies, 266
affirmative action
  and blacks
    do not all benefit, 172, 182, 184
    can end segregation, 171, 172,
      176, 183
    can harm blacks, 176, 218
  as compensation, 169-72, 176
  is ineffective, 182
  connection to diversity
    management, 217
  denies basic rights, 181-82, 185
  Executive Order 11246, 192
  harms the community, 181-82, 185
  promotes equality, 168-76
    con, 177-85
  rationale for, 169-70
  as reverse discrimination, 174,
    178-81, 183-84, 215, 217
  undermines self-respect, 176, 184
Age Discrimination in Employment
  Act of 1967
  effect on business, 77
Agile Corporations, 149-51
Aid to Families with Dependent
  Children (AFDC)
  as necessary, 249-51
  problems with, 242-43
  reforms for, 251-52
air-traffic controllers
  and labor unions, 115, 118
Amalgamated Clothing and Textile
  Workers Union (ACTWU), 125
American Airlines
  unions for, 114, 118
American Business Collaborative for
  Quality Dependent Care, 259-60
American Federation of Government
  Employees, 152
American Federation of Labor–
  Congress of Industrial
  Organizations (AFL-CIO), 92
  changes in leadership, 119
  and Clinton administration, 131-32,
    160
  and labor law, 110
  Organizing Institute, 114
American Federation of State, County,
  and Municipal Employees

(AFSCME), 115, 118
American Federation of Teachers, 115
Americans with Disabilities Act, 77
Ansberry, Clare, 76
Applebaum, Eileen, 84, 85, 87
Apple Computer Inc.
  diversity management in, 214
Apprenticeship for Adulthood
  (Hamilton), 220
apprenticeship programs
  benefits of, 72
  costs of, 229
  as effective, 29-33, 222-27
  as ineffective, 34-40, 229-36
  should begin in high school, 221-22,
    227
  teach work ethic, 224-25, 227
  would increase opportunities for
    youths, 219-27
    con, 228-36
AT&T
  discrimination cases, 207
  labor agreements, 152
  work-family programs, 259
Australia
  comparable worth in, 195-202
Autrey, James, 261
Avon Products Inc.
  diversity management in, 205, 214

baby boomers, 23, 284
Baby Bust: A Generation Comes of Age,
  The (Dunn), 284
Bailey, Thomas, 233
Baird, Zoe, 279
Bakke, Allan, 175
Baltimore Works, 46
Bandow, Doug, 91
Bane, Mary Jo, 243
Bank of America, 83
Barr, Edward E., 219
Becker, Gary, 35, 39
Belsky, Jay, 284
Belz, Herman, 177
Benn, Jim, 125
Bensinger, Richard, 114
Bernstein, Aaron, 140
Beyond Race and Gender (Thomas),
  215, 217
Biller, Moe, 118
Birnbaum, Philip, 208
Bishop, John, 44

Bittker, Boris I., 170
blacks
  affirmative action for
    can be harmful, 176
    is justified, 168-76
      con, 177-85
  difficulty finding work, 231, 233, 234
  discrimination in job market, 233
  unemployment rates, 231, 234
Blackstone, William, 171
Blake, Stacy, 204, 208
Bluestone, Barry, 117, 137
Bluestone, Irving, 137
Boxill, Bernard, 171
Bravo, Ellen, 283
Brazelton, T. Berry, 282
Brimelow, Peter, 181
Brown v. Board of Education of Topeka, 169
Bullen, Martha, 282
Bunzel, John, 215
Bureau of Labor Statistics (BLS)
  college degrees and jobs, 52
  contingent workers, 83, 85
  immigrant workers, 124
  unions and wages, 129
  women in workplace decreasing, 281
Bush, George
  and labor unions, 118, 133, 134
business
  contingent workforce benefits, 85
  diversity management benefits, 203-11
  government regulations hinder, 75, 77
  and permanent striker replacements
    should be allowed, 158-63
      con, 154-57
  supports work-family programs, 254-61
      con, 262-68

Canada
  comparable worth programs, 192
Card, David, 97, 98, 99
Cardozo, Arlene Rossen, 282
Carey, Ron, 116, 118
Carter, Jimmy, 134, 136, 192
Catalyst, 267
Catchings, W., 60
Center for Employment Training (CET), 45
Chapman, Stephen, 91
child care
  government-supported, 90
  and job training, 45
  and men, 265, 282-83
  on-site programs, 256, 259-60, 265

problems with, 283, 284
and women, 265, 282-83
children
  benefit from stay-at-home mothers, 281-85
  benefit from working mothers, 269-77
  should visit workplace, 20
  support needs better enforcement, 242, 245, 252
  in welfare families, 242, 245-47, 251-53
Chusmir, L.H., 208
Civil Rights Acts (1964, 1991)
  effect on business, 77, 179, 216
  and equal opportunity, 178
  replaced, 185
  Title VII, 77, 179-82
Clarke, Kevin, 122
Clerical-Technical Union, 124
Clinton, Bill
  on apprenticeship programs, 35, 220, 229
  cutting government jobs, 152
  and diversity management, 213
  education programs, 25, 30, 31, 32, 46
  Family and Medical Leave Act, 78
  health benefits program, 80
  on jobs and wages, 49-52
  and labor-management relations, 134
  and labor unions, 114, 115, 118, 131-35, 160
  and minimum wage, 92, 94
  welfare reform, 242, 243, 247, 249
COBRA (Consolidated Omnibus Budget Reconciliation Act), 77, 88
Coleman, James, 226
collective bargaining
  government promotes, 134
  necessity of, 155-57
  as outdated, 132, 136
contingent workforce
  benefits business, 85
  government regulations create, 74-81, 87-88
  government regulations should protect, 82-90
  increase in, 75, 83, 84, 90
  is exploited, 83-90
  laws, 89, 90
  makeup of, 83, 90, 281
  problems of, 83-84
  receive no benefits, 84, 87-88, 258
  types of jobs, 84
  and unions, 86-87, 89
  wage rates, 84
Commission on the Future of

Worker-Management Relations,
134, 135
Communication Workers of America,
118, 120, 152
comparable worth
in Australia, 195-202
in Canada, 194
can be effective, 186-93
con, 194-202
in government jobs, 190-92
and job evaluations, 188-89, 195,
198-200
Minnesota-type plan, 188-90, 195-98,
200-201
negative effects of, 189, 192, 196-202
"pay for points" plan, 188-89
in private jobs, 192-93
in United Kingdom, 195-202
computers
and illiteracy, 26-27
in the workplace, 26-27, 42, 43
Congressional Budget Office
on minimum-wage employees, 92,
95, 98
Consolidated Omnibus Budget
Reconciliation Act (COBRA), 77, 88
contract work, 69, 83
Corning Incorporated
diversity management in, 207
labor-management relations, 117,
141-42
work-family policies, 266, 267
Cornwall, John, 70
Couch, Kenneth A., 34, 36
Cox, Taylor, 204, 208
Crichton, Michael, 213
Cross, Elsie, 215
Cuban, Larry, 26
Curry, Theodore H., II, 205

Dahl, Robert, 120
Decter, Midge, 176
Deming, W.E., 149
Denmark
apprenticeship programs in, 223
work organization in, 18
Dertouzos, James, 79
Dickens, William, 106
Digital Equipment Corporation
diversity management in, 214
Dineer, Greg, 128
discrimination
age, 77
blacks in the workplace, 233-34
cases, 207
economic, 187, 195
reverse, 174, 178-81, 183-84, 215,
217

see also affirmative action;
comparable worth; diversity
management
DiTomaso, Nancy, 208
diversity management
as beneficial, 203-11
connection to affirmative action,
217
consultants on, 213, 214-15, 216
as counterproductive, 212-18
drawbacks of, 214, 215, 216, 217
and employee satisfaction, 208
training for, 214-15, 216-17
Dixon, Carlie Sorensen, 279, 280, 285
Dogan, Pierre, 27
Donahue, Thomas R., 156
Donnelly Corporation, 140-41
Dority, Doug, 117
dropouts, 20-21, 234
Dunn, William, 284
DuPont Company
diversity management in, 214
work-family policies, 257
Durand, D.E., 208

Earned Income Tax Credit (EITC),
244, 252
Eastern Airlines strike, 140
economic discrimination, 187, 195
Economic Policy Institute (EPI), 117
education
basics must be taught, 25, 28, 40,
224
certificate of initial mastery, 21, 229
college degrees
costs of, 226
and employment, 52
as unnecessary, 32, 225, 226
continuing, 22-23
decline in, 25-27
and dropouts, 20-21, 234
general
increases employability, 35-36
German-style apprenticeship
program
would be effective, 29-33, 222-27
con, 34-40, 229-36
government funding of, 20-21, 22
higher
increases earnings, 35, 40, 42
leadership programs for minorities,
210-11
"Nation at Risk" study, 224
reasons for, 26-28, 35
system should emphasize work
skills, 17-23, 31
con, 24-28
technical should be restructured, 20

304

work-study is outdated, 220
Edwards, Richard, 104, 132
Eisenberger, Robert, 208
elder care, 256, 259-60, 265
Ellwood, David, 243
Employee Involvement programs, 147
Employee Participation programs, 147
Employee Retirement Security
  Income Act of 1974 (ERISA), 87
employee stock ownership plans
  (ESOPs), 134
employers
  affirmative action violates rights,
    172-73, 179
  and comparable worth, 189, 199
  and creation of contingent
    workforce, 83-88
  effect of government regulations
    on, 75, 77, 78
  effect of increased minimum wage
    on, 92-94
  opposition to labor unions, 89, 111,
    118-19, 123-29, 133
  right to replace strikers, 134-35,
    158-63
  is harmful, 154-57
  try to exploit workers, 123-29
  violations of workers' rights, 89
  work-family issues are important,
    256-57, 266
employment
  affirmative action is justified, 168-76
  con, 177-85
  data bank, 44
  by merit standards, 173-75
  and personal connections, 175
  reasonable cause for firing, 174
  and seniority, 89, 175
  and tax credits, 44, 73
  and young people, 20, 22, 38-39, 45
Ensuring Minority Success in Corporate
  Management (Thompson and
  DiTomaso), 208
Equal Employment Opportunity
  Commission, 77, 78
Europe
  labor-market regulations, 78
  new jobs created in, 133
Ezorsky, Gertrude, 168

Families and Work Institute, 256,
  257, 265
family
  business supports programs for,
    254-61
    are inadequate, 262-68
  care of elderly, 255, 256, 259-60, 264
  changes in, 255, 258, 263-64

two-career benefits, 274-77
two-career problems, 270-74
working mothers benefit, 269-77
  con, 278-85
Family and Medical Leave Act
  effect of, 75, 78, 279
  importance of, 256
family-leave programs, 259
Family Research Council, 281
Family Support Act of 1988, 243, 249
Farber, Henry, 110, 111, 112
Federal Housing Authority (FHA),
  169-70
Federal Reserve System, 58, 61
Federation for Industrial Retention
  and Renewal, 125
feminism, 213, 282
Fierman, Jaclyn, 262
Fifth Amendment, 178
Filene, Edward, 60
flexible scheduling, 259, 265, 283
Food Stamp Employment and
  Training Program, 44
Ford, Henry, 60
Formerly Employed Mothers at the
  Leading Edge (FEMALE), 279
Foster, W.T., 60
Fourteenth Amendment, 178, 182
Freeman, Richard, 106, 110, 111,
  117, 120
Friedan, Betty, 282
Friedman, Dana, 265
Friedman, Sheldon, 43
Fromstein, Mitchell, 78-79

Gallaway, Lowell, 57
Gans, Herbert U., 69
Gardenswartz, Lee, 216
General Motors, 76
  Saturn division, 117, 129, 134
Generation X, 284
Generous, Diane, 75
German Socio-Economic Panel
  (GSOEP), 37, 38
Germany
  apprenticeship programs
    benefits of, 31-32, 227
    costs of, 32-33, 226
    drawbacks of, 36-37, 233-34,
      235-36
    how they work, 30, 222-23, 229
    education in, 30, 32, 37-40
    unemployment in, 32
    work organization in, 18
Gilbert, Neil, 248
"Glass Ceiling Report," 216
Glass Ceiling, The New Leaders, The
  (Morrison), 215

Glazer, Nathan, 185
Golden, Lonnie, 84, 85, 87
Goldman, Alan, 174, 175, 183
Gore, Al, 152
government
  and comparable worth policies,
    190-92, 193
  and contingent workforce
    regulations create, 74-81, 87-88
    regulations needed to protect,
      82-90
  growth in, 58
  intervention
    causes unemployment, 57-65
      con, 66-73
    in employment issues, 89,
      172-73
    in labor-management relations,
      135
  racism fostered by, 169-71, 176
Great Depression
  caused by government intervention,
    61-62, 63
Greene, Linda S., 180
Griggs, Lewis, 217
Gross, Barry, 183
G.T. Water Products, 260
G2 Securities, 79
Guidelines on Leadership Diversity
  (GOLD) Project, 204

Hamilton, Stephen, 220, 221, 224-26,
  233
Haney, Craig, 180
Harrison, Bennett, 117
Hartwig, Eugene, 77, 80
Hayes, Charles, 120
Hayghe, Howard, 281
Head to Head (Thurow), 220
health care benefits
  and Bill Clinton, 80
  and COBRA, 88
  and contingent workers, 84, 88
  reform, 244-45
Hecker, Daniel, 52
Heflin, Julie, 285
Henderson, David, 78
Hobson, John, 60
Hochschild, Arlie, 267
Home by Choice, 280
Home By Choice (Hunter), 284
Hoover, Herbert, 59, 60, 61
Hudson Institute, 204, 216
Hughes Aircraft Company
  diversity management in, 214
Hulbert, Ann, 276
Hunter, Brenda, 284, 285
Hyse, Richard, 226

immigrants
  in the workforce
    changes in, 204
    exploitation of, 83, 124, 127
    labor unions protect, 124-25, 127
Immigration and Naturalization
  Service (INS), 124-25
infrastructure investment program,
  73
Institute for American Values, 280
International Brotherhood of
  Electrical Workers, 221
Irving, John, 161, 162
Ivarra, Carmen, 123

Japan, 18
Jenkins, Howard, 160
Job Corps, 20, 45, 46
Job Link Center, 47
Job Opportunities and Basic Skills
  (JOBS) programs, 242, 245-46
job search assistance, 45-47
Johnson & Johnson, 259
Judis, John B., 48, 113
Justice for Janitors, 115-16, 125

Kane, Thomas, 45
Kantor, Harvey, 228
Kassebaum, Nancy Landon, 160, 163
Katz, Lawrence, 52, 97, 117
Keith, Damon J., 185
Kelly Services, 76, 77, 79, 80
Kendall, Frances, 217
Kennedy, Randall, 180
Key, V.O., 120
Keynes, John Maynard, 63, 70
Kiester, Edwin, Jr., 221
King, Coretta Scott, 115
Kingston, Paul, 282
Kirkland, Lane, 110-11, 115, 119
Kirschenmann, Joleen, 233
Kochman, Tom, 214
Krueger, Alan B., 96

labor
  market growth in, 133
  is poorly managed, 139
  shortages, 19, 199
  surpluses, 192, 199
labor laws
  affirmative action
    is justified, 168-76
      con, 180
    comparable worth
      can be effective, 186-93
        con, 194-202
    and contingent workers, 89, 90
    discharge for reasonable cause, 174

reform of, 89, 134-35
  on striker replacements, 135, 156,
    157, 159-60, 162
labor-management partnerships
  are beneficial, 71, 117-18, 137-45,
    155-57, 163
  con, 146-53
  and Clinton administration, 134
  must be restructured, 138-45
  three-track system of, 143-44
Labor-Management Reporting and
  Disclosure Act of 1958, 135
Labor Policy Association, 75
labor unions
  are outdated, 130-36
  con, 122-29
  and ban on striker replacements, 135
  benefits of, 120, 142-43
  and blacks, 120
  and contingent workforce, 86-87, 89
  government intervention in, 135
  health and safety issues, 128
  history of, 120
  and immigrants, 124-25, 127
  influence is declining, 104-12
  con, 113-21
  leaders are changing, 116-17
  membership is decreasing, 52,
    105-108, 114, 131, 163
  con, 114
  reasons for
    change in industry, 109-10, 132
    employer opposition, 111,
      118-19, 133
    failure to recruit, 105-109
    global competition, 131-32
    ineffectiveness of, 111
    lack of organizing, 110
    leaders have poor image, 112,
      142
    legal restrictions, 110
    workers oppose, 136
  minorities in, 123, 126
  and North American Free Trade
    Agreement (NAFTA), 114, 131-32,
    133, 135
  partnership with management,
    141-43, 155
  is harmful, 146-53
  percentage of jobs represented by,
    105
  private-sector, 131, 132, 134
  problems to overcome, 118-19,
    142-43
  public-sector, 105-106, 131
  reasons for growth in, 115-18
  recruiting new members, 106, 107,
    108, 109
  support from liberals, 117
  Supreme Court decisions on, 135,
    156, 159
  Teamsters strike, 114, 117
  and wages, 52
  women in, 109, 123-24, 126
Lancaster Laboratories, 260
Lawrence, David, 213
Lawyers at Home Forum, 280, 285
LeMay, Ronald, 265
Leonard, Jonathan, 106
Lerner, Steve, 116, 125, 126, 127
Levering, Robert, 140
Levin, Michael, 196
Liebow, Elliot, 67
Lips, Alan, 162
Lopez, Julie Amparano, 257
Lorenzo, Frank, 140
Losey, Michael, 79
Louisville Plate Glass Company, 159,
  162
Loury, Glenn C., 184
Love and Profit (Autrey), 261
Lynch, Frederick R., 212

MacDonald, Heather, 214
Machine That Changed the World, The
  (M.I.T.), 148
Mackay doctrine, 156
MacKinnon, Catharine, 213
Manpower, Inc., 76, 78-79
Manpower Demonstration Research
  Corporation, 45
Mansfield, Harvey C., Jr., 184
manufacturing
  changes in, 109-10, 132, 225
  loss of jobs in, 68
Marshall, Ray, 17, 223-24
Marshall, Thurgood, 176
Mathematica Policy Research, 45,
  49-51
Mattox, William, 281
McDonald-Pines, Jane, 43
McEntee, Gerald, 118
McGinnis, Jeff, 75
Meany, George, 119
Medicaid, 242, 244, 252
Medoff, James, 110, 111
Meisinger, Sue, 77
men
  and diversity management, 215,
    217-18
  family responsibilities, 265, 282-83
  time spent in workplace, 265, 267
  in workforce
    changes in, 204, 205, 258
    rates of pay, 187, 190-91, 195,
      200, 202

types of jobs, 187, 201
Mencimer, Stephanie, 98
meritocratic principles, 173-75
Meyer, Bruce, 46
minimum wage
  and Clinton, 92, 94
  Congressional Budget Office on, 92, 95, 98
  employees who receive, 92-95, 98
  increase in
    reduces employment, 91-95
      con, 96-100
    would not help poor, 92
  nonpayment of, 89, 126
  for part-time work, 90
  studies on, 97-99
  and teenagers, 32, 93-95, 97-99
Minimum Wage Study Commission, 95
Minnesota
  comparable worth program works, 188-90
    con, 195-98, 200-201
minorities
  apprenticeship programs would benefit, 227
    con, 231-32
  creating jobs for, 230-31
  difficulty finding work, 231, 233, 234
  and diversity management, 204-11, 214
  educational leadership programs, 210-11
  and labor unions, 123, 126
  unemployment rates of, 64, 231, 234
  in workforce
    changes in, 204
    contingent, 83, 90
Moms Club, 280
Montgomery, Mark, 44
Morrison, Ann M., 203, 215
Morrison & Foerster, 267
Mosley, Sherry, 267
mothers
  stay-at-home benefit families, 278-85
  working benefit families, 269-77
Mothers at Home, 279
Mothers First, 279-80, 284
Mothers of Preschoolers (MOPs), 279
Moynihan, Daniel Patrick, 243
Murray, Charles, 184
Myers family, 269-77

Nagel, Thomas, 172
National Abortion Rights Action League (NARAL), 120
National Alliance of Business, 31

National Association of Manufacturers, 75
National Association of Mothers' Centers, 280
National Association of Temporary Services, 76
National Association of Working Women (9to5), 283
National Education Association, 115
National Labor Relations Act (NLRA), 89, 110, 134, 160
National Labor Relations Board (NLRB)
  promotion of unions, 135
  reinstating workers, 119
  replacement workers, 161, 162
  and union elections, 107-12, 116, 136
National Labor Relations Board v. Mackay Radio & Telegraph Company, 156, 159
National Longitudinal Surveys of Youth (NLSY), 38
National Partnership Council, 152
National Rifle Association (NRA), 120
National Study of the Changing Workforce, 256
Neckerman, Kathryn, 233
Neuman, Elena, 278
New York City Bureau of Motor Equipment, 142
9to5 (National Association of Working Women), 283
Nock, Steven, 282
North American Free Trade Agreement (NAFTA), 49
  and labor unions, 114, 131-32, 133, 135
NOVA program, 46
Nozick, Robert, 172

Office for Federal Contract Compliance, 192
Okin, Susan Moller, 272
Omnibus Trade and Competitiveness Act, 50
on-the-job training, 21-22, 45, 46, 49, 72
Organization for Economic Cooperation and Development (OECD), 70, 197
Osborne, Beth, 280, 284
Osterman, Paul, 230, 232
Overworked American, The (Schor), 265

Parker, Mike, 146
part-time work, 68
  minimum wage for, 90

trend towards, 69, 75, 83
see also workforce, contingent
Payroll Options, 80
Penello, John A., 160
Peterson, Wallace C., 66
Pfister, Peter, 267
political correctness (PC)
  effect on workplace, 213, 217-18
Porter, Sylvia, 255
Posner, Richard A., 182
Postal Workers union, 118
poverty levels, 72, 92, 243-44, 258
Prager, Jeffrey, 180
Preston, James, 205
Prewo, Wilfried, 29
Professional Air Traffic Controllers
  Organization (PATCO), 118, 156
Project Independence, 245-46
Prudential Insurance
diversity management in, 214

Quality of Work Life programs, 147
Quayle, Dan, 279

racism
  and merit, 180-81
  as public policy, 169, 176
Rae, Douglas, 183
Rand Corporation, 79
Randolph, A. Philip, 120
Reagan, Ronald
  and air-traffic controllers, 115, 118,
  140
  and comparable worth, 192
  and diversity management, 215
  and labor unions, 118, 133, 134
Reen, Bruce, 243
Reich, Robert B., 41
  on high-value enterprise, 150
  and labor unions, 117, 118, 131-35
  and minimum wage increase,
  92-95
  on striker replacements, 154-57,
  160, 161
  and training workers, 25, 49, 51
reverse discrimination, 174, 178-79,
  180-81, 215, 217
Reynolds, Alan, 94
Rhoads, Steven E., 194
Richards, Chuck, 152
Riley, Richard, 35
Ringer, Benjamin, 180
Rockefeller Foundation, 45
Rothstein, Lawrence E., 141
Rouse, Cecilia, 45
Rowe, Anita, 216, 217, 218
Rush, Linda, 279
Rustin, Bayard, 120

Sabo, Martin, 94
Sandroff, Ronni, 207
Scardelletti, Bob, 117
Schneider, Debbie, 129
Schor, Juliet, 265
Schwab, Donald, 199
Sears, 114
Second Stage, The (Friedan), 282
Seidman, William, 142
self-employment, 75, 83
Seligman, Daniel, 184
*Sequencing: A New Solution for Women
  Who Want Marriage, Career, and
  Family* (Cardozo), 282
Service Employees International
  Union (SEIU)
  growth in, 115, 126, 127
  and Justice for Janitors, 125
  strike by, 61
  temporary workers, 75
sexual harassment
  in the workplace, 123, 207
Shaiken, Harley, 117
Shalala, Donna E., 241
Shaw, Peter, 24
Sheflin, Ned, 108
Shelley, Kristina, 52
Skanche, Steven, 142
Skills Development Fund, 22
Slaughter, Jane, 146
Social Security, 63, 90
Society for Human Resource
  Management, 77, 79
Sorensen, Elaine, 186
South Coast Air Quality Management
  District, 87
South Korea, 20
Sowell, Thomas, 176
Spencer, Leslie, 181
Spock, Benjamin, 285
Sprint International, 265, 266
St. Antoine, Theodore J., 79
State Farm Insurance, 207
*Staying Home: From Full-Time
  Professional to Full-Time Parent*
  (Bullen), 282
Steele, Shelby, 170
Steinberg, Bruce, 76
Stern, Andrew, 126
Stieber, Jack, 80
Stigler, George, 97
Stoll, Michael A., 231
Stone, William A., 159, 162, 163
Strauss, George, 197
strikes
  Eastern Airlines, 140
  Justice for Janitors, 115-16
  Professional Air Traffic Controllers

Organization (PATCO), 118, 140,
  156
and replacement workers, 118
  ban on, 134, 156-57
  employers should be allowed to
    permanently hire, 158-63
    con, 154-57
  Teamsters, 114, 117
  workers' right to, 156-57
Sturdivant, John, 152
Styring, William, 77, 78
Suarez, Joan, 125
Supplemental Security Income (SSI),
  242
Supreme Court
  on right to permanently replace
    strikers, 135, 156, 159
Sweden
  work organization in, 18
  Youth Centers, 20
Sweeney, John, 75
Swiss, Deborah, 283-84

Tandem Computers, 263
taxes
  and contract workers, 75
  credits
    Earned Income Tax Credit (EITC),
      244, 252
    and employment, 44, 73
  cuts in, 73
Teamsters, 114, 115, 116
technology
  and educational decline, 25-27
  and job creation, 72
  in the workplace, 18, 86, 222, 225
teenagers
  in contingent workforce, 83, 90
  and minimum wage, 32, 93-95,
    97-99
temporary work, 69, 71, 83
  is exploited, 84-90
  see also workforce, contingent
Texaco, 207
Texas Commerce Bank, 259-60
Thiederman, Sondra, 214
Thomas, R. Roosevelt, 215-18
Thompson, Donna, 208
Thurow, Lester, 220
Total Quality Management (TQM),
  149
Trade Adjustment Assistance (TAA),
  50, 51
Trade Expansion Act of 1962, 50
Trade Readjustment Allowances
  (TRAs), 50, 51
training programs
  will benefit U.S. workers, 41-47,

71-72
  con, 48-52
Transportation Communications
  International Union (TCU), 117
Treybig, James, 263
Troy, Leo, 108, 130
Truman, David, 120
Trumka, Richard, 116
Tucker, Marc, 17
Tucker, William, 74
Turner, Brian, 117
Tyson, Laura, 117
Tyson Foods Inc., 128

underconsumptionism, 60-62
unemployment
  blacks, 231, 234
  caused by government intervention,
    57-65
    con, 66-73
  changes in system, 46
  and contingent workers, 88
  in Germany, 32
  history of, 58-63
  insurance for, 63, 69, 90
  minorities, 64, 231, 234
  "natural rate," 63, 71
  rates of, 32, 62-64, 68-69, 72, 133,
    234
  and training, 45-46
  women, 64
  worldwide, 70
unions. See labor unions
United Auto Workers (UAW), 118,
  119, 120, 134
United Food and Commercial
  Workers (UFCW), 115, 117, 124,
  128
United Kingdom
  comparable worth in, 195-202
United Mine Workers (UMW), 114,
  116, 119
United States
  competition in world market
    and diversity management, 206
    and education, 18-19, 25, 38,
      225-26
    and labor-management relations,
      138, 155, 163
  Department of Labor "Glass Ceiling
    Report," 216
  economic superiority lost, 138-39
  high school graduates, 32
  is pro-college, 32, 225, 226
  productivity decline, 138-39
  should restructure education
    systems, 19-20, 220-27
U.S. Steel Workers, 118, 129

310

U.S. West
  diversity management in, 214
  labor-management relations, 117

Valente, Judith, 269
Van Alstyne, William, 182, 183
Vedder, Richard, 57
veterans
  employment preference for, 171-72,
    174, 176
Virtual Corporations, 150-51
vocational education, 21, 220, 235
Voos, Paula, 110, 117

wages
  buying-power decrease in, 67-68
  controls, 196
  laws covering, 63, 89
  market driven, 199-200
  real
    decrease in, 114, 120, 126
  temporary work, 84
  see also minimum wage
Wagner, Kathleen, 283
Wagner Act, 159
Warner, David, 158
welfare reform
  costs of, 249-50
  and health care reform, 244-45
  should require recipients to work,
    241-47
    con, 248-53
welfare state, 63-64
What Do Unions Do? (Freeman), 117
Whitehead, Barbara Dafoe, 280-81
Whitehead, Jay, 80
Williams, Chuck, 82
Williams, Lynn, 129
Williams, Walter, 183
WMX Technologies, 266
women
  and AFDC reform, 251-52
  and child care, 90
  choosing to stay home, 278-85
  and discrimination cases, 207
  economic discrimination of, 187,
    195
  family responsibilities, 265, 266,
    282-83
  in the workforce
    changes in, 204, 209, 258, 263-64
    changing attitudes about, 278-85
    contingent work, 83, 84, 90, 281
    decrease in, 281
    and diversity management,
      204-11, 214
    and feminism, 282
    harassment of, 123

  increase in, 109, 258, 263-64
  and labor unions, 109, 123-24, 126
  pay inequalities
    comparable worth can help,
      186-93
    rates of, 187, 190-91, 195, 202
    reasons for, 67, 84, 258
  time spent in workplace, 265, 267
  types of jobs, 123-24, 187, 200
  unemployment rates, 64
  working mothers benefit families,
    269-77
    con, 278-85
Women and the Work/Family Dilemma
  (Swiss), 283
Wood, Regna Lee, 25
work
  bad job
    definition of, 68
  contract, 69, 83
    see also workforce, contingent
  economy should create jobs, 67, 70,
    71, 73
  ethics, 224-25, 227
  full-employment policy needed,
    70-73, 234
  good jobs
    decrease in, 69-70
    definition of, 67, 71
    importance of, 42, 67
    loss of jobs in U.S., 68
  organizations, 18, 19
  part-time, 68, 69, 75, 83
    minimum wage for, 90
    trend towards, 69, 75, 83
    see also workforce, contingent
  skills
    education system should
      emphasize, 17-23, 31
      con, 24-28
  temporary, 69, 71, 83
    is exploited, 84-90
    see also workforce, contingent
  values, 69
  week reduction, 88-89
  welfare recipients should be
    required to, 241-47
    con, 248-53
Worker Adjustment and Retraining
  Notification Act, 78, 88
work-experience programs, 20
Work-Family Directions, 264, 265
work-family programs
  as necessary to business, 259, 263,
    265-66
  business supports, 254-61
    con, 262-68
  types of, 259

311

workforce
changes in, 109, 204, 216, 258, 263-64
contingent
benefits business, 85
government regulations create, 74-81, 87-88
government regulations should protect, 82-90
increase in, 75, 83, 84, 90
is exploited, 83-90
laws, 89, 90
makeup of, 83, 90
problems of, 83-84
receive no benefits, 84, 87-88, 258
types of jobs, 84
and unions, 86-87, 89
wage rates, 84
contract, 69, 75, 83
employee input is valuable, 129, 140-45, 155
firing practices, 79-80
full-time
benefits of, 84
as too costly, 75, 84
illiteracy in, 26-27
immigrants in, 83, 124-25, 127, 204
men in
changes in, 204, 205, 258
rates of pay, 187, 190-91, 195, 200, 202
time spent in workplace, 265, 267
types of jobs, 187, 201
minorities in, 83, 90, 204-11, 214
paid vacations for, 89
participation in companies
is beneficial, 140-45, 155
part-time, 69, 75, 83
rates of growth, 106, 133
right to strike, 156-57
self-employed, 75, 83
self-management, 140-41
share in profits, 142
temporary, 69, 71, 83
increase in, 75-76, 83
is exploited, 84-90
women in
changes in, 204, 209, 258, 263-64
decrease in, 281
harassment of, 123
increase in, 109, 258, 263-64
pay inequalities

comparable worth can help, 186-93
rates of, 187, 190-91, 195, 202
reasons for, 67, 84, 258
time spent in workplace, 265, 267
types of jobs, 124, 187, 200
Workforce 2000 (Hudson Inst.), 204, 205, 216
Work of Nations, The (Reich), 150
workplace
children should visit, 20
continuing education in, 22-23
employee participation in
is beneficial, 139-45, 155
programs for, 147-48
equality in
affirmative action promotes, 168-76
con, 177-85
comparable worth can be effective, 186-93
con, 194-202
gender inequalities in, 186-93, 194-202
job evaluations in, 188-89, 195, 198-200
racism in, 169-71, 176, 180-81
reengineering of, 149-53
sexual harassment in, 123, 207
technology in, 18, 86, 222, 225
and educational decline, 25-27
youth training in, 30-32
Workplace Fairness Act, 156, 157, 159, 160
Workplace of the Future agreement, 152
wrongful termination
legal definitions, 79
Wynn, William, 117

Xerox Corporation, 129

Yeager, Daniel, 160
Young, Coleman, 120
Your Staff, Inc., 80
youth
jobs after high school, 221, 222, 229-30

Zenith, 114
Ziller, Robert, 208
Zycher, Benjamin, 93